BE PURE!
BE VIGILANT!
BEHAVE!

2000AD AND JUDGE DREDD:
THE SECRET HISTORY...

PAT MILLS!

MILLSVERSE
BOOKS

Created with Vellum

To 2000AD readers,
for your incredible loyalty to the comic.

Thank you.

CONTENTS

AUTHOR'S NOTE

I have tried to give a fair and balanced account of the turbulent, complex and exciting history of *2000AD* and *Judge Dredd*. I've done my best to be even-handed in my portrayal of people and events, giving credit where it's due.

However, these are my memories; my point of view—although they are often confirmed by other's recollections, wherever that is possible or important.

I recognise that some people portrayed in this book may have different views, and a different recollection of events that took place over the last forty years. In certain cases I haven't included names, and identifying details have been changed to protect the privacy of individuals.

Pat Mills
2017

INTRODUCTION

"Through a minefield of imbeciles and chimps."

The creation of *2000AD* and *Judge Dredd* was a tortuous and protracted process. In this, it was not unusual. I understand most great comic book heroes, such as *Superman* and *Batman*, go through a complex process of changes, revisions and modifications before the final iconic product is achieved. But *Dredd* was more tortuous than most, because its two creators, writer John Wagner and artist Carlos Ezquerra, reluctantly and understandably walked away from their embryonic creation, leaving myself and others to develop it, rather than let it be stillborn. In making their exits, ultimately because of their lack of intellectual property rights over their character, they had my sympathy. In their situation, I might well have done the same. But I could not allow their character to die. *Dredd* had to survive because its potential was so obvious and so enormous.

It was not just the creators who wanted *Dredd*, or even *2000AD* itself, to fade away. Leading fantasy artists loathed us because we were published by IPC Magazines, who were responsible for the past desecration of beautiful artwork by Frank Bellamy and Frank Hampson, creator of *Dan Dare*. For instance, one young fantasy artist, John Bolton, came in to bollock me personally for over an hour for IPC's past "crimes" over the way they'd treated Hampson, Bellamy and other stars, losing, destroying or not returning their artwork. It was known that the store men regularly used priceless masterpieces of comic art kept in the vaults of Fleetway House in Farringdon Street, to bung up leaking drains and use as dart boards, also slicing bits off the pages so they would fit the shelves better. A shameful story. I completely understood how he felt. I was suitably repentant on behalf of the browncoats, who were probably—even as we spoke—stubbing out their fags on a page of *Dan Dare*, while they rested their mugs of tea on *Heros the Spartan*. John said he couldn't work for me because of this appalling past, and because we didn't return original artwork. He clearly had only come into the office to let off steam. After I had been suitably tongue-lashed and castigated, he left, and I turned to my staff: "Okay, guys—get the shredder out and let's cut up some more old artwork. Who's got the Stanley knife?"

Art agents also didn't want their leading artists—like the great Brian Lewis—to be associated with our low-grade publication printed on cheap bog paper in black and white, as at least one of them made very clear to me. Comic fans hated us because we weren't their glossy and colourful image of science fiction—whether it was superhero comics, *TV 21* or *Heavy Metal* magazine. One super-fan would come into IPC HQ at Kings Reach Tower, and patiently explain to me at great length where I was going wrong, why I needed the benefit of his expert advice and why *2000AD* should be more like *Heavy Metal* or *Metal Hurlant*. I'm so glad I didn't take his advice because I understand he ended his days sleeping under a railway viaduct.

IPC comic editors, too, wanted our publication to die because they sensed it was the crest of the new wave that would eventually shut down their publications and end their careers. The managing editor, Jack Le Grand—oozing passive aggression—would tell me with great relish the latest sales figures, which suggested *2000AD*, after its initial huge popularity, was on the slippery slope to disaster. We're talking about a drop of maybe 2,000 sales, of week after launch sales of 200,000 copies a week. Actually, nothing to worry about, but he could dream, couldn't he? He and his unpleasant ilk did everything to undermine my confidence and throw a spanner in the works. For example, "losing" a potentially ground-breaking strip and withholding information on cool artists. But that was a tactical error on their part, because it just brought out the "screw you!" in me.

SF writers like Michael Moorcock derided us for our story about a Soviet Union invasion of Britain. Newspapers like *The Guardian* agreed. We made their front page with our futuristic story about the Russian invasion, quickly changed at the last moment to a Volgan invasion on the instructions of the IPC board of directors. The reporter disapproved of my irreverent tone when I claimed the Russians—whom we had depicted with authentic uniforms and hardware—were not Russians, but actually fictional "Volgans". There's a river Volga in Russia, the reporter pointed out. There's a Volga republic in Africa, I replied unconvincingly, trying hard not to laugh. But your Volgans are white, insisted the reporter, finally cornering me.

My response to the avalanche of criticism and negativity, as always, was very measured, calm and reasonable. A typical Pat Mills response was a large sign I placed above the entrance to the *2000AD* offices. It said, "Piss off all *Heavy Metal* Fans."

For most of *2000AD's* history it was to be disliked and misunderstood, not just by these various factions, but even by its owners. This explains why IPC Magazines sold *2000AD* and other juvenile publications to Maxwell, who sold it to Egmont, who sold it to Rebellion—the current publishers—where it finally, *finally* received the TLC it deserves and is, as a result, now celebrating its 40th year of publication in 2017! An astonishing achievement which you, the readers—staying with us through its bad times as well as the good—are responsible for, and I thank you for your loyalty, tolerance and fortitude. Thus a typical optimistic comment in the late '90s, when the comic went through its infamous Dark Age, was "It's really crap at the moment, but it's got to get better soon. It's *got* to." You are stars, all of you!

On the positive side, our pariah-like nature gave us a cult status and ensured there was no danger of us selling out. But our critics' hatred was actually useful, because the more pissed off I got, the stronger it made me. I used their negative energy to my advantage, riding a wave of passive and not so passive aggression to produce a product of such quality it would confound them all. I couldn't afford to fail with so much defeatism in the air and so many wanting to dance on our graves, waiting to say, "You see? I knew *2000AD* would die. Because science fiction doesn't sell. Especially when it's so violent, fantasmagoric (stupid) and breaks all the rules."

As *2000AD* art editor Kevin O'Neill commented, "Yes. This was how Britain's favourite comic was created. Through a minefield of imbeciles and chimps."

This is my personal journey through that minefield and others may have an entirely different experience from their time on the Galaxy's Greatest Comic. I've called it a secret history because much of what I'm about to relate is not widely known. I hope to reveal and explain many of the mysteries that have fascinated readers. I'll leave calendar dates and exhaustive details to Wikipedia, because what matters most—to me at least—are the passions, the personalities and the key stories that shaped the comic.

It's a recreation of events and conversations based on my memories and therefore some dialogue may not be 100% verbatim and the exact sequences of events may not always be 100% accurate. But what is 150% accurate is the truth they represent.

I've used Torquemada's legendary exhortation to guide me. Torquemada was the Grand Master of Termight, Earth, thousands of years in the future, the fanatical adversary of Nemesis, an alien warlock, who looked like the Goat of Mendes on a bad day. They were the main characters in my galactic space opera, *Nemesis The Warlock*, co-created with artist Kevin O'Neill. It became one of *2000AD*'s most successful stories. It's why Torquemada's famous words ended up being painted on the Berlin Wall: "Be Pure! Be Vigilant! Behave!"

So my *2000AD* story breaks down as follows:

Part One: Be Pure!
Creating *2000AD*'s identity and stories, maintaining a purist approach in order to give the comic its unique identity.

Part Two: Be Vigilant!
The comic's launch and how it went from strength to strength, against all the odds.

Part Three: Behave!
The Dark Age of the '90s. The disastrous reinvention of *2000AD*. Its rescue by Rebellion shortly after the millennium, a return to sanity, and the beginnings of a new and long Golden Age. Well—*Goldenish*.

The story begins in a garden shed in Scotland sometime in 1971
...

PART I

BE PURE!

1. ORIGINS

Actually, the story probably begins a few months earlier, on a bus going up the Lochee Road in Dundee, heading for the tenement flat where I lived with my young family. John Wagner and I both worked on the editorial side of *Romeo*, a teenage romantic weekly and one of numerous publications produced by DC Thomson's, the great powerhouse of British comics. We had just finished work and John was mad keen for us to get home in time to watch *Star Trek*, of which he was a big fan. He assured me I would like it ,and I think I tried, and enjoyed it. Sort of. I don't recall liking any TV science fiction. But favourite films included *Fahrenheit 451*, *Privilege*, and *Clockwork Orange*.

John went on to introduce me to other books that he said were essential reading. One was *The Hobbit*, followed by *The Lord of the Rings*. John had taken several days off work to read them cover to cover. Once again, I tried, but again they didn't do much for me and —after getting about a third of the way through *The Hobbit*, I gave up. But John persevered and passed on his copy of Luke Rheinhardt's *The Diceman*. It was about a guy who makes decisions on the roll of a die. Ah! Now this was more like it! I loved it. He also introduced me to *Stranger in a Strange Land*. I grokked that.

So, you may ask, what other kind of books did I like? Well, here are some of them and you will doubtless see how they influenced me in creating *2000AD*.

First of all, *Maddened by Mystery: or The Defective Detective*, written by the great Canadian humorist Stephen Leacock. Here's a brief excerpt:

The great detective sat in his office. He wore a long green gown and half a dozen secret badges pinned to the outside of it.
Three or four pairs of false whiskers hung on a whisker-stand beside him.
Goggles, blue spectacles and motor glasses lay within easy reach.
He could completely disguise himself at a second's notice.
Half a bucket of cocaine and a dipper stood on a chair at his elbow.

The edition I read had brilliant illustrations in a Ronald Searle-style and cruelly mocked the establishment and the Church of England. I was eight years old. My mother looked at what I was reading and said, "Hmm. I'm not sure that story is very suitable for you." But it was too late. The damage was done. I'd read every word of it, and I loved it.

Other titles I loved included *Gulliver's Travels* and *Erewhon* by Samuel Butler, about a world where illness is a crime punishable by imprisonment and criminals are treated in hospital. And of course, *Catch 22*, *1984*, *Animal Farm* and *Flashman*.

But where most of us would enjoy Conan Doyle's *Sherlock Holmes*, I preferred his *Brigadier Gerard*. Brigadier *who?* Okay: it's about a pompous French hussar in the Napoleonic Wars. To quote Wikipedia, "Gerard's most notable attribute is his vanity—he is utterly convinced that he is the bravest soldier, greatest swordsman, most accomplished horseman and most gallant lover in all France." I remember him as a pompous prat, who somehow wins thanks to his idiotic behaviour.

You can begin to see a pattern emerging.

I was also a rabid reader of *Jeeves*, because he makes a fool of his upper class boss. And *Don Camillo*, about a Catholic priest in post-war Italy, because I was rooting for his "frenemy": the communist mayor.

I was never into comics as a kid, but I was a total fan boy where cartoons were concerned, notably by Ronald Searle, Steadman, Raymond Lowry and Heath; plus the *Esquire* collections and *Mad* magazine. I loved *The Ecologist* magazine, *Oz* and *International Times*, but it was the weekly *Punch* and fortnightly *Private Eye* I bought religiously, at a time when the latter was amazing, and was regularly being sued for daring to reveal the truth about the corruption at the heart of British society.

It's only in later years I can see the pattern myself. Satire questions the world we're in and reveals the truth. And, thus, it's a key constituent of *2000AD*. But John—whilst also enjoying satire—actually has broader tastes in science fiction than I do.

But note how working class fictional heroes like Jeeves are thin on the ground in the list above. Then—and now—there aren't enough: Harry Potter and Oliver Twist are the only names that spring immediately to mind. Instead, we are indoctrinated with brilliant but upper-class heroes: Holmes, Hannay and Bond. The fact that it doesn't seem to concern most people is a measure of how strongly we have been socially conditioned to look up to our "betters".

You doubt it's deliberate indoctrination? I can't agree with you. I'm not even convinced it's always a subconscious response by the servants of the State. Richard Hannay, after all, was the creation of the great and pernicious spin doctor of World War One: John Buchan, who easily outclassed Alastair Campbell in justifying Britain's war crimes. See, for example, the on-line article entitled: John Buchan: The Secret Elite's Special Propaganda Weapon.

Buchan's role as popular novelist and head of British propaganda is no coincidence. I could cite numerous other examples of state-connected authors of popular fiction. For example, Ian Fleming and Dennis Wheatley.

But there is a clincher for me. Back in the early '80s I was commissioned—with John Wagner—to write a *Doctor Who* TV drama entitled *Song of the Space Whale*. It featured a working class space captain of an abattoir in space, slaughtering alien space whales as food for the colony planets. "Everything is used. Nothing is wasted. Everything but the song." (John's brilliant line, adapted from a similar American advert for pigs where every part of the animal is used, "Everything but the squeal.")

Our space captain was based on the captain of a dredger John had worked on. The BBC script editor insisted that we could not have a working class space commander. He was adamant that it was out of the question. There could be no debate. He wasn't keen on the castaways inside the space whale being working class either, who were also based on real working class people. They, too, had to go. Mainly for these reasons, the TV script proved abortive. It was used later as a Big Finish *Doctor Who* audio play *The Song of Megaptera*. Most fans agree that the working class captain works just fine. And it cannot be dismissed as the unfortunate attitudes in the '80s. I can think of more recent examples of where the covert class war continues and the fictional media is deliberately manipulated by the State. I studied it in detail before giving my findings at a *Charley's War* lecture at the University of Liverpool, when I was an Honorary Professor there. In summary: no anti-war dramas or comedies have been shown on terrestrial TV during the centenary years of the Great War.

This also explains my dislike of most superheroes—because they are invariably upper middle class: arms dealers; tycoons; lawyers; scientists and so forth with establishment values, generally pursuing terrorists, or psychopaths, or street scum. No social commentary. No questioning of the status quo in any real or meaningful way. And featuring men we're supposed to look up to, rather than identify with.

It's offensive and shameful and if I could have found working class heroes as a kid, I would have read every one of them. So—as soon I had the opportunity—I featured working class heroes in all my stories. It's why you'll find very few officers as heroes in the early issues of *Battle,* the war comic John and I later created. That was something *I* was adamant about. Then came my *Action*—"the comic of the streets" (that line speaks for itself), and it was loved by its readers for this reason. I was determined to continue the theme in *2000AD*. I think you'll find, for the most part, that it's the working class heroes and villains, the under-dogs, the aliens, the robots and the mutants, who are the long-term favourites. Mega City is filled with a rebellious underclass, hence the popularity of John's *Chopper* and *Block Wars*, and *Judge Dredd* himself is a foot soldier. The theme is often oblique rather than polemic, but it's there. I suspect readers sense there is something out of place with the alternatives where there isn't this subtext, and I'm glad about that. In my opinion, such stories have little place in *2000AD* and run the risk of diluting the comic, steering it away from its roots.

But I'm getting ahead of myself. Let's return to that garden shed.

I had moved across the water from Dundee, to Wormit in Fife, and there John and I made our plans to make a living as comic book writers. We had a great time working at DC Thomson's. I have fond memories of the two of us walking the corridors of the DC Thomson building, known as the Red Lubyanka, wearing dark green visors with 'HACK' written on them in white letraset. But we both wanted more from life. The garden shed was to be our office. Almost everything we wrote together clicked with the editors we submitted scripts to, ranging from *War Picture Library* to *Cor!!.* I left DC Thomson's and John followed shortly thereafter.

It's hard to imagine how we never killed each other back then. Two strong personalities sitting in a shed, writing and arguing about comic stories through all-night scripting sessions, because John was an insomniac. Relieving the tension with intermissions where we played football (in the shed) at three o'clock in the morning. Breathing in the evil green fumes from a solitary oil lamp, so we would regularly have to take fresh air breaks outside in all weathers. Keeping our pet spider suitably fed with dead wasps until the spider finally gorged itself to death. Playing volleyball over the washing line until John broke his ankle during the game. I've always felt guilty about that, because my garden was on a steep slope and John jumped back to hit the ball and … Krak!

We would do anything to relieve the moronic tedium of writing for *Whizzer and Chips*, *Whoopee*, *Shiver and Shake*, *Cor!!*, *Lion*, and *Valiant*.

If you'd like to know more about that truly awful, but also rather funny era, check out *Serial Killer*, the first book in the *Read Em and Weep* black comedy thriller series I co-wrote with Kevin O'Neill. *Read Em* is also a fictional version of the story of British comics in the 1970s, where life in the shed is described in chilling detail!

But our frustrations showed us that if we didn't like the comics or stories we were working on, we would ultimately have to create our own, which would culminate in *2000AD* and *Judge Dredd*. One example of the stories we wrote together illustrates what the comic world was like back in the early '70s.

With our love of satire, we had created *Yellowknife of the Yard*, the story of a Red Indian detective who is sent to Scotland Yard on an exchange scheme. We submitted it to the *Hotspur* editor, who wrote us a furious rejection letter, claiming we were insulting Scotland Yard by having an American Indian as a police inspector. Seething with rage, he said our story was potentially libellous by giving Yellowknife an incompetent British police sergeant as his dumb sidekick.

So we then submitted it to *Valiant*, who accepted it straight away. The story wasn't great, but there was one excellent scene John had come up with which we both loved. It showed Yellowknife approaching his wigwam in the American desert and the text waxed lyrical about the romantic life of an Indian living a timeless life in harmony with the earth and nature. Yellowknife steps inside his wigwam and there are steps leading down which lead to … an underground disco. It was Saturday Night Fever down there.

That was the one change they wanted. Satire not required. But we had some fun on a later story where we featured Yellowknife up against the Fat Gang. And should you have any old copies of *Valiant* from that era, you'll see the obese villain has a belly wheel to support his massive gut, something I think I dreamed up, and Dredd fans will know all about. Great fun!

But we weren't happy writing conventionally humorous comic strips. We did get one break, when we wrote *Boo! Peter*—a *Mad* Magazine-style piss take of *Blue Peter*, which, it will come as no surprise to you, both John and I loathed but were forced to watch for our research, noting how Noakes, Singleton and Purves spoke in linked trio dialogue, invariably ending with "Super!" Our piss-take was hugely popular with test-audiences. In fact the kids liked it so much, they wanted *Boo! Peter* to appear every week. They couldn't get enough of it and, well, I think we had enough bile about *Blue Peter* to oblige them. But IPC didn't have the bottle to go ahead and do a British *Mad* Magazine, just as later they would turn down *Viz*. I imagine our story's probably been published in an annual or something and I like to think it holds up well to this day. Super!

But we weren't happy bunnies and things just got worse and worse. We were commissioned to write a text Yellowknife story for the *Valiant* annual, but we were so skint, we couldn't afford a ream of typing paper. So I hit on the brilliant idea of typing it on tracing paper, of which I had a plentiful supply. Shortly afterwards, my Trimphone trilled and the assistant editor of *Valiant*, Steve Barker, was on the other end. He was furious—no, he was demented … he was *deranged*. He proceeded to tongue-lash me for half an hour for submitting an unreadable story. My lame suggestion that if he put it on white backing paper it would be okay, only worked him up into a greater, foul-mouthed froth that left me trembling on the end of my Trimphone.

Eventually John left to work for IPC in London and I continued writing *Yellowknife* and various other stories and cartoon strips. I needed the money, but ultimately I had to admit to myself, 'I am writing absolute crap here. This is awful. The readers must feel the same way. I've really got to bring this to an end for my sanity's sake." So I rang *Valiant* up, fully prepared to sack myself.

Thankfully, it wasn't Steve Barker who answered the phone. In fact, I believe he had died around this time. (I'm told he was found drowned in a swimming pool.) Instead, a new, chirpy young chap answered and I explained my serious misgivings about *Yellowknife*. "Oh, no," the friendly lad reassured me. "It's great stuff. Keep up the good work."

So, somewhat reassured—but not entirely convinced—I carried on with *Yellowknife* for a miserable while longer before finally kicking it into touch. That chirpy young chap was Steve MacManus, later to be the editor of *2000AD*.

2. DARK SATANIC MILLS

At this point, it's necessary to explain the factory system through which Britain's comics were produced, often resulting in flat, ephemeral, disposable stories and art, because nobody cared, and then to jump forward in time to show how creators, including myself, fought our way through to find Jerusalem and produce work of lasting value on *2000AD*. Because that problem and its solution is at the heart of its success, and it explains many of the tensions between editorial and writers and artists and why some of the Galaxy's Greatest Comic's stories succeeded and others bombed.

Often it really was like that scene in *Metropolis*, where the enslaved workers, heads down, trudge their way to the factory machines and operate them for endless hours. It *was* a factory and when I describe it to my colleagues in French comics, they shake their heads in disbelief. In France they have a benign system, which favours the comic creators and the publishers, and as a result they produce amazing and beautiful comic books, which are wildly successful. (Japan is the world leader in comics. France is second. The United States is third.)

Why we had—and still have—a Lowry-like factory system in comics, albeit greatly improved—is something to do with British culture, the "them and us" attitude of management and workers, a hangover from the days of Britain's harsh industrial past and, sadly, it's deeply ingrained in our national psyche. This is how it manifests itself:

As comic writers and artists, we do not own our characters: instead we sell all rights to the publisher. So any fees from films, reprints or merchandising go to the company and are not shared with the creators. In the beginning, none of it was ever passed on. Today, we receive a small percentage, although it's below industry standard. Back then, and perhaps even now, they could also employ cheaper replacement writers and artists if we protested or became *difficult*, as I was frequently described. Worse, we had no credits on our work. This was a deliberate policy of the publishers to stop individuals from building up a fan following, and creators getting together, so any artist's signatures on their work were ruthlessly whitened out. This policy worked for many decades, until Kevin O'Neill sneaked credits onto *2000AD* stories and the industry was changed forever. Publishers' lack of shame for these restrictive practices is something to be marvelled at.

Long running serials for both boys' and girls' comics were generally dreamed up in three days, and seasoned writers boasted that they could write at least one or two episodes a day. A synopsis or outline was rare, and often a story idea would be accepted on the basis of a quick conversation with the editor. This is how a story I wrote for *Jinty*, *Girl in a Bubble* was commissioned. It featured a heroine who has no immunity to disease and lives inside a giant plastic bubble. She hasn't been told, by the sinister woman who looks after her, that she is actually well again. She's being held in a secure environment and used for experiments. Then one day a girl from the nearby council estate climbs over the wall and becomes her friend, encouraging her to leave the bubble. I worked the story out fully and showed Mavis Miller, the editor, my outline. She was alarmed. She thought at first I had submitted *Girl in a Bubble* as a text story, and was relieved and surprised that it was actually just a full synopsis.

So everything was about speed. Creators were forced to sacrifice their creative integrity to just "bang a story out". If it was a subject the writer was very familiar with and loved: football for example, it might just work. But invariably it would be rushed and shallow because it's simply not possible to create a story in that time without there being weaknesses. Research was a dirty word, regarded as unnecessary or even pretentious—we were writing *comics* for *kids*, after all—who cares about them? Are they really going to notice the difference? I can recall the managing editor, Jack Le Grand, looking suspiciously at me when I put in an expenses claim for science fact books to help me create stories for *2000AD*. I had no time for his passive aggression and all the time-wasting forms I had to fill in, so I just paid for them out of my own pocket. I believe John and I were the first to research backgrounds to our stories.

We did try the other option of making things up out of our heads and it never worked for us. Thus we were commissioned to write *Ann's Animal Sanctuary* for *Sandie*. We tried to "wing it" and realised, after an abortive attempt or two, that it was impossible to write about an animal sanctuary unless you have been to one or have files on the subject. In the pre-internet days I kept copious newspaper clippings for possible stories as well as scrapbooks full of exciting visual images that might feature in stories. I recall *2000AD* staff, still sadly imbued with old school thinking, sneering at the mountain of references and photocopies I would supply artists with. In their minds it was not necessary. They were totally wrong. The writer often has to act as director in my view. It's no good leaving it to editorial or the artist unless you are absolutely confident of their interpretation. For quality results, it's important to go that extra mile.

For the standard of stories I was after on *2000AD*—especially as they were high concept, but possibly for all comics—I estimate a writer should spend a total of four weeks thinking about his characters and plot, researching them, writing an outline, probably a revised outline, and then two drafts of episode one *before* scripting the entire serial. Plus maybe two weeks in total looking at character designs, altering the story to suit them, talking to the artist, sharing visions, and later editing the story against the art, so it fits like a glove. Similarly, an artist needs two weeks, maybe longer, to develop his interpretation and research visual aspects of the story and characters.

To spend six weeks developing a story was unheard of and it's still unusual today. The reason being that the creators are not paid for those six weeks. So the publisher is getting all that work for nothing. Due to the poor story fees, then and now (Rates have been fixed and most of us haven't had a pay rise in the last twenty years.) no one can afford to give a publisher six weeks of their time for free. Equally none of us want to piss a story off, the standard solution in British comics, before John and I, with our purist attitudes, came along.

So in creating *2000AD*, I found various ways of ensuring that every story had the equivalent of six weeks spent on it, one way or another, and that's why the comic is still around today. It's not rocket science. It's just hard work.

Here were my solutions and you will see how they informed some of your favourite stories:

* I spent ten days approximately writing first drafts of each *2000AD* story. As I was being paid on staff, I could afford to then write subsequent drafts until I was finally happy with them. And to then assess them against the artwork.

* By making the stories longer—six pages instead of the customary three—it meant the writers were paid twice as much.

* Sometimes the story plot, characters or designs would be supplied by editorial. Thus on *Judge Dredd: The Cursed Earth*, Kelvin Gosnell, the editor who followed in my footsteps, gave me the plot, based on the film *Damnation Alley*. He also provided the vehicle that Dredd uses to get through the radioactive hell.

* *The Cursed Earth* is also a good example of making up a story as you go along, another solution to the problem, although it would never be allowed today. I had no idea what was going to happen next. On this occasion, it worked and there is something to be said for a

flexible story rather than a tightly defined outline with no wiggle room.

* On *Ro-Busters*, Kevin O'Neill designed the spaceship and the various robots, going through two versions of Ro-Jaws and Hammerstein, so I didn't have to think about the hardware, just the characters. The artist's input could sometimes make a big difference, notably with Kevin and especially on *Nemesis*.

* *Judge Dredd*, as we shall see, had the equivalent of six weeks development time. Easily. But this was something John, as a freelance, could *not* afford to do. It would have been grossly unfair. Hence my level of involvement as developer.

* After his Dredd experience, I think John did take up to six weeks, perhaps, creating *Strontium Dog* with artist Carlos Ezquerra. So this time he and Carlos weren't beholden to, or overshadowed by developers. I know he spent a week coming up with the brilliant title. It's well worth it. But imagine if he'd asked IPC to pay him for that week for coming up with a fantastic title that has stood the passing of time? He should have been paid for his development time. It's utterly wrong that writers should ever have to subsidise publishers.

* One solution was to pay writers unofficially "through the back door", by paying them for an extra story that I might have written in my staff time. I did this whenever I could. And subsequent editors would undoubtedly have done the same. The problem with this one is it is open to abuse, but that's to be expected if publishers don't acknowledge the need for paid development time.

* Cross-pollination: using material from one story to help create another. So I spent at least six weeks dreaming up *Mekomania*, a robot history of the future, which proved abortive. But I'd spent so long researching and thinking about robots I was able to use some of the ideas in *ABC Warriors*, a robot "Meknificent Seven", and in *Metalzoic*, a story where humans are almost extinct and robots live a tribal existence in an electronic jungle. Similarly, significant aspects of *Flesh*, my story about dinosaurs, appear in *Judge Dredd: The Cursed Earth*.

* Formula stories. These were very successful in girls comics. Once you find the winning formula, you repeat it endlessly, so it doesn't take up too much time to come up with a new variant. On *2000AD*, my *Harlem Heroes* followed the formula I had created with Geoff Kemp with *Death Game 1999* on *Action*. I had told Geoff we had to devise our own version of *Rollerball*. Geoff came up with spinball, based on a giant pinball table. It was phenomenally popular and I devised aeroball, an aerial version with jetpacks for *Harlem Heroes*. I could pass the story over to Tom Tully who had written *Death Game*, knowing he would follow the same successful formula.

Arguably, *Shako*—my story about a man-eating polar bear— follows the same formula as *Hookjaw* in *Action* about a great white shark.

* Using the writer as typist for my stories. I'd tried this method when I created *Action*. I would outline the story, get a writer to add some ideas of his own and type it up. Then I would rewrite it. I briefly tried it on *2000AD*, notably on my first version of *Dan Dare*, but I wasn't happy with the results, so decided it would be quicker for me to write the story in its entirety, which I could eventually afford to do as I was personally well paid by the publisher, as I'll go on to explain.

* A later and more successful solution I employed was to write with a co-writer who might be an expert in his field, so no research time was necessary. The most prominent was Tony Skinner, of whom more anon. Other writers have used this approach successfully, too. Hence John Wagner's later long term writing partnership with Alan Grant.

* Occasionally, there would be a story that required minimal research, as I already knew the subject so well. Such a story is my *Greysuit* about a rogue secret agent, a variation on my original *Mach One*, the most popular *2000AD* story for some two months before *Judge Dredd* took off. Thus the opening sequence, where the Iranian secret police arrest kids for break-dancing half way up a mountain, is based on a scene I actually witnessed when I spent three months in

Iran. Similarly, the main plot—about incriminating photos of a paedophile Tory minister discovered in a safe deposit box by robbers during a bank heist—was told to me by the late John Hicklenton and actually happened. The robbers were so disgusted by the photos, they considered paying the minister "a visit", but they were too afraid of "the Greysuits". So they left the photos on the ground for the police to discover. In my fictional version, the British secret service send in a Greysuit (our equivalent of the American Men in the Black) to liquidate the robbers. It's a similar but separate event to the film *The Bank Job*, also based on real life events.

———

I don't think any of us, today, would closely imitate films like *Rollerball* or *Damnation Alley* in a way we did back then. We were on the right side of plagiarism but it's still not aesthetically or morally pleasing. It's why I don't take kindly to anyone copying my own stories as "homage". But sometimes it was the only way back then to produce comics at the required, sweatshop high speed. So we had *Mach One* looking like the *Six Million Dollar Man* and the computer in his head "inspired" by a character from a Marvel comic. Some of the cool hardware in *Flesh* was similarly "inspired" by vehicles in a Marvel comic and so on.

So there are solutions, but they're not easy, they're often not right, and—all too often—the writer can still take six unpaid weeks to produce a story, in which case he is bankrolling the publisher, which is outrageous. To give you an idea of their intransigence and stubborn short-sightedness, let me recount what happened on *Charley's War*, my anti-war saga for *Battle*, described by journalist Andrew Harrison as "the greatest British comic strip ever created."

On this occasion, I planned to continue *Charley* from World War One into World War Two. But I needed a research budget—e.g. that vital six-week development time again—to think long and hard about the story, to interview veterans and to sustain its anti-war quality. It was possible, but it would not be easy because so many aspects of World War Two have been censored to this day. A Suit, Gil Page, managing editor after Jack Le Grand, turned me down. I think he was glad to get rid of me. He had suggested I drop *Charley's War* years earlier when the story was at the height of its success.

I believe he was uncomfortable with its critical message. And it contrasted with the bland, meaningless, merchandising stories in the comic, even though those stories alienated readers and ultimately destroyed *Battle*. Making money from license fees was always more important. So my long running saga was given to another writer who, impressively, screwed it up in record time. From being the number one story, it bombed overnight. Despite Joe Colquhoun's continuing fantastic artwork, the readers hated the new, non-challenging storyline. So *Charley's War* came to an abrupt end. They gave Joe some of those one-off merchandising stories to end his career on, and he died at his drawing board.

When our partnership split up, I did say to Joe that I would love him to draw *Slaine*, and I could get him into *2000AD*, but he said he didn't think he had the imagination for a science fiction comic. But Joe had a subtle imagination that is all too often unrecognised or even cared about in male comics, although widely appreciated in female comics: he could imagine and create memorable characters without the shortcut of making them look like freaks. That is *supreme* imagination.

I wish I could say this was an odd, one-off event, but it's not. It is a typical example of British comic thinking and its negative effect on readers and creators that exists in one form or another right through to recent times.

But there was some hope even in this Victorian publishing nightmare. I say Victorian because DC Thomson's art studio was laid out like a Victorian counting house with its high desks contrasting with the ultra low wages paid to staff.

One man, and one man alone, has taken on the British comic system and won.

He was the late, great Leo Baxendale. As it states in Wikipedia, in the 1980s he fought a *seven-year* legal battle with DC Thomson for the rights to his *Beano* creations, which was eventually settled out of court. His earnings from that settlement allowed Baxendale to found the publishing house Reaper Books in the late '80s.

I recall that battle going on earlier and I know he had to sign an NDA, so he couldn't talk to us about it. But we knew it was going on and it inspired many of us.

We were kindred spirits. I once went on a signing tour with Leo, Alan Moore and Steve Bell promoting political comics (in my case *2000AD*'s spin-off *Crisis* and *Third World War*.) Leo told me that his first *Bash Street Kids* featured the kids stealing a tank and attacking a police station with it. Imagine putting that in a scene today.

Following Leo's example, I—and some other writers—challenged IPC and tried to get a better rights deal. For a brief period, after a long battle, I won. I was given copyright on a number of my *Ro-Busters* stories. Notably *Yesterday's Hero*, a *Defiant Ones* story where a war robot and a robophobic human soldier are forced to become friends; and *The Terra Meks*, based on *High Noon*, where one giant robot takes on an army of demolition robots bent on destroying his city.

The *Terra Meks* is regarded as an all-time favourite by readers, but there is no way I would have written it and sold all rights. Because I retained the copyright, it was worth my while to take my time developing the characters and the story. Sadly, the publisher then changed his mind and ended the copyright deal and a great opportunity was lost. Think of all the other *Terra Meks*-style stories I and other writers would have created had we been given a fair deal.

Once again, this is why the French system is superior to the British. French creators can afford to take their time creating their stories. We can't. It's why their books are so successful and why British adventure comics have almost disappeared, apart from *2000AD*. Other explanations—such as changing demographics and tastes and the rise of computer games—only play a minor role and are used as an excuse to justify doing nothing. But the real explanation for the decline in comic sales is the lack of rights which forced many of us to work elsewhere. In my case, France. For most of my peers, who don't share my dislike of superheroes, the United States. Plus a lack of affection by many writers, artists and editors for the mainstream tastes of younger or more middle of the road *2000AD* readers. Of which, more soon.

3. ALL FOR ONE

Jenny McDade, a key writer on *Tammy* and the writer of TV's *Super Gran* once described myself, John Wagner and Gerry Finley-Day as "The Three Musketeers" because the three of us always hung out together. Every lunchtime, we'd leave Fleetway House in Farringdon Street, head along Fleet Street and linger over long lunches in a restaurant in the Strand. (In the days when comic editors had expense accounts and regularly entertained creators as part of their emotional relationship with them.) There we discussed the state of British comics, which was dire. The awful policy of Hatch, Match and Despatch where a comic is created, matched to another and then merged into it to boost sales. The terrible stories such as *Paddy McGinty's Goat*, a kid who has an alien friend who disguises itself as a goat. The writer certainly didn't spend six weeks developing *that* script. And we planned the next stage of the Comic Revolution which Gerry had started. He began the revolution by creating *Tammy*, which was radically different to the staid girls' comics that had gone before.

And as boys' comics sank like a stone, we talked about how to save them by applying girls' comic thinking to them. Because, by 1975, boys' comics seemed about to die, and everyone believed it was inevitable. There was nothing anyone could do. That defeatist attitude was prevalent in British comics then and now. We aimed to prove them wrong.

Our "girls' comic" thinking and use of emotion would sometimes work well. For example, *Charley's War* is really a girls' comic story in terms of plotting, emotion and characterisation. But there are gender differences I would discover the hard way. Girls love stories involving jealousy: *Cinderella Spiteful*, for example, in *Tammy* was a mega-hit. *Green's Grudge War* by Gerry, about competitive male soldiers in *Action* didn't fly. Similarly, girls love mystery stories such as *School of No Escape* in *Sandie*, written by John and myself. They love discovering the secret of what's hidden in the locked room. Boys didn't give a shit, as we found out when John and I later wrote the mysterious *Terror Beyond the Bamboo Curtain* for *Battle*. Girls aren't interested in weapons, whereas we found boys love big guns, the bigger the better.

Whether we were "all for one and one for all" is open to question. Certainly Gerry was all for John and myself. He was very supportive of us. He encouraged me to move down to London. He introduced me to his mortgage broker so I could buy a property. He found me a freelance job on *Tammy* so I could develop my girls writing skills. I certainly needed a change of direction as I couldn't face more *Whoopee*, *Whizzer and Chips*, *Shiver and Shake* or *Cor!!* I've talked to cartoonist Steve Bell, who had an equally "joyous" experience working for them. He created *Doobie Doo the Back to Front Man* for *Whoopee*, which he didn't think really fitted the criteria of IPC's so-called "humour" department. I'm sure he was right. In the text novel *Serial Killer*, Kevin O'Neill and I describe just how soul-destroying it was working for the "humour" department, so I won't pursue it further here.

Gerry also facilitated John being made editor of *Tammy's* younger companion comic, *Sandie*. Later, when John had given up on comics and was caretaker of a house in the Highlands, Gerry and his wife

Linda, an editor of teenage girls magazines, made a special trip to see him and persuaded him to come back.

Even before I met Gerry, his reputation had preceded him. His eccentric ways, his rough and ready scripts, and his fierce arguments with management because he didn't toe the line, were the subject of much negative gossip. In other words, he was a creative. Suits can never relate to people like Gerry, John or myself. They understand creativity like a hospital manager understands surgery. And for them the rule of order is always more important. It may amuse you to know that Gerry told me he had a theory that the neater the script (in those pre-computer days) the more likely it was to be flat and boring. I looked at some pristine submissions and there was something in his theory. They were, indeed, deadly dull.

By comparison, Gerry's dog-eared, badly typed documents, full of crossings-out, and illegible scrawls were also full of life: *The Camp on Candy Island* (girls version of *The Prisoner*) and *Slaves of War Orphan Farm* (featuring the brutal Ma Thatcher who laid man traps to stop her young slaves escaping. It appeared before Steve Bell's *Maggie's Farm* but maybe the song inspired Gerry and his left wing co-author). Gerry also devised and got me to write *School for Snobs* (with John); *Aunt Aggie:* A cruel, phoney TV personality who pretended to be "salt of the earth" with "a heart of gold." Very Jimmy Savile and almost certainly inspired by him. And *Sugar Jones* for *Pink* magazine. An ageing *Absolutely Fabulous* TV star, a phoney in a pre-botox age, who thus has to rely on layers of make-up. Her cruel tricks and bitchy comments have something in common with Julia Davis in *Nighty Night,* although I could never hit her genius high notes. I remember female magazine staff on *Pink* objecting to an episode I wrote where Sugar appeared at Wimbledon wearing an outrageous "tennikini" which consisted of a bikini with strategically crossed tennis racquets. A true *Nighty Night*-style character. The series was often drawn by Ramon Sola, the star artist on *Flesh.* The guys at Rebellion, who now own the rights, tell me some of the art on *Sugar Jones* still looks pretty good. The story is written in that condensed three-page style that I did away with on *2000AD* by spreading the same story content over six pages. But if there are any fans of *Sugar Jones* out there who would like to see it collected, do let Rebellion know.

Thankfully, Gerry had sales: *Tammy* was a runaway success. If it wasn't, the Suits would have done for him. Later, on *2000AD*, his rough, "first draft" *Rogue Trooper* scripts and now "old school" approach would result in his departure. As someone said recently on Facebook, he wasn't cool enough for *2000AD*'s new "hip" image. But I and many "mainstream" readers are not convinced it was justified. To prove my point, in recent years, I revised one of his *Rogue Trooper* scripts and got Gerry back into the comic. I felt I owed him that. He was, after all the mentor of John and myself. It was well received by the readers, who were delighted to welcome him back. It wasn't that difficult for me to edit, so I think it could have been done, back in the day, and, if necessary, deduct the cost from Gerry's script payment. There's always a way to facilitate talent—unless you *want* to get rid of someone. The readers preferred Gerry's *Rogue* to subsequent versions; which is understandable; he had served in the territorial army and he understood comradeship, a key element in the story with Rogue assisted by the chips of his dead comrades. And they were *his* characters.

In any event, Gerry was entitled to rather more respect than he received. For example, I observed, when Gerry and I visited the *2000AD* offices during the Dark Ages, that he was totally ignored. Like he was invisible in the office. Like his many great contributions to *2000AD* didn't matter. Shameful.

Thanks to Gerry's behind the scene efforts, John and I were commissioned to produce *Battle*, the first of the new wave boys' comics. John and I created *D. Day Dawson*, which Gerry wrote and made the number one story for several years. Today, fans would probably despise it, but ordinary readers loved it at the time and they are the difference between success and failure in publishing. He also created *Rat Pack* with Carlos Ezquerra and *Bootneck Boy*, a precursor to *Charley's War*.

His military background served him in good stead, especially when he wrote *Hellman of Hammer Force* for me when I created *Action*: the story of a good German soldier in World War Two. It also helped to make a success of *Rogue Trooper*, *VCs*, *Harry on High Rock* and *Fiends of the Eastern Front*.

So Gerry is a crucial figure in the secret history of *2000AD* and I don't like to see his contribution minimised or even whitened out of the picture. Thus I've been less than happy in later years to see his role on *Rogue Trooper* being chipped away; for example, when his name and others, including myself, were missing from the Fleetway film and TV presentation packs, intended to create interest for *2000AD* in Hollywood. Steve MacManus, then the editorial supremo, told Gerry and I that he "forgot" to include credits. You can probably guess my response, so we won't linger on it.

The other key figure is John Sanders, the publisher and remarkable character who gave me a free hand to turn British comics upside down. After John Wagner and I produced *Battle*, he tried to make me Managing Editor of Boys' Comics. ("Do you possess a tie, Patrick? And a suit might be a good idea, too.") But the Board of Directors didn't like my views and ideas for the Comic Revolution. They wanted a Suit, so they turned me down. Instead John commissioned me to produce *Action*.

John Sanders and I endlessly argued, mainly about copyright and a proper deal for creators, but I have huge respect and even affection for him, because he had style, he had passion and a dark sense of humour, he was a character, not some humourless Suit and that made him a pleasure to work for. Sometimes.

He also came up with some great ideas: *Day of the Eagle* for *Battle*, about a British assassin sent to kill Hitler. (The Suits were concerned that it would set kids a bad example.) He actually painted some red blood on *Hook Jaw's* teeth and encouraged our excesses. He had to take it when a pre-disgrace Frank Bough ripped up a copy of *Action* in front of him on Nationwide. He came up with the title *2000AD*, because he said this was a future the readers would be living in. And he wanted me to do the story of a Russian Invasion of Britain, tempting me by saying that Prime Minister Thatcher could feature in it, shot on the steps of St Paul's Cathedral.

I had six weeks to produce the stories for *Action* and not much more to produce the final product. The tone was everything and the readers responded positively to my "comic of the streets." The tone was spot-on, apart from *Coffin Sub*. The premise had potential but the writer and artist were middle of the road and the readers turned on the story savagely, in a way I've never forgotten. My editor designate, Geoff Kemp, was very talented and I felt I needed to move over to give him space. But then he left and John Smith, previously the managing editor of the nursery group, took over. He made determined efforts to adjust to the new thinking. Too determined, in fact.

I was a bit shell-shocked by the fall-out over *Action*. I had passed control over to an editor far too soon. I hadn't commented on some of the changes even though they were not to my liking. They wouldn't have thanked me if I had. And they rather enjoyed the fact that my face went white when I saw the cover that got *Action* banned. They were too "tough", even for me. Nevertheless, *Action* was my baby and I made a mental note that I wouldn't make the same mistake again. And if I saw my creations being screwed up, it would be incumbent on me to speak out whether they liked it or not, (generally *not*) a policy that I continue to this day.

Kelvin Gosnell from the IPC competitions department had tipped off myself and John Sanders that science fiction was going to be the next big thing, with *Star Wars* just over the horizon. John Sanders gave me the green light to create a science fiction comic and that was my cue to exit *Action*. A few months later it was banned.

In my view *Action* should still be around today. It was potentially much stronger than *2000AD* with an overlapping, but still separate, readership. Some of the stories in *2000AD*'s *Crisis*, that would appear over a decade later, like my *Third World War*, *Skin* and *Troubled Souls* bear this out (*Skin* was commissioned by *Crisis* but the printers refused to print it and it was eventually published by Tundra). They're close cousins to *Action*. It was a tragedy it went under and many readers were upset by its loss.

But I realised there was a way to avoid all this censorship and aggravation by retreating into the escapist world of science fiction.

4. THE MAN IN THE HIGH TOWER

IPC Magazines had now moved to King's Reach Tower and I spent many long months alone on the semi-deserted top 30th floor, writing the first episodes of the science fiction comic. Here's a run-down, in approximate chronological order:

SHAKO

A polar bear swallows a top secret deadly capsule and is pursued by the CIA who want it back. My thinking was to create another *Hook Jaw* and I spent some time researching polar bears and decided they had the necessary savagery and visual power.

HARLEM HEROES

I was keen to repeat the success of *Action's Death Game 1999*. So I devised aeroball with players hurtling through the air on jet packs, desperately trying to avoid the lethal spikes around the goals and, inevitably, being impaled on them.

DEATH BUG

This was a disaster story about insects who set people alight. It has to be seen in the context of the times. Disaster movies were huge, but I knew it was no good doing a repeat of the *Towering Inferno* or the *Poseidon Adventure*. Comics can't compete with such spectacle. *Death Bug* was more intimate, designed to make your skin scrawl. I ditched the story later when I didn't like the artwork, but I still believe there is something in a disaster movie story if I could just get the right angle.

DAN DARE

I got John Sander's okay to bring *Dan Dare* back and I spent long periods of time going through the back issues of *Eagle* and discussing a suitable approach with my proposed *Dan Dare* writer Ken Armstrong (creator of *Hook Jaw*) who also designed an excellent NASA style spaceship. My initial thinking was to apply the same realism as in the original series, but not to attempt continuity with it. Ken wrote one version, which I then rewrote, adding a scary sequence when a space suit is punctured in a vacuum. I felt we needed the publicity of bringing back *Dan Dare* to help our launch and we undoubtedly benefited from it.

VISIBLE MAN

Originally, I was looking for a Spock-style companion for *Dan Dare* and I considered a man whose entire inner organs were visible. Then I thought it had enough potential to have its own series. (So Dan was later given Mr Monday, a Martian, as his companion.) John Wagner later added a great line to the story when a scientist looks at Frank, the Visible Man. "You're so ugly, Frank, only a mother could love you. From now on, I want you to think of me as mum."

PLANET OF THE DAMNED

I was interested in the Bermuda Triangle, so I used it as a gateway to an alternative Earth with a barbarian hero. I wasn't that keen on the artwork and the story later appeared in *Starlord*.

MACH ONE (Originally called *Probe*.)

My premise was to have an ultra-violent *Six Million Dollar Man*, because I knew that's what our readers wanted and I didn't give a damn what *Heavy Metal* fans wanted, despite their constant lectures on where I was going wrong with my new sf comic. If *Mach One* sounds rather superficial today, it's worth stressing that it was the number one story in *2000AD* for the crucial first two months. We owe *2000AD*'s initial success to *Mach One*. It was also a perfect example of why stories need a development time of six weeks because it went through several drafts and modifications. The stories I produced were strong enough in themselves, but they were a killer to write, because they required a great deal of research and thought. I had the time and I also like writing secret agent stories, but it's a high maintenance story and it was uneconomic for subsequent writers to produce similar stories, so it eventually lost popularity. It's why you'll see very few "present day" sf stories in *2000AD*. They require far too much research and a taste for authentic hardware and realistic scenarios. It's easier to write stories in a galaxy far, far away. But, at that time, readers definitely preferred *realism*. They were hostile to anything "stupid" to quote a kid's comments from a later market research report. I suspect we lost some of those readers as *2000AD* became more fantasy orientated. Or "stupid", if you prefer. Such readers even thought *Charley's War* was "stupid" because it featured a dog wearing a gas mask, which they said was "totally stupid and unbelievable". Not only did dogs wear gas masks but horses did, too.

But the character needed sexing up. John Wagner had read Marvel's *Deathlok the Demolisher*, about a manic cyborg, a series we were both fans of, and suggested giving the secret agent a similar dictatorial computer, wired into his brain. That was an excellent addition. And IPC juveniles art supremo, Doug Church, whose lair was also on the top floor, suggested the story was called *Mach One*. A much better title than my own.

JUDGE DREAD

This was the original *Judge Dredd*: Britain's last Hanging Judge. I had taken the name from a popular reggae band at the time. The hero was a kind of occult Doctor Who, with the visual image of Peter Cushing or Christopher Lee. This Judge, famous for being Britain's last "Hanging Judge", before capital punishment was abolished, had sentenced to death many of Britain's most notorious and vicious murderers. I wrote a first episode where the Judge and his companions pursue a group of black magicians who are holding a sabbat at Stonehenge. It ended with a sensational revelation: Judge Dread discloses he last met the leader of the Satanists when he stood before him in the dock at the Old Bailey; and sentenced him to be hung from the neck until dead!

I wanted to tap into the sub-genre, which includes Dennis Wheatley black magic thrillers, *Quatermass*, *Doctor Who*, *Sherlock Holmes*, Hammer Films and many more. I didn't commission artwork for it (a version that appears later in an annual did not involve me) because John had discussed the script with me and said he thought the occult angle should be dropped from the sf comic. Foolishly, I agreed with him. Normally, I stick to my guns and maintain my own very strong and purist views, but I must have had an off day, a moment of tiredness or weakness, because I went along with his recommendation.

Looking back, there's clearly huge potential in this much-loved, British sf/horror/occult sub-genre and—if I'd spent the mandatory six weeks developing it like my other stories—I think something pretty special would have emerged.

I tried reviving my original *Judge Dread* for *2000AD* about ten years ago, giving it a new title. Set in an alternative 1960s Britain, with a kind of Hammer Horror feeling, the story I outlined showed all the men the Judge had sentenced to death returning as zombies, intent on vengeance! They were led by a manic and evil mod, straight out of *Quadrophenia*, who was the last person to be hanged in my alternative Britain. The rebellious mod sings The Who's *My Generation* as he's dragged to the execution chamber. Dread's own niece is driven away on a scooter by this leering, Sting-like zombie mod, whom the Judge had sent to the gallows for killing a rocker.

The current editor, Matt Smith, rejected it as being too nightmarish. Matt felt it needed more science fiction/fantasy to remove the story from the horror reality I had presented. He suggested it was set in a fantasy nether-world which just killed the story stone-dead and, in any event, I'd already done something similar for *Doctor Who* audio plays with my *Dead London*.

As Matt admitted on my later development of *Visible Man*, also set in modern times, he saw such *Quatermass*-era stories as "old fashioned", even though there is clearly a market for this sub-genre amongst today's sf audience. John Wagner and Alan Grant explored aspects of it in their hilarious *Doomlord* for *Eagle*. However, I could see I was beating my head against a wall so I gave up. I think from these examples and his recent shutting down of *Greysuit* he's just not into science fiction set in the modern world. So if there's something amiss, it's dead in the water, rather than overcome. Or banished into fantasy.

I agree it is more difficult and more time-consuming to get this sub-genre right. You can do anything on an alien world, or with futuristic characters, and the rules of drama can be and are often broken, but realistic sf in 2017 is more restricting, it needs cool but conventional writing and cool but realistic art and the right support to really appeal to the readers. Not easy. But I believe we have to try. Yes, Alan Moore's excellent *Skizz*, set in Birmingham, was not as popular as his fantasy series *Halo Jones*, but we must keep experimenting and encouraging new directions in sf, and, sooner or later, such a story will click. In the meantime, it was a waste of a potentially excellent series and a considerable waste of my unpaid time.

So, back in the day, when John said to me that as *Judge Dread*, my Hanging Judge, was dead, could he have the title for his planned future cop story, I shrugged and said, "Sure. Why not?"

FLESH

By now, having the luxury of time, I was able to reflect on the way the comic was developing and I realised that *Shako* didn't have what it took to be a number one story. The science fiction element in the comic was growing ever stronger and I felt a polar bear wasn't in the same top league of monsters as *Hook Jaw*. Instead, I decided to go for dinosaurs.

John was very fond of *Shako* and I was happy for him to take over scripting it from episode two. I had introduced a character called Falmouth characterised by having a really foul mouth and I still chuckle as I remember some of John's dialogue in episode two when

Falmouth sees *Shako*. "Christ on a bike! Look at the size of that fucking bear!" Obviously deleted from the final cut. But we would regularly write in our own variants for our own amusement.

I knew I didn't want my monster story to be like any dinosaur saga that had gone before. It needed to involve time travel, but why would men travel back to the Cretaceous? "Maybe to *eat* the dinosaurs?" John suggested. That set me thinking and resulted in the high concept world of *Flesh*. I provided references for all the vehicles and figured out what the Fleshdozers looked like. They were based on the cover of Harry Harrison's *War with the Robots*, illustrated by Angus McKie. Angus is a fantastic artist, who did an excellent strip in *Heavy Metal* at that time and produced a later sf cover that inspired my character Charlie in the *Terra Meks*.

It took forever to work out the world of *Flesh* and the characters. And to come up with the title. I agonised over calling it *Flesh* for some time before deciding it was right.

I'll come onto John's *Judge Dredd* in a future chapter, but there's an important note to add here about titles. By now, I was aware that the most popular stories always had the hero's name in the title. I was beginning to realise it should be the rule but decided to break it with *Flesh*. It is well regarded as a title to this day and I am personally very fond of. However, it means that the story is unlikely to ever be a number one story. *Flesh* was very popular, but never top of the polls, unlike *Mach One*. But if I'd called it "Gorehead" or "T Rex" (after the hag tyrannosaur Old One Eye) or "Claw Carver", it could well have been even more successful. Hence *King Kong, Godzilla* and so forth. This is a rule indicated by studying reader feedback and—to this day—we simply do not pay enough attention to it. It's why Matt Smith quite rightly said, when we brought back *Invasion!*, that it should be called *Savage*. It's a rule I've talked about before and I don't know why it's ignored, especially as it was learnt the hard way.

If you want a story to be as successful as *Batman, Spiderman, Superman, Judge Dredd* or *Strontium Dog*, get the hero's name in the title. If you want a cult success, rated at conventions, but not with a wide audience of regular readers then by all means don't take any notice of what I'm saying.

The logic behind this rule is that it *forces* the writer to concentrate on his main character, not on his clever concept, as I did on *Flesh*. If I'd named the story after the protagonist I'd have rewritten the first two or three episodes of *Flesh* so he—or she—was introduced much earlier.

We come back to that six-week development time rule again. I'm afraid readers love characters and heroes more than they do our ingenious ideas. It's annoying, but true, and, unfortunately, it's an inflexible rule. I know this rule doesn't apply to Arthur C. Clarke, Olaf Stapledon and many other sf novelists, who write about situations first and people second, but we're talking comics here, not books or films. It's why I read and ditched such sf novels quite early on in my research to produce *2000AD* because I could sense they were leading me in the wrong direction.

5. "OH, BRAD ... "

I was now focusing on the art look of the comic and I wasn't very happy with the results that were coming in. I didn't like Trigo's *Harlem Heroes*, apart from the final page, featuring a player as just a brain, so we used that later. I wasn't impressed by *Dan Dare* art—it was slick: cool even, the kind of things "aficionados" might like, but not kids. The characters were weak and I just found it boring. *Mach One* was okay, but lacked "something". *Shako* seemed fine, but didn't have the thrill power I was after.

I had made the stories six pages each, so the visuals could have more impact, but I wasn't getting results. This was partly because the artists were Argentinian so I couldn't explain what I was after. There were cultural differences, but I'm sure they could have been overcome because they were master draughtsmen. But traditional British sf artists wouldn't touch us with a barge pole. We were seen as far too scummy.

For a while, I thought being printed on high quality web-offset or even glossy paper was possible. I was assured by John Sanders' co-publisher, Johnny Johnson, that it was no problem. It would have made all the difference; I could go down the *TV21/Eagle* road. It would take the pressure off the scripts and the art, because both would look so much better on glossy paper. I was delighted! But I'd crossed an invisible demarcation line and was severely tongue-lashed by John Sanders for interfering in the printing process. My sf comic was to be printed on the cheapest, humblest bog paper. Get used to it!

While I was on *Action*, I had very occasionally used the services of Doug Church, the art supremo. No one really knew what his real job or official title was, he just sort of floated around the juveniles "doing a bit of this and a bit of that". He made a real difference when he laid out title pages of *Action* and I started to involve him, semi-officially in my sf comic. Before I knew it he was laying out every page, every picture, indicating with stick figures what the artists should draw and where the visual emphasis should be. And also telling me why artists shouldn't use pens, only brushes, and other pearls of wisdom, most of which he was right about. He was also very knowledgeable about science and full of creative ideas.

Doug didn't like my first version of *Flesh*, he felt my opening was wrong visually, so I went away and rewrote it. I had no problem accepting his criticism because the guy clearly had talent. Doug's subsequent layout was great. And the artist—Boix—needed it. Even the later *Flesh* artist—the genius Ramon Sola—benefited from Doug's dynamic layouts. Most of that first *Flesh* serial was designed by Doug.

Doug was also responsible for the entire *2000AD* look, designing that brilliant first logo (easily superior to all the conservative logos that followed), and composing the promotional adverts, and his importance to the comic cannot be stressed enough. He's barely known today, because he was "old school", but he was actually cooler, and more imaginative and talented than so many who followed in his footsteps. This might well explain changes of logo, etc, as subsequent staff wanted to put their own mark on the comic, rather than Doug's.

We tried to get Doug on the *Future Shock!* documentary about *2000AD* and nearly, *nearly* succeeded. Maybe next time. He's a smashing guy and if anyone wants to know what he's like, I based Smith 70, the machine gunner in *Charley's War*, on Doug. He chattered faster than Smith '70's machine gun and drove everyone crazy, which endeared him to me, as I talked fast and drove everyone crazy as well. You can see my obvious and great affection for Doug by the way Smith 70 is portrayed.

Specifically, Doug came up with:

- The idea of Mega-City One. To escape controversy, the publisher had suggested I change *Dredd's* world from New York to a galaxy far, far away. I didn't like that at all, so I insisted it had to be New York. But when Doug saw Carlos's first amazing image of the city, he said New York was too limited ('No. No. No, Pat. That's no good. That's no good.") and suggested a Mega City stretching down the whole of the Eastern seaboard. I thought it was a brilliant idea, and I went for it.

- *Mach One*. Doug came up with the title of the original number one story in *2000AD*. He also designed the slow-mo special effects on *Mach One*, which none of the artists could have created on their own. They're sensational. When has anyone attempted anything that brilliant since? But if we'd hung onto Doug he would have come up with more incredible visuals.

- Layouts. He designed the early issues of the comic, so the work of traditional artists suddenly looked cool. He made the pages look dynamic in a very different (and far superior) way to Marvel and DC, with a focal image on each page. He was a great visualizer. Compare the first six progs designed mainly by Doug with the six progs that followed, and you'll see what I mean. Doug was literally sketching every picture out for artists. This is probably why he's not remembered with great affection by some artists today, who maybe saw his work as intrusive, but it was absolutely the right thing to do. Often their work would otherwise have been somewhat flat and even dull. If I could have twisted

Doug's arm, I'd have got him to design many more stories.

Nearly every story was choreographed by Doug. He was like a film director, and I try with my own stories to imitate what he taught me, stressing to the artists certain visual approaches he used.

Those layouts on the first six to twelve issues are of great—even historic—significance and really should still be studied today by some artists and art editors, because there is much Doug could teach them.

John Wagner and I hired Doug specifically to visualise and layout the artwork on another (abortive) comic project. It featured graphic novel versions of famous stories. Specifically James Herbert's *The Rats*, drawn by a Spanish artist, possibly Ortiz, and Sven Hassel's *Legion of the Damned*, drawn by Carlos Ezquerra. Once again he did a brilliant job. If you know *The Rats*, Doug laid out that creepy house where the rats festered. He had previously designed the first amazing *Death Game 1999* cover on *Action*.

Doug was a great adviser on the comic. He was my Obi-Wan Kenobi. He suggested Jesus Blasco for *Invasion!* I had previously suggested another artist who Doug didn't rate. I'll try and capture Doug's speech pattern here, so you can get a sense of what he was like. I think there's a touch of David Jason in *Only Fools and Horses* in Doug:

"No, no, no, you don't want him. You don't want him. He's no good. He's rubbish! No! What you want, Pat, what you want, is someone like Jesus Blasco. Yes. Yes. Blasco! Steel Claw. Yes. Steel Claw. I'll see if I can get him. You see you need someone with a bit of class, Pat. A bit of class. Cos comics are a funny old business. A funny old business. You leave it to me, Pat. You leave it to me."

I still miss Doug and his endless energy. He was the only "developer" on *2000AD* I could never replace. Doug alone of my colleagues was indispensable. That said, we didn't agree on everything. Doug was keen on *2000AD*'s editor being a giant-brained kid:

"See he's got this giant brain, Pat? This giant brain. And he knows everything. He knows everything."
"You mean he's a bit like the fucking Mekon?"
"No. No. No. He's a kid, see? He's just a kid. But he's so intelligent, right? He knows all the secrets of the Universe."
"I'd just want to kill the little shit."

So, in conjunction with Kelvin Gosnell and assistant art editor Kevin O'Neill, I dreamed up Tharg as the alien editor, whom I later came to loathe. Primarily because of the Tharg stories, which I thought were empty rather than funny, and a mask to hide appalling editorial screw-ups, and rarely in an amusing way. *Private Eye's* Lord Gnome Tharg is not. But most readers today, regrettably, would disagree with me. To quote one of them who read an early draft of this book, "Tharg is cool when you're a kid, so piss off." Rather different to the early days, when I voiced my loathing at a convention and there was a huge round of reader applause. And many of those readers were kids. It even inspired a petition to get rid of the Mighty One, which obviously the Mighty One ignored. So I will move swiftly on.

Covers were crucial. Especially because we were to be printed on such crappy paper. My solution was to use Lichtenstein-style pop art images for the cover. Lichtenstein had taken from comics, so it seemed fair to go full circle and take from him. As Ken Parille says in *The Comics Journal*, April 24, 2017:

"For decades, comic-book fans have bristled at the mention of Roy Lichtenstein. They believe he should have given some credit—and a lot of cash—to the artists whose work he swiped. They resent the fact that our culture celebrates millionaire fine artists, yet ignores lowbrow draftsmen who laboured in assembly-line obscurity. Lichtenstein's defenders—his

fans—respond to attacks on the artist by invoking "all art is appropriation"".

Back then, I felt the same way as the fans. It was time to appropriate Roy.

Images inspired by his style would have given us a unique identity that would have suited bog paper. It would have provided a distinctive brand look on the newsstand at a time when there were rival comics. *Private Eye* stands out on the newsstands for this reason. It would have been cool, yet still appealed to kids, because of its graphic simplicity combined with Lichtenstein's famous emotional charge. And furthermore, at a time when I didn't have any great cover artists, it would have disguised them. Almost any artist could follow the Lichtenstein approach. In a similar way, Doug was often disguising some boring artists, faking mutton into lamb with his layouts.

In the pre-internet days, I'd based this cover idea on a luxurious coffee table book about Lichtenstein I'd seen in Colchester art college library. But when I went to borrow it to show Doug, I discovered it had been ... appropriated. So I had to explain Lichtenstein to Doug who only half-understood what I was talking about. That's why the early covers have a touch of Lichtenstein, but only a touch. It wasn't the defining brand I was after.

So when I write the fictional equivalent of *2000AD* (*Space Warp*) in my *Read Em and Weep* series, I shall have the hero, Dave, appropriating that Lichtenstein book from a library.

6. THE KILLING MACHINE

My revival of *Dan Dare* led to meetings with Paul de Savary, who had the film rights to the character, and was interested in what I intended to do with the comic version. I had several meetings with Paul and his designer, previously *Space 1999*, who I recall didn't like Ken Armstrong's design because it had "too many bits sticking out from it" (the solar panels) and thus wouldn't make a good toy. This connection resulted in John Sanders approaching me with an interesting business offer. He suggested that I produce *2000AD* as an outside contractor, supplying IPC with the final finished product. In some unspecified way, Paul de Savary would be part of the equation, probably helping to finance it. Paul was definitely part of the equation. I think the interest for Paul was primarily *Dan Dare* and guiding its return to comics, although as time went on, I recall him also enthusing about my other stories

The outside contractor idea would have neatly bypassed all the problems John Sanders was having with the old editorial regime as they dug their heels in, refused to change, and waited for their retirement or redundancy as boys' comics slowly died. In addition to a fixed fee, it would have given me a percentage of the comic's profits, so naturally I agreed. But it was too big a task for me to handle alone; it would involve hiring an office and staff. Therefore, as a first step, I brought in John Wagner. I paid him to review the first drafts of my scripts and he agreed to create a future cop story for me as part of the package. The deal would have given us both some intellectual property rights over our stories.

With the prospect of a better and fairer future ahead of us, John and I enthusiastically talked about including his idea about a cop of the future. We were both impressed by a one-page black comedy, American underground strip called *Manning*, that appeared in *Comix: A History of Comic Books in America*, by Les Daniels. It featured a ruthless cop who shoots a fleeing criminal in the back. To quote from the strip:

"Some call it police brutality, he calls it justice."... "Crime in the streets ... people going wild ... somebody's gotta do something about it ... That's my job ... I'm a cop. My name is Manning, special agent attached to the bureau of nocturnal traffic. My job ... Justice. They say that this is a world of many colours or shades, that there is no black and white ... They're wrong. Just as sure as there is a good and evil I am good and if they get it from me they got it coming."

Does that sound like Dredd? John also liked a story in *Creepy 73* (1975*)* called *Purge!* by Bruce Bezaire and Jose Ortiz. In *Purge!* a futuristic cop hunts down and executes a suspect for a terrible crime, which we discover on the final page is reading a copy of *Creepy!*

We also rated science fiction movies like *Fahrenheit 451*, where cops burn books, *Logan's Run*, where cops shoot old people, *Death Race 2000*, where crazy drivers run over pedestrians in legalised death races, and *Rollerball,* where death is turned into a sport. John suggested, "What about a future New York cop who executes people for the smallest infraction of the law, such as dropping litter?"

It sounded brilliant. And if the idea of the death penalty for dropping litter seems unconvincing or ridiculous now, then consider the situation in modern Iran. That incident I mentioned earlier when I saw teenagers breakdancing halfway up a mountain outside Tehran.

The mountain is where everyone goes on their day off to relax, sightsee, and—if you're a teenager—secretly drink, fight, make love, or breakdance, all of which are illegal. They believed they would be safe from the law, but the secret police were also watching, and moved in to arrest them. *Dancing* is against the law there. The teenagers would probably have been beaten in jail or—if they behaved like rebellious kids the world over and fought back—a far worse fate awaited them.

Or consider the recent brilliant *Handmaid's Tale* TV series based on Margaret Atwood's novel, about an authoritarian America. It seems scarily plausible, particularly today, that democracy could be overthrown and biblical fascists take over. But the United States came close in the 1930s to being taken over by corporate fascists, were it not for the actions of Major General Smedley Butler. Thoroughly documented, the attempted *coup d'etat* is barely known or cared about today, which indicates just how Orwellian our society really is.

So this future cop worked for me. Of course, the tone had to be absolutely right. To resolve whether such a man should be a villain or a hero would take considerable thought and development. Traditionally, comics have characters the readers want to look up to. I was to encounter this problem again on another *2000AD* hero, *Finn*, as I will describe later, where some readers were concerned about his moral compass swivelling from the path of righteousness. He was not following the unwritten code of traditional heroes best symbolised by that arch-bore *Superman*. I have to be honest, I wanted to tell them to swivel.

I know we all look for role models in life, but movies and novels often don't have sympathetic protagonists, and I was moving away from tradition. There are various ways extreme characters can work with a readership. Manning actually comes over to me as funny, because it satirises the murderous cop and slyly mocks him and, ultimately, it is an underground strip. But we're in dangerous territory here. For a mainstream and young audience, a strip can be humorous, and it can mock the hero's world, but it can never mock the hero himself. That would be a serious mistake. As one Marvel comics editor said to me, "Laughing at their favourite comic book hero is like laughing at the reader's dick." But I knew John would be suitably respectful of the readers' genitalia.

I was reminded of this on a more recent *Dredd* story I wrote. I had Dredd saying, in exactly the same style as *Manning*, 'I get my fun polishing my gun." There were several angry letters from readers criticising this line because they felt it was taking the piss out of their hero. They were *not* amused, although I was, because I was drawing on my role model for Dredd, who I've always had in my mind when I'm scripting Dredd and how I imagined his private life. More on him later. And without dark comedy from time to time, there's a danger of appearing to glorify a fascist.

If you think that's not a danger, let me say there were readers who seemed to genuinely think my Torquemada in *Nemesis* was right to deal with the "alien problem". I was so incensed by this, I went out of my way to show him up as the prat he truly is. We may fear these guys, but we also need to mock them, to show they are human, that they are not all-powerful, they can be challenged and they *can* be destroyed.

But, to get over the humour problem, Mega-City is full of total loons, while Dredd himself is austere and righteous. On occasion a good guy (as in *The Cursed Earth*); on other occasions a bad guy.

And I'd seen, time and time again, how readers preferred extreme characters. To my surprise—and even alarm—a psycho with no feelings would regularly win out any day over a hero who had humanity or vulnerability. That was initially hard for me, as a girls comic writer, where powerful emotions are paramount, to comprehend. I became increasingly frustrated by the readers' preference for inhuman heroes. For example, a well-written and drawn story I commissioned for *Action*, *The Running Ma*n (Writer: Steve MacManus. Artist: Lalia.) had been poorly received. It featured a *Fugitive*-style hero with a proactive objective to find who had framed him, being chased across America by mad axe man, Crazy

Luigi. But the readers didn't like it, despite some revisionist memories to the contrary, because the hero was seen to be *running away*. I suddenly realised that if we'd made Crazy Luigi the hero it would have gone down a storm.

Dredd was clearly in the Luigi class but—most importantly—there was enough satire to stop the story being a humourless and gratuitous slugfest. John needed a title for his cop story and I gave him *Judge Dread*. Later, I would change it to *Judge Dredd* in case the reggae band complained.

My expectation at that time was that *Judge Dredd* should have *some* emotion and humour and it's worth lingering for a moment on these expectations and whether they were really valid or not. They would lead me later to introduce Maria, the Judge's Italian landlady. She would worry about him being wrapped up warm enough when he was out on those cold Mega-City streets. Similarly, John himself would later create Dredd's humorous companion, Walter the lisping wobot, who once bought "Judge Dwedd" a stick to beat Walter with, so that the Judge would not "hurt his hand on Walter's wuff metal skin."

I thought John's Walter was great—as someone for the Judge's emotionless persona to bounce off—and so did the readers at the time, as was confirmed by their letters and a sudden surge in the popularity of Dredd. Walter, a vending machine robot, was brilliantly designed by Kevin O'Neill and was so successful he even had his own one page strip, drawn by Brian Bolland. I recall a mum writing in to say how her young son was upset at the prospect of Walter going to the smelter and could he please be spared that awful fate?

But the late great *2000AD* artist, John Hicklenton, who drew a *Judge Dredd* serial of mine—*The Tenth Circle*—told me, "As a thirteen year old I was blown away by Dredd. I turned to my dad and said, 'I'm going to draw that one day.' But I didn't like Maria and Walter the wobot. I *just* wanted Dredd to be a killing machine. I imagined him sleeping in a cryotube."

John Hicklenton made a really important point that goes right to the heart of the debate over what is *Judge Dredd*, and many readers today will wholeheartedly agree with his verdict. This is the Dredd they preferred and I can understand why. As a teenager, I remember preferring a secret agent film that was just full-on violence and mayhem, with zero characterisation and minimal dialogue, in preference to the relative complexities of Bond. Others will disagree and point out Walter the Wobot is still remembered with great affection to this day. And so many of them value John's superb humorous stories like the *Oxygen Board* or the emotions in my Rico story, or the traditional heroism in my *Cursed Earth* saga. I think it was a dilemma for many years before Dredd as a killing machine finally won out. As it is John's hugely successful and established character, it is his call and it is absolutely right that he should take the character wherever he wants it to go.

But in the late summer of 1976, as editor of the new sf comic, I had a very different perspective. I read John's first draft and found, surprisingly, it did not have the science-fiction tone or the other elements I was expecting, although he did have a special science-fiction gun, inspired I think by Dick Tracy. Instead, Dredd was hunting and burning anonymous "communist subversives". There were no surprises and no executions for dropping litter, no satire as in *Manning* or the *Weird and Eerie* future cop. The tone was dead straight. Dredd was, literally, a killing machine.

I added a satirical element, described in the later chapter *Joe Dredd*, where I was drawing on my role model for the character and Dredd rescues and then executes a perp, but—for me—it still wasn't quite right.

The killing machine concept is fascinating from a recent perspective because this means his very first draft—John's primary vision of the character—is the closest to the second Dredd movie, which is also somewhat lacking in humour. It's far closer than the drafts that followed, or the Dredds that would appear in *2000AD* in the first few years. Watching the film, I was struck by this, and how the dialogue felt so like John's. The film is a vindication of John's approach and is very much his movie.

Whether a simple killing machine would have worked in the comic at the time is questionable. I personally doubt it, because it would have seemed out of place in *2000AD* as a whole, which had stronger elements of futurism, characterisation, humour and plot development. So I revised the first draft and introduced an element of satire, although I felt it still did not have enough edge for my taste. In retrospect, I think what I was really looking for was the black comedy that comes through in the *Terminator* movies. Arnie is a comparable and scary killing machine, but there is more humour. I'm sure James Cameron had a lot more time than John and I to get the character right.

John and I then wrote a third version together, which more closely resembled what he originally described to me. It featured a sequence where Dredd executes bank robbers, then a jaywalker steps off the pavement in his excitement to see "justice" done. So the Judge turns and executes him as well. That worked for me.

7. I AM THE LAW

We gave the script to artist Carlos Ezquerra and included a reference of David Carradine in *Death Race 2000* as the basis for Dredd. Carlos, born in Zaragoza, Spain, but living in Britain, had impressed John and I by his work on *Battle*, co-creating two impressive series, *Major Eazy* and *Rat Pack*. So I knew it was going to be good. But I was still not prepared for the fantastic images Carlos and his agent later brought into the office.

They were extraordinary! The lawman of the future I was staring at was unbelievable! I was blown away by them, and so was everyone else—including my middle-aged mother-in-law who said, "That character is going to be famous". It was obvious we had something really special here and it confirmed Carlos's status as a world-class comic creator.

This is Carlos' view of the success of his first visualisation:

"I drew him before the 1977 punk boom of black leather and chains [...] I have always believed that successive generations went to the opposite extreme of its predecessor. In this case I thought the peace-loving, flower-wearing hippies would be superseded by a spiteful, black anarchic generation. The Dredd generation."
(*The Making of Judge Dredd*, 1995)

I agree with this totally. And it's good to hear Carlos refute the punk connection. I get so tired of writers claiming *2000AD* grew out of the punk movement. Sorry, but that's wishful retro-thinking. It certainly featured punk artists like Mike McMahon, but it wasn't punk from the point of view of the *primary* creators. Although it's fair to say we definitely all had *very* punk attitudes even if we didn't have spiked hair. And Carlos has also said that the uniform was inspired by growing up in Franco's Spain. It quite clearly has a strong fascist/Nazi feeling as well.

This was my reaction as recalled by Doug Church, my art director:

"When Pat Mills first saw Ezquerra's sketches of this surly bloke sitting on a massive motor-cycle—he was orgasmic."
(*The Making of Judge Dredd*, 1995)

That sounds like me. Those first sketches of a tall, elegant, remote, *mysterious* Judge of the future on a Bike out of Hell have never—in my view—been matched by any of the subsequent Dredd artists. Indeed they have rarely been matched by Carlos himself. I think this was because he later felt it necessary to follow the powerful, but more "gritty", down to earth, street-cop versions of his successors, possibly because this was what John Wagner preferred.

As Carlos recalls, he had combined, *"a basic motor-bike helmet with a fifteenth century executioner's hood … I added elements from an ancient Greek Warrior's helmet to give Dredd's helmet that distinctly rounded full-face look."*
(*The Making of Judge Dredd*, 1995)

It's worth stressing at this point that there are great creators and great developers, but as the creator comes first, in my opinion, he— or she—is the one that truly matters. Without them, all you have is a blank piece of paper. So often in comics, it's the developer who gets the recognition and the praise and I think this has happened more than a little in Carlos's case. I'm pleased to see that's changing in recent times.

I still prefer everything about Carlos's original: the character, the bike and the city—which I'll discuss a little later—and in this, I feel I am somewhat in a minority, at least among my peers who rate the versions by Bolland, McMahon or Jock, possibly missing the point that none of these three artists—brilliant as they are—have ever, to my knowledge, designed human heroes with the same iconic status as Dredd. It's important to recognise this and thereby reinstate the importance of creators

I showed the designs to John Wagner who, to my dismay and disappointment, tossed them angrily to one side and said in his dour Dredd-like voice, "Fucking hell! He looks like a fucking Spanish pirate! I'm not writing him, he looks fucking stupid!"

I can totally understand why he felt this. After all, John was visualising a cop of the near future: Carlos's version was of a *very* distant science fiction future.

Ironically, Dredd's flamboyant, heavily padded, "busy" look, which John was referring to, whilst unusual in the 1970's, is now commonplace amongst riot police the world over. I once observed some riot police in Serbia preparing for a football match and their kneepads, shoulder pads and fabulous, futuristic boots were extremely "Baroque"—as John would put it—and actually put Dredd *in the shade*. So it was prophetic of Carlos to have anticipated all this. In 2017, cops the world over often look scarier than Dredd. The dark and sinister future of science fiction, I'm afraid, has arrived.

Dredd's look was something John would take some adjusting to, as is evidenced by the art changes he later required for his stories of the Judges on the Moon. He was clearly still uncomfortable with the futuristic design and was trying to find a way to modify it. Against art editor Kevin O'Neill's advice, he insisted on the Judges wearing cloaks and made other uniform changes. Then when he saw the cloaks, he was unhappy with them, and asked for them to be taken out again which would have been problematic, so Kevin refused. Actually, I quite like the cloaks myself. But then I'm a huge Bolland fan, too, and, for me, he can do no wrong.

All this passion and dissent is actually very healthy and is no criticism of any of us, because it shows how much we *cared* and how we wanted the very best for our comic and our readers. It is very different to sf author Michael Moorcock's view of *2000AD*. Apparently, he had worked in comics some years before I arrived on the scene and was therefore consulted by the media for his opinion. Having initially criticised us in *The Guardian* when *2000AD* first appeared, for my story about a Soviet-style invasion of Britain, he then went on to say in *The Sun* newspaper September 8 1978, nearly two years later, *"The men who used to produce comics were very creative and they really cared about what they gave the kids. Now they just do it with a supermarket mentality, like producing tins of beans."* It's a pity he didn't actually look carefully at comics at that time and reflect, before giving his opinion which often applied more to his era than mine. Not only were we passionate and caring about what we were doing but so, too, were the Comic Revolutionaries on *Battle, Tammy, Jinty,* and *Misty* as well as the people responsible for brilliant comics from D. C. Thomson's like *Jackie, Commando, Bunty* and *Warlord.* I think we all deserved a little better from Mr Moorcock.

This is John's generous recollection of his reaction to the Dredd designs:

"I was unhappy with them. I thought they were way over the top. I was looking for somebody with much cleaner lines. I saw Dredd more like smooth glistening metal rather than Carlos's baroque Judge. But he was obviously right—it's a look that has lasted. Carlos is a great character creator; he was right and I was wrong."
(*The Making of Judge Dredd,* 1995)

Yet interestingly, in the 2012 movie, the character *has* actually moved back to the streamlined look John was originally after. Dredd is now *much closer* to the *Death Race 2000* reference we sent Carlos. And, arguably, this is better from a movie point of view in that Dredd looks more convincing, more functional. *Robocop* also went for that clean, metallic look John describes and that was, of course, very influenced by Dredd.

Staying with the art, we now come to the city. I considered the background of one of Carlos's illustrations, which showed a tiny but curiously curved skyscraper, very different to anything I had seen before in science fiction. John and I had not paid any attention to the visual look of the city, which we imagined would be similar to today's architecture. This was not unusual in British and American comics, where backgrounds are rarely a priority. But I was becoming increasingly aware of their impact from studying old science fiction books and European comic art and I saw the potential immediately. Accordingly, I asked Carlos to draw a full-page poster based on this small image.

Carlos recalls:

"The first strip was set right in the middle of New York City, some years in the future—so I decided to make the buildings rounded and soar into the air, to house the many millions of people."
(*The Making of Judge Dredd*, 1995)

Here is Doug's recollection of me showing him Carlos's New York page:

"Pat was in raptures over it—but I thought it was a horrible piece of work, but he wanted to feature it as a full-page colour poster."
(*The Making of Judge Dredd*, 1995)

Here I have to disagree with Doug. It was *not* horrible and I am *still* in raptures over that poster.

With hindsight, I realise Carlos might have been influenced a little by Gaudí, whose architecture is equally wild. Or perhaps not. In any event, nothing takes away from the uniqueness of his vision, which is his alone. All I contributed to the city was encouraging Carlos to bring out its potential. I looked at that city for hours and hours and could still do so today. I do not believe any other artist's subsequent version of Mega-City has matched it. In fact, they have often detracted from it. The original city has almost skeletal, insectoid, *mile-high* buildings, rather than the broader, more plausible, and less interesting blocks of his successors. Inspired by this image, I planned a Dredd story where these "starscrapers" were so high, they ran out of air on the top floors.

There was a remote, sinister, *mysterious* quality to Carlos's metropolis. In my view, it has more originality and magic than even the beautiful cities in *Blade Runner* and *Fifth Element*. I do not recall going into comparable raptures when I saw those cities on the screen. Carlos's city also included CCTV police cameras, at a time in the 1970s when they were unknown. It was this poster image, with Dredd riding across the future landscape, which inspired me to write his triumphant catchphrase, "I am the Law."

The city was also important to me for two crucial reasons. Firstly, along with the other images Carlos had drawn, for the first time it suggested my comic might eventually break into the European market and/or appeal to those incredibly critical fans of *Metal Hurlant*, *Heavy Metal* and similar comics. Secondly, it gave the comic a classy, fantasy look, which it desperately needed to offset the very crude bog paper we were printed on. So we could legitimately call ourselves a science fiction comic at a time where everyone believed sf comics must have the glossy paper and full colour of *Eagle* or *TV21*. This poster was therefore crucial to my plans.

But, above all, these beautiful, mysterious starscrapers of Mega-City One showed a world where kids could dream about the world of tomorrow. There was an aesthetic quality to them, even an optimism about the future that I felt could inspire our readers.

That said, to this day, I don't feel any of us—writers or artists—

have ever really done justice to Carlos's sense of *mystery* in Mega City. That aspect has been simply ignored.

Interestingly, looking at the movie city in 2012, the deliberately drab, functional city block has won out over the starscrapers. And it works—especially the exciting scene in the film where the block goes into lock-down, which is brilliant. And if it works, and sells, that's what ultimately matters. But I still carry a torch for Carlos's original city and I dream of what might have been.

Certainly we lost some of our European appeal with the direction *Dredd* took and it's why, at least until recently, *Dredd* comics have not majored in Europe, except for some Bolland and McMahon classics. But clearly there is a market and an interest there for British work, as is shown by the huge popularity of *Slaine* and *ABC Warriors*. European comics are very inspiring. I was motivated to write *Nemesis* after reading Caza, Druillet and Lob's *Lone Sloane Delirious*. I'm sure Kevin O'Neill's Baroque view of Termight, the underground world in *Nemesis*, was also partly inspired by the Europeans. Although—in a typically Brit way—he has gone so much further and darker. And I based my overall vision of *2000AD* on European comics. But I feel that Kevin and I—and other great artists like Brendan McCarthy— were relatively alone in our love of European artists and our desire to be part of that artistic universe. For others, the move was always towards American art, but to the functional and basic imagery of superheroes rather than the beautiful art of Mike Kaluta, Bernie Wrightson and Barry Windsor-Smith.

Even though we lost something, perhaps we gained something at the same time: that very British celebration of the dark. Or maybe we just reinforced our unique, isolationist Brexit cultural identity. A friend of mine, Serbian film director and comics festival organiser Dejan Kraljacic sums this up well.

"Dredd is American. But in the right way. A very convincing future in which you can feel the stamp of the author. By comparison, American superheroes seem compromised. Dredd is more radical, more punk rock, more on the edge. But he's too alternative-tough for America and not

artistic enough for Europe. For our taste, the art is too realistic and too simple, compared to European styles, which have more backgrounds, more details, more mystery. Such as the art of Moebius which is very cool, very seducing. I really think Dredd is Great Britain; a reflection of Britain's unique identity, neither American or European."

Wise words. So now I had the story, the art, and all should have been well. Unfortunately not. In the space of a few short weeks, John, Carlos and myself would all resign for different reasons, and all of us insisted we would never, *ever* return. Now that is *very* British!

PART II

BE VIGILANT!

8. BETTER DREDD THAN DEAD

John Wagner soon had another reason for being unhappy about *Dredd*. John Sanders could not get his revolutionary plan for my sf comic to be produced by outside contractors past his board of directors. I know he did his level best but it was not to be. I never found out why.

Although I don't think I had endeared myself to the board a year earlier, when Sanders had put me forward as the new managing editor of the boys' comics, and his directors interviewed me for the job. They asked me what changes I would make if I got the job. I told them with great enthusiasm how I'd like to do away with merging two comics together in a bid to artificially boost sales: the wretched policy of "hatch, match and despatch", which was insulting to readers and I knew they absolutely hated. "Great news inside, readers – *Lion* is joining forces with *Valiant.*" I also talked about comics appearing on better quality paper and—most important of all—treating the readers with more respect, making the stories more sophisticated, more cool, more real. If I had the power of managing editor, I would also have sacked many of the old regime, and made a new start with the talent I knew was out there and had been suppressed. Unfortunately, I rather fear I revealed as much to the directors. Big mistake. It was not what they wanted to hear.

What they wanted, and eventually got, was a "yes man", a Suit, not a long-haired comic revolutionary, with a guillotine waiting for all those who were driving British comics into the ground. My fictional version of this scene appears in *Serial Killer*. I deny I turned up for that interview, as the fictional Greg does, wearing a velvet Austin Powers suit, with a frilly shirt open to the waist, although my suit was also, er ... a little off-beat.)

So, in the autumn of 1976, John Sanders sadly informed me I would have to go back to creating my sf comic as work for hire, and selling IPC all rights. The deal was off. I had no choice but to resign. At the time I was being paid a very basic sum. It was a lot of grief for a poor financial return. It involved commuting to London every day from Colchester, working long hours, numerous personality clashes, and missing out on my family life. I wanted to go back to freelancing, having fun and enjoying my kids growing up. So my mind was made up. Goodbye to all that. It was a pity, but I was very serious. Sanders was worried, because he knew there was no one else he could hand the project over to. They'd screw it up. And we both knew, by now, from the dummies and artwork produced, that this comic was potentially very special indeed. But there was a limit to how far I was prepared to work to breathe new life into IPC juveniles. And so I happily returned to my writing.

———

Two days later, John Sanders telephoned me at home. Realising there was no-one who could take over from me, except the old regime with their 100 per cent track record of endless failures, he offered to pay me £250 a week to continue to produce my science fiction comic. In 1976 this was serious money—about £1400 a week today—and I readily accepted. But it was on offer to me *alone*, because as John Sanders made clear: I was the *sole* creator. They could hardly afford to pay both of us that kind of money.

I felt pretty bad about it, but the private contractor deal was dead, whatever I decided. Aware also that, not just *Dredd*, but my other stories: *Flesh, Harlem Heroes, Mach One* etc., were really starting to take shape, and were *equally* special and shouldn't fall into the unloving hands of the old regime. If you think I'm being paranoid about the old regime, take a look at the censored version of *Action* when it returned after being banned. It was just awful. "Look what they done to my comic, Ma!" Readers still complain today about that shameful comic castration.

John Wagner was naturally bitterly disappointed when he heard the news and, understandably, decided to have nothing more to do with Dredd, as he makes clear in the following:

"We'd been promised to be allowed to do 2000AD as a contracting-out job (not in house) and would have more than a writer's interest in it - a profit motive. Pat [...] called me in to talk over lots of stories and we developed one or two of them. I had been involved for a few weeks, I'd done Dredd and put a lot of imagination and creativity into it - more than just the usual work for hire deal. But the IPC board turned it down [...] I was jarred off by it and thought to hell with it. I won't be writing for it anymore—I've had enough."
(*The making of Judge Dredd* 1995)

John and I never fell out over this. We were both sensible enough to know the target of our anger should not be each other or John Sanders, who was just as gutted as we were, but the system, in the shape of his antique board of directors. It was such a pity. John Sanders was a great visionary—he'd anticipated the idea of contracted-out creativity decades before it happened.

Losing John Wagner was a setback, but I was used to setbacks. It was just another one to overcome, and although I was sad on a personal level for John, it wasn't a problem creatively. This was because my vision of what I wanted from the comic was now crystal clear and I was not going to let anything get in the way of achieving it. Particularly on the money I was being paid, which I felt I had to justify.

And, in truth, by this stage, no one was indispensable with the notable and unique exception of my art director, Doug Church.

And now Carlos was unhappy, as well as John.

"I was very angry that I wasn't able to draw the first Dredd story ever published, having done so much to create the visual look of the character, the city and other elements. I had made up the character, so why not be allowed to draw the first one? I was very angry, which was maybe a bit childish, but I returned to Battle."
(*The Making of Dredd*, 1995)

Actually, he went to *Battle* first. I would have loved Carlos to have drawn the first episode, but by the time the first script was finalised, he had already gone. When he left, *Dredd* was not a "house character" open to other artists, so no other artist had appeared to copy Carlos's unique style. Everyone would have thought it impossible. If Carlos had been prepared to sustain a high weekly output, which he was easily capable of (as regular *2000AD* readers are well aware) it might never have happened. After all, there would have been no reason to look for other artists when I was completely crazy about *his* version. *Why* would I go elsewhere when I was, and still am, his biggest fan?

It's possible Carlos was unhappy at the prospect that other artists might *eventually* follow him, which was the normal policy on long running, number one stories. After all, it still happens today. But that was not the key reason he left. As with most things in life, it was about money.

He was unhappy with the money he was being paid. I remember him complaining about it vehemently, especially the money for the city design, although I paid him as much as I could within my budget limitations. Looking back, I wish I'd found a way to pay him more: he really deserved it. But I was stuck with a fixed page-rate for artists, and my accounts were carefully audited by the old regime, who were constantly finding fault with what I was doing. Perusing accounts was about all they were good for.

He was also unhappy with the comic itself, which I sensed he, and/or his agent, did not like and did not think would succeed. In this he was not alone—everyone in comics seemed to think so.

Carlos was unhappy with me personally, from the angry Spanish words he muttered under his breath to his agent, which a colleague translated for me later. We never actually sat down and talked it all through, and in retrospect we should have done, but it was impossible with his agent watching over him. My recollection is of Carlos standing alongside his agent, Barry Coker, and looking very fed-up as Barry translated his grievances.

I rather think something got lost in translation.

Financial security was important to Carlos and, even more so, to his agent and this was a risky new comic. I wonder if Barry, looking at it from a business point of view, confirmed his concerns and advised Carlos, directly or indirectly, against continuing with *Dredd*. That's certainly how it came over to me at the time and the odd Spanish words my colleague could understand. Agents are not known for their foresight or for their understanding of the—er—complexities of the industry. A leading comic agent at the time believed DC Comics of America were the same company as DC Thomson of Dundee!

Also, this is how agents work. Any creative will tell you agents always want their clients to avoid dangerous new projects and stick to "bread and butter" work. It was understandable: so many new comics had failed at that time. Why should my sf comic be any different? Ultimately, of course, Carlos was unhappy for the reason we were all unhappy: because he did not have control over the intellectual property rights to his character and in this he had—and still has—my sympathy.

My friendly rival on *Battle*, the excellent editor Dave Hunt, for whom I have the greatest respect, saw his opportunity. I say "excellent" because, after John Wagner and I created *Battle,* Dave took over from us and did a superb job. He patiently put up with John and I, endlessly breathing down his neck. Subsequently, we often competed in a friendly way for artists and ideas. I remember, a year before *2000AD*, I gave a passionate speech to John Sanders on why there should be a German hero for *Action*: *Hellmann of Hammer Force*, a daring, even controversial concept at the time. John was concerned there might be trouble from the British Legion. I argued that it was time Germans were seen as human beings, not "nazi schwein" or "sausage noshers" as in *Captain Hurricane*. I think John agreed in the end just to get me out of his office. When Dave heard about my breakthrough, he quickly gazumped me with *Fallmann* about a German paratrooper in *Battle*, who thus became the first German hero to appear in comics. Damn!

Now, in an adroit move, which still amuses me, he once again beat me to the draw and poached Carlos in the autumn of 1976. He offered Carlos the opportunity to create and exclusively draw *any* serial he wanted, if he would just come back to *Battle*. Believing, like everyone else, that *2000AD* would die, and wanting more creative control, Carlos went off to create an American Civil War serial, *El Mestizo*, for *Battle*.

This is Dave's perspective:

"Pat was in charge of all new comics and seconded Carlos from my Battle Picture Weekly to draw the preliminary Dredd sketches. Carlos was very happy working on Battle Picture Weekly with such characters as Major Eazy and the Rat Pack and, to be honest, I was a bit loath to see him go ... Luckily for me, he seemed quite happy working on Battle."
(*The Making of Dredd*, 1995)

So, as Dave makes clear here, this was the real reason Carlos left *Dredd*.

El Mestizo was a mixed-race hero who fought for neither North or South in the tradition of the Eastwood character in *The Good, the Bad and the Ugly*. The serial would later bomb. It was an interesting idea, but it was obvious to me why it would bomb because the scripts, by Alan Hebden, lacked real spaghetti-western stylish humour; the modern war elements needed playing up and the western element playing down for a World War Two comic. More grim trench war, as in *The Good, The Bad And The Ugly,* just might have persuaded the readers. However, it must also be recognised that cowboy stories are usually *hated* by comic readers in this country. Yep, I'm afraid so. And that goes for the brilliant Western series *Blueberry* by Giraud, too. They've never worked in the UK. "No cowboys, please, we're British." And when British readers hate a story or a genre, oh, boy, they really hate it! You have to brace yourself for the hate mail.

It's worth stressing this hate mail. It's one of the reasons we all got rather good at what we did, because we feared the readers' wrath! I recall on *Action,* I commissioned one story that turned out to be a turkey, compared with seven hit stories, and got my arse kicked for it. The abuse I received from readers on that turkey story, *Coffin Sub,* about a haunted submarine was unbelievable. Don't anyone try a comic strip version of *Das Boot!* You have been warned! But Westerns were—and I suspect still are—particularly high on the readers' hate list.

The concept of a hero fighting for neither side in a war also needs careful handling. El Mestizo's role seemed unclear and fuzzy. Mixed-race may have been a problem, too. Although it was extremely hard to prove, especially at the dawn of the politically correct era, I was aware of some reader resistance to my later black characters *because* they were black. Certainly the old regime warned me against using black characters because they told me the readers would object. Instead, they suggested I should have white heroes with black sidekicks. *Hi yo Tonto!*

There were problems with the art as well. *El Mestizo* didn't come over as a visual icon. He looked cool, but he was a little short and ordinary, IMHO. If I was in the editor's chair, I would have asked for him to be larger than life; *more* Jimmi Hendrix in his stature, posture and facial expression; more power; more oomph; more expression; more hip. Oh, yes, and less moustache.

If all that sounds incredibly picky, and even anal, let me tell you, this kind of post-mortem and in-depth analysis is what is required to make a comic hero *work*. There is so much at stake if you want to produce a top character.

And that analysis is what John and I were trying to do in our separate and sometimes competing ways on *Dredd*.

Unfortunately, Dave, if he agreed with this analysis, could hardly tell Carlos he'd got it wrong, having just lured him back with a creative freehand, away from that difficult bastard Mills he'd been working with on the sci-fi comic. Dave was an excellent editor, the best I have ever worked with, but he was a nice guy. Most editorial were, in fact, nice guys, but in comics nice guys don't finish first.

And this leads me to another important diversion, which explains the Comic Revolution. Staff editors are paid a modest salary and do a good job but there's only so much grief they need in their lives. They want to relax at the weekend and forget work and have a life. And that's absolutely right. In the immortal words of American editor Archie Goodwin: "Keep telling yourself every day: it's only a comic … It's only a comic …" By comparison, the publisher was paying me: an outsider; a freelancer, huge money and expecting huge results. John Sanders said I was being paid more than he was! And he was paying me *not* to be a nice guy: to *be* difficult, to rock the boat, to dissect stories and art, to agonise over them, to argue with creators, to endlessly reject scripts and art until it was right, to figure out exactly why stories worked or did not work, to change my mind, to change direction, and tell talented contributors things they did not want to hear, and to revive an industry that was dying, where many of the staff *wanted* it to die, so they could get their redundancy.

He was not paying me to be popular.

In other words I needed to be a complete monster. Which, in creative terms, is okay *if* you know what you are doing. I did.

Returning to *El Mestizo,* it was a bloody shame it didn't fly, because I would have liked to see historical stories, my first love, succeed in *Battle*. There are so many historical sagas I'd love to have written myself because I am crazy about the genre, as readers of *Charley's War* and *Slaine* will know. But it was not to be. It stiffed at the box office. And, as a history-buff, I'm sad it did.

However, the reason I have gone into such detail on *El Mestizo*, Dredd's rival, is this: If it had been popular, I have absolutely no doubt Carlos would never, *ever* have returned to *Judge Dredd* and *2000AD*.

There's a footnote I should add here. Carlos tells me he does not entirely agree with my version and I'm sure there are some details I may have got wrong. The good news is that Carlos lives fifteen minutes down the road from me from where my wife, Lisa, and I live in Spain, so we're intending to meet up soon. If it's anything important, I'm sure he will put me straight and I will amend it in the next version of this book. His English is now very good and Lisa speaks Spanish, so there's no risk of details being "lost in translation".

Anyhow, with no writer and no artist, I had to find both, or the Lawman of the Future would die. It would prove to be no easy task.

9. JUDGEMENT DAY

Carlos had a gritty, even grimy, style. It looked like he drew with a felt tip and yet it was aesthetically pleasing at the same time. It is a style I have always liked, although I think he has had a little resistance to it in Europe and the States.

I invited a number of comic artists to submit samples. I told them I wanted a modern, challenging look, which they sometimes took just a little *too* literally. I recall doing a double take when one artist, Bill Ward, a staff artist on IPC juveniles, submitted a leather-clad, camp, gay interpretation of *Dredd*. It was good, but a bit too YMCA, if you know what I mean. Another artist drew a wonderfully over the top, sadistic Nazi version of *Dredd* who was clutching a whip, rather than a lawgiver. This guy had serious talent, he was an important find, and I felt if he took out the whip he might have worked. Unfortunately, I took too long making up my mind about him—it was that *whip* that made me hesitate—and when I finally got back to him and asked him to do a one-off *Dredd*, he rather grumpily turned me down. He disappeared from comics so I don't recall his name, I'm afraid. A great loss, and my bad. And then along came the answer to an editor's prayers in the form of young Chelsea art school graduate Mike McMahon.

The surly punk look now associated with *Dredd*, the emphasis on the chains and the kneecaps, was developed by Mike and stemmed from his own surly punk persona, an ideal qualification for drawing Dredd. Attitude was never a problem on my new wave comics, as long as talent came with it, and Mike had plenty of both. In this, I should add, he was not alone. With the notable exception of the very easy-going and affable Dave Gibbons, some of the new generation of young artists had "interesting" attitudes towards either myself or *2000AD*, but as long as they produced great work, which they did, they could be as "interesting" as they liked.

Mike captured the Ezquerra *Dredd* style perfectly, though the elegant sharpness of his sample portfolio, that I infinitely preferred, quickly gave way to a less appealing, rougher, scruffier style, almost as rough as Gerry Finley-Day's scripts. He had the grit and the grime, all right. A little too much for my taste. But Mike's incredible ability to out-Ezquerra Ezquerra was astonishing and I am sure it dismayed Carlos, who must have believed his creation would go down the toilet without him. And he would have been right. Without Mike, *Judge Dredd* would have died. End of story. We owe Mike a lot.

However Mike's scruffy, semi-underground style didn't meet with John Sanders' approval. John rightly didn't want *2000AD* to be swamped by unclear, fuzzy art showing characters at dramatic, odd and occasionally incomprehensible angles, the polar opposite of what was known at our rival DC Thomson's as "front seat of the stalls" art. After all, our potential readers were middle of the road kids, not fans. But Mike's style was just, *just* on the right and healthier side of fandom, and was getting more reader-friendly all the time. So whenever John ordered us to dump him, his artwork would be hidden away for a while until John had calmed down and forgotten about Mike.

We had our character and our artist. The next objective was to get the script right. By now, the script I'd written showing Dredd executing a litterbug had been vetoed by the board of directors. *Action* was being heavily censored and we were getting the same treatment. It was clearly too violent. In an attempt to get the board off our backs, John Sanders suggested that I relocate Dredd to a galaxy far, far away, but I insisted Mega-City must be a futuristic New York.

I'd looked at a number of possible *Dredd* scripts from writers and bought a few, but none of them quite had the ingredients for the *first* episode which had to be *definitive*. With no sign of John Wagner relenting and returning to *2000AD*, I decided to write *Dredd* myself. The result was a story about the Judge recognising a face-changing perp by his unique voice-print and leaping off his robot bike to arrest him. It was drawn in a rather crude style by McMahon, which I wasn't that happy about; the script was okay; but it didn't have the *extra* element needed for a first episode. So I relegated it to episode two and continued hunting.

My final choice for episode one of *Dredd* came from a most unlikely source: an unpublished writer named Peter Harris, who had previously submitted a war serial to me and John when we were producing *Battle*. This rejoiced in the unsexy title of *Four Green Tank Men* and we didn't proceed with it. I talked about *Dredd* to Peter over the phone and sent him my briefing sheet with examples of script and art, never expecting anything worthwhile back from him. But now from Peter—to my astonishment—came an exciting and very un-*Green* story about a criminal gang of mutants hiding in a derelict Empire State building with a highway running through the middle of the upper stories. The defiant punk-like mutants murder a Judge whose corpse is sent back to Justice H.Q. chained to his bike. Dredd insists on going in alone to deal with them; to show the citizens of Mega-City that a Judge is never afraid. Inevitably he blows the mutants away and executes their leader, Whitey.

As this is a style of Dredd story that isn't always emulated today, let me say why I especially liked it. It had architecture with the Empire State Building, but showed there were starscrapers dwarfing it. It had a sense of *wonder* and futurism. It had *emotion*—the death of Dredd's buddies—and courage: Judge Dredd goes in alone to show the mutant scum that Judges are not afraid of them. Wow! I think that's as powerful today as it was back then. But he *couldn't* execute Whitey, alas, with the board breathing down my neck and I felt then —and still do—that a standard prison sentence is pretty boring if we're in an sf future.

My editor designate, Kelvin Gosnell, with his invaluable love of science fiction, came up with a different ending, suggested by a J.G. Ballard story. Instead of being executed, Whitey is sentenced to be marooned on Devil's Island, a massive traffic island, surrounded by high-speed motorways. Impossible to escape from, unless you wanted to be smeared by a juggernaut. I loved it and I still do. I'm told Whitey is no longer on that roundabout and was dealt with by John Wagner in a later story. What a shame. I like to think Whitey is still there, chewing the grass verge, begging for food from passing trucks, and fighting and eating other castaways.

But the most curious aspect of this story is the writer himself. Peter Harris disappeared and never surfaced again. I believe he was an accountant and wrote comics in his spare time. A Suit! That will teach me to show them more respect! I often wondered what happened to him and imagined what other incredible Dredd stories he might have come up with which—at this early stage—may well have eclipsed those written by John Wagner and myself.

Peter's story still holds up really well today, and confirmed the important elements for *Judge Dredd* scripts for other writers to follow: the justice system of multiple Judges; the science fantasy; and a proactive, ruthless, yet *human* hero, on this occasion avenging his dead fellow Judge. It was a key moment in Dredd's development.

In recent years, I heard that the *Future Shock!* director tracked Mrs Harris down and I learnt the sad news that Peter had passed. But his widow was thrilled to hear of her husband's success.

I've asked the *Future Shock!* director to pass on her details to Rebellion, as his estate may be due some royalties for that first Dredd episode.

Thank you, Peter, for your vital contribution to the Galaxy's Greatest Comic by developing the *Judge Dredd* world.

You, most of all, need to be remembered by us in this 40th birthday year.

Until this stage, the serial might still have gone in any number of other directions. For instance, with the easy luxury of hindsight, Kevin O'Neill, myself and others have sometimes wondered whether the series should have been about just *one* Judge for Mega-City: Judge Dredd.

Or at least more of a Justice elite, supported by regular cops. After all, Ezquerra's original illustrations and my third draft script itself make it very clear there were support *police* for the Judges. They're still around in later stories. And there is only *one Lone Ranger, Batman, Robocop, Zorro* and (Thank God) *Superman*. Also, a solo role for Judge Dredd might have been more in keeping with the science fiction *mystery* of Ezquerra's initial design, which our scripts *didn't* do full justice to. Perhaps none of us were sufficiently marinated in sf to take full advantage of that starscraper world. Imagine what Philip K. Dick would have done with them!

And on the subject of those starscrapers, it raises an interesting point in comics. The writer creator can respond to the artist's vision; or the artist can respond to the writer's vision. On most stories, I respond to the artist's vision. In John's case, the artist responds to his vision. It's a choice and it usually can't be both.

There are casualties either way. Thus, I've gained enormously from responding to Kevin O'Neill's vision on *Nemesis* and *Marshal Law* and letting his art inspire my stories. Ditto Clint Langley on *Slaine*, *ABC Warriors* and *American Reaper*. In fact I'm well known for this approach and it does bring out an artist's best work and makes it a truly collaborative process in which the artist is a true co-creator. But I can think of other occasions where I've let the artist set the pace, tone and direction and it's been a big mistake and cost me, big-time. So I can understand John's perspective that it's the *writer* who should be in the driving seat. It makes a lot of sense. Many other writers follow a similar policy to John.

Mike McMahon drew the first episode of *Judge Dredd*, which was excellent, apart from the first page showing the Empire State building. I'd been expecting something at least as enthralling as Ezquerra's Gaudi-esque fantasy city. But his city view, the first time the readers would see Mega-City, looked scruffy and depressing. So I asked Mike to draw it again. The second version was equally unimpressive and I think we reluctantly ended up with the first version, as there was not enough time for him to do a third version. Instead, the page was "sexed-up" in the office by Doug Church.

But in the context of the 2012 movie, perhaps Mike was right after all. The tower blocks featured there are equally dark, grim and depressing, like some future version of a hellish council estate. Maybe Mike was just too far ahead of his time.

And it also comes down to interpretation. Mike's vision is so much closer to John's Dredd-like pessimism than my optimism. Thus when Mike worked on *Slaine*, it was brilliant, but he saw a very realistic, downbeat and grim "mud hut" world, whereas I wanted the Celtic world to look how they *imagined* their land to be. A glorious fantasy world.

In any event, I'd run out of time, it was now Judgement Day. *2000AD* was about to be launched and the readers would decide whether I'd got it right or wrong.

10. MILLS AND BOOM!

Dredd was not the only problem strip. There had been last minute additions, changes and alarms. John Sanders had suggested *Invasion!*, which I scripted a couple of weeks before Judgement Day.

I had to turn down a seriously proposed idea by a senior IPC staff member for a science fiction gorilla version of Idi Amin as a villain in *2000AD*. This intelligent gorilla was the President of a fictional African republic and had to be executed by a British assassin. Idi Amin was always popular in comics: for instance in one memorable American comic strip, Idi's spirit is inside the body of a luscious, almost naked heroine roaming through the jungle (Esteban Maroto and Bill Dubay, *Idi and Me*, issue #4 of the *Warren* magazine, 1984) Bill Dubay simply wrote new Idi dialogue to a conventional Red Sonja-style story. And there was later an excellent evil space captain in *Strontium Dog*, based on Idi, but this was going too far. By comparison, the Russians—sorry, *Volgans*—invading Britain was a walk in the park.

And, awed by the Paul Da Savary film version of *Dan Dare*, I decided to write a more compelling story with my editor designate, Kelvin Gosnell. We focussed it on Jupiter's red spot with huge alien life forms living there, the Biogs, based on microscopic life I'd seen in the National Geographic. Story-wise I think its basic plot is in the

Dan Dare tradition. Despite the very different artwork, I followed the approach of the original Frank Hampson *Voyage to Venus* adventure in *Eagle*, which I really rate, with Dan descending—in a high gravity suit—into Jupiter's mysterious Red Spot. I wanted to feature a familiar planet in our solar system, where something very strange and alien is happening. I tried out various artists—I believe two Italian brothers—but their version still looked dull to me.

Then, Italian artist Belardinelli submitted a wild version on spec. At least it was exciting and eye-catching and—most important— helped us over the poor quality paper. His black line was the best in the business. I knew his work from the past on *Battle* and *Action* and there his figure work was not bad. But on *Dare* his weak anatomy started to show. This would get worse throughout his subsequent career (on *Slaine* etc) possibly because of his origins as an excellent inker, not a penciller. I tried to ignore it because I like his work so much. So did most readers. Fans didn't.

His basic character design was also wrong—an over-reaction against the old Dan images and a misinterpretation, or even a mistranslation, of my character notes to him. We really should have designed *Dan* for him, but we had run out of time. Kevin O'Neill my art editor pointed the flaws out to me. I think he was quite dismayed by them. I completely saw Kevin's point, and I arranged a quick straw poll to see what everyone else on the comics floor thought: some thirty or more people. They (I was told by my pollster) liked it, apart from Jack Le Grand who thought it was a bit "fantasmagoric". It's a good example of where a purist view is valid, but—at the end of the day—we have to accommodate the ordinary reader, the kid in the street, who ultimately matters more, because they are the ones who keep us in business.

This was a theme in *2000AD's* history which was going to endlessly haunt us and came close to destroying us, when later editors put fans first and ordinary readers *third*. It's something hard-core fans fail to appreciate, or don't care about, even to this day. It reminds me of the French maxim about arthouse films: "The smaller the audience, the better the film." They're entitled to their view, but we dare not let it influence us. In any event, it was just two weeks to press date, so I was stuck with Bellarinelli's version.

With all these intense situations going on, I was greatly helped by Kelvin. Amongst his many achievements on the comic were getting the hardware and the science right. This was incredibly important at the time. Before *2000AD*, many readers *hated* comic science fiction stories, calling them "stupid" and "unrealistic", with some justification. So Kelvin gave many of the stories technical details that would make them seem real and convincing. But, increasingly, we would discover that *2000AD* readers weren't as passionate about reality and conventional hardware as *Battle* and *Action* readers. That came as a surprise to us and so the comic moved towards science fantasy.

Kelvin and I wrote the final version of *Dan Dare* together and episode two of *Invasion!* "Laugh this off, Twinkletoes" is Kelvin's memorable line! He was also keen to bring the influence of science fiction novels into the comic. He was widely-read, and a big fan of Harry Harrison, perhaps the only sf writer who wrote the kind of heroes that would work in *2000AD*. Arthur C Clarke writes memorable scenarios like his *Rama* saga, but I couldn't tell you anything about his characters. As a result, Kelvin later commissioned the excellent *Stainless Steel Rat* adaptions drawn by Carlos Ezquerra. He then went on to create *Starlord* and *Tornado*.

I also wrote *Flesh* and many of the *Mach Ones*, with further important contributions by Kelvin and others, but I couldn't continue to write or rewrite everything in the entire comic.

Then *2000AD* hit the streets! Prog One was a smash hit and *Dan Dare* was popular —— about 3rd or 4th in the vote charts. Certainly not at the bottom in a comic where the readers liked *all* the stories. They can be very critical if there's a lame story and I always remembered negative letters. I don't recall any critical letters apart from things along the lines of "my dad doesn't like it, but I do". And sometimes, "my dad likes it, too." Lot of criticism in the press, however, but the papers were also criticising my "Volgan" invasion of Britain with *The Guardian* deciding that readers would dislike its political subtext. They were so wrong. I'm still writing this story today. A drama about a foreign power invading our homeland will always work.

I paginated the first issue, which needed lots of space for each story to give them the visual impact I wanted. So I held *Dredd* back for the second issue because I was confident that my first issue stories were strong enough to sell the comic and also because I wanted something to intrigue the readers and persuade them to buy the second issue. As one reader wrote in after looking at the advert for Dredd "coming next prog", "Who or *what* is Judge Dredd?"

In retrospect, I'm glad I did this for other reasons, too. Because it confirms that *2000AD* was a hit *without Dredd* and also sold well *before Dredd* became popular. It stops all those—then and now—who attempt to rewrite history, inflate *Dredd's* role and downgrade the importance of the other stories in those crucial early months.

During the first two critical months, during which the fate of a comic is irrevocably decided, *Dredd* was popular with the readers, but no more so than any other heroes. It had good weeks and bad weeks in the popularity polls, depending on who was writing and drawing it and—equally important—what the competition was like.

But *Mach One*—a *Six Million Dollar Man*-style secret agent—was always the number one character, as I had expected and planned for, and the publication owes its huge initial success primarily to him, with the other heroes, including *Dredd*, not too far behind.

The comic's phenomenal sales—selling out everywhere—confirmed we had our mix absolutely spot-on and its future looked bright. My plan to have a comic of *all* number one heroes was working. There were no *Coffin Subs* here. Neither was there one lead story with supporting stories, which I was against. If you wonder why, look no further than *Valiant*, which had *Captain Hurricane* plus supporting stories. It's not the way to do things and it encourages complacency—with the star story being favoured and often carrying the others, which are not given the TLC, the attention, and the priority they should have. It's taking the easy way out: unfortunately a very British trait, and does not give the readers value for money.

The free gifts went down well. There was the "Space Spinner" with prog one, although I'm not keen on that first cover—I don't know why I let Doug Church talk me into that one. I guess I was getting tired. And the Red Alert survival wallet with prog three (designed by Doug, myself and Kelvin) is still highly rated by readers to this day.

My plan to give away free "Brain Bags"—pulsating brain paper bags that the reader stuck over their heads—was vetoed as being in too much bad taste. I'd already clashed with Peter Lewis, the head of free gifts, and a handlebar-moustached, military cross winner, when I wanted to give away tin-foil German iron crosses on *Battle*. He threatened to resign if I got my way. I told him bikers would love them. He said, "We don't want to attract those kind of readers."

But my next idea, Biotronic Stickers, went down well in Prog Two. They made it look like the readers' flesh was cut away, revealing *Six Million Dollar Man* bionics inside. After our launch, when the readers tried to remove them, the stickers would, on occasion, remain adhered to their flesh. A mother wrote in to say her young Billy had started crying when she tore off his biotronic sticker. Naturally, my staff and I were most concerned.

It was a great time, with sacks full of enthusiastic reader mail, and I look back on it with huge affection.

I was heavily editing stories, so much so, and so bizarre, that John Sanders would show them to his colleagues as curios. The scripts would be written on, rewritten, then rewritten again, so you could barely read them through all the crossings-out, in a high-octane, anarchic work environment, totally at odds with the mausoleum-like comic offices surrounding us. Loud music, louder script discussions, even louder laughter, and bad taste comedy from *Derek and Clive* ("Cancer? ... Cancer.") was the order of the day and drew many complaints.

In this wonderfully juvenile environment there would be script-writing jam-sessions where I—and others—felt it was necessary to physically act out the stories. We played air lawgiver (*Judge Dredd*), air shotgun (Bill Savage in *Invasion!*, working out how he would kick down toilet doors), air death games (*Harlem Heroes*), and even air tyrannosaur (*Flesh*). Figuring out exactly how Dredd would leap from his bike onto a car; or how Mach One would punch through walls or ski an avalanche, required a lot of swearing, and exuberant action, to the dismay of our funereal peers next door on *Buster*. It was comic rock 'n' roll. Leo Baxendale, creator of the *Bash Street Kids*, recalls the creative atmosphere in the *Beano* being similar in his day.

John Wagner, seeing his character successfully up and running, thankfully came back to *Dredd*. It was a huge relief! He wrote a *Dredd* serial where the robots of Mega-City One rise up in rebellion, which proved his excellence as a writer. This achievement was even more impressive because it was drawn by multiple artists: some cool and some not so cool, but they were all that were available to me in the time. The rebellion was led by robot messiah "Call Me Kenneth" whom John dryly pointed out to me at the time was a carpenter by profession. Three months after *2000AD* had hit the newsstands, Dredd finally became its most popular character.

For me, the key moment in the robot revolution came when the menacing Heavy Metal Kids appeared. Beautifully designed by Kevin O'Neill, they were powerfully and humorously illustrated by Mike McMahon. It's that scene where they look at the readers and say, 'Hello, Fleshy Ones". I knew then we'd cracked it, especially when the board of directors, who were looking at every single issue after the *Action* debacle, expressed concern that the readers were being addressed as "Fleshy Ones".

It's a great story and perhaps there should be a remake, just as I wrote a remake of the Rico story to tie in with the first *Dredd* movie.

However, soon after I left *2000AD,* Judge began to drop in the popularity poll. This would be after the *Robot Rebellion*, but before Brian Bolland drew the *Dredd* on the Moon saga. This sheds some light on just how important Brian was to the development of the character. In order to hide the drop from the powers-that-be, the votes were rigged to make *Dredd* seem more popular than he actually was, to ensure he stayed in the comic. Especially as someone in authority thought it would be a good idea to "rest" the Judge for a while, even though I had designed all *2000AD* serials to be ongoing.

The voting system must seem rather curious and obsessive today, and some fans prefer to ignore the objective evidence they provided. Editors had the most elaborate graph charts, recording the success or failure of individual stories, and the episodes where they were especially popular or unpopular were noted and analysed. But it was surprisingly accurate, albeit biased towards action, which usually meant subtle episodes would not go down so well. The system worked until the split between younger mainstream readers, who still filled in the forms, and fans who didn't, made it difficult to interpret them correctly. Or rather for some fans to claim they were inaccurate because they didn't reflect their own purist preferences. I'm not convinced, and I think it's somewhat indicative of an unspoken disdain towards younger readers or mainstream readers. What do they know? They're only the majority of the readers. Today, the forums provide some feedback, but it's not a complete guide and ultimately it's now down to editorial judgement and preference.

11. EXIT WOUNDS

My plan was to stay with the comic until it was rock solid, so it couldn't be destroyed the way *Action* had been destroyed; see it through its first important twelve weeks; plan and edit—where possible—the stories for the following three months; ensure I had the right staff, and then move on. I'd already discussed my next creation in the Comics Revolution with John Sanders and he was keen for me to start. It was to be called *Misty,* (I took the title from the film *Play Misty For Me),* a girls' comic version of *2000AD*, with the emphasis on the supernatural, rather than sf.

But I was leaving *2000AD* and *Judge Dredd* alone in a toxic and hostile desert and expecting the comic to thrive. It would not be easy.

We're back to that sad British comic thinking that Dez Skinn, creator of *Warrior* magazine, who once worked on *Buster,* describes:

> *I was around 25 when I was told that no matter whether my ideas were any good, I could not become an editor until I turned 30. The thought of another 5 years as a sub-editor, regurgitating the same tired old 1950s formulae, coupled with my 1975 proposal of a horror weekly named CHILLER being turned into THE BUSTER BOOK OF SPOOKY STORIES was enough! I was out.*

When I told the editorial director, John Sanders, that I was resigning, he asked how long I'd been at IPC. "Five years," I replied.

To which he said, "I'm surprised you didn't leave years ago".

Here's a similar view that Annie Parkhouse related to me:

I started on Lion with Geoff Kemp as editor. Initially he was not happy to have a girl on his staff, but I felt we had a great working relationship. Then he was also editor on Jet and Thunder, where I was the only art staff.

When Jet and Thunder failed, [it was cynically just more of the same], I was sent to Valiant, which I hated. Geoff protested to no avail. It was like being at school. All joy was sucked out of the job.

I was only at IPC for 2 years before going freelance, but because I was young it seemed like ages. The resistance to change was why most of the young creatives left within about 6 months around 1972. I left in the October, Steve (Parkhouse) the following April.

Like the previous comics in the Comic Revolution (*Battle* and *Action*), *2000AD* was hated by the old regime. Thus when John Wagner and I created *Battle*, we were told it had to be top secret so they couldn't interfere and make trouble with the union. We worked on it in an office kept locked at all times and when other editors asked what we were doing, we said—in those politically incorrect times—we were working on a braille comic for the blind. When the managing editor, Jack Le Grand, eventually discovered what we were really up to, he saw it as a huge betrayal and cut me dead in the street.

The same attitude continued on *2000AD*. Then there was the tragically "lost" strip by Ken Reid. Long before *Monty Python*, there was the brilliant Ken Reid. His surreal cartoon strips, such as the original *Frankie Stein, Georgie's Germs, The Nervs, Jonah* and *Face Ache* are often Pythonesque, and sometimes even more insane, yet equally funny. Importantly, they show that dark comedy is not the sole property of the Cambridge Footlights, as some of its elite members like to think. Ken's working class humour, easily up to the standard of Python, was out there long before it.

A few weeks before *2000AD* was due to go to press, I learnt that there was a brilliant Ken Reid cartoon strip he had produced for a dummy that had never been published! Jack Le Grand thought it was disgusting and had condemned it to the vaults. It concerned the hideous mutant survivor of a nuclear war who had a horrible "thing" on his back and every week he would try and kill himself. But each week the thing on his back would prevent him. So if he jumped off a cliff, the thing would turn into a propeller and fly him to safety etc. You can just imagine how Ken would have drawn it! How deliciously foul, and what a wonderful contrast to all those ghastly, saccharine, formula strips in *Whoopee! et al.* Just what I needed for the back cover of *2000AD*. I had 100 per cent power to do what I wanted with *2000AD*, so I requisitioned the strip from the vaults. But the old regime told me that it had mysteriously "disappeared" and could not be found. Yeah, right.

Later, after I'd left and was safely out of the way, there were also serious plans by the old regime to revamp *2000AD*, giving it traditional *two page* stories and featuring a celebrity column: like Dick Emery, who hosted the Airfix page in *Valiant*. I know they invited astronomer Patrick Moore, host of *The Sky At Night*, to write the celebrity column in *2000AD*, because I was shown the postcard he sent them where he agreed to write for "this wretched little comic". Thankfully none of this ever happened. It could have been worse: it could have been Jimmy Savile they invited.

But whatever sabotage the counter-revolutionaries were planning, I knew *Judge Dredd*, at least, was in safe hands with John.

Dredd's success was not just due to Carlos's stunning art and the quality of John's writing, but also because the standard of some of the other stories—which had merit and unique qualities of their own, and should have also been number one characters—began to slip more than a little when I couldn't find writers of John's calibre.

Ultimately, *Dredd* won out over all the other stories because of the quality of the *writing*, the brilliance of Carlos's design, plus the *vital* boost it received by being drawn by Mike McMahon and later by Brian Bolland. Their artwork *also* helped pushed *Dredd* into the stratosphere where it has remained ever since, as well as creating a merchandising, reprint and foreign edition boom, especially in Brian's case.

So this is probably a good time to cover the gorilla in the corner that publishers and editors usually don't like to talk about. The subject of "creator" and "developer", which was never a problem for John Wagner or me, but sometimes seemed to be a problem for others.

Thus, from time to time, I'd see references stating I was only the co-creator of *2000AD*. This re-writing of history seems to have originated from someone at Titan Books, whom I tried hard to track down, but he never had the courage to reveal himself and justify his mischievous fantasies.

"The Historian", as I will call him, was always just out of my reach, rather like General Public, that mysterious character my robot Blackblood is endlessly pursuing. But "The Historian's" clearly inaccurate opinion seems to have been endorsed by staff at Rebellion when they first took over *2000AD*, as they repeated the same claim in their publicity. So I rang Rebellion up and asked, "You must know I produced the comic alone. So who is this so-called co-creator?" No answer. I pressed them. "Come on. Who is my mysterious co-creator? And where the Hell are you getting your information from? Is it from Titan? And why don't you have the courtesy to check with me first?" A long pause before the staff-member at the other end went into less than convincing denial mode. "Oh, we—er—made a *mistake.*" There was some hasty, fancy footwork behind the scenes. "We'll change it."

So I expressed my opinion directly to the Rebellion publisher,

Jason Kingsley, who was very understanding. It has never happened again.

In comics, you have to fight your corner or they *will* walk all over you, as Gerry Finley-Day found out.

It should be obvious, if you've read this far, that there is no co-creator of *2000AD*. But there was, in fact, one key developer: Doug Church, whose importance can't be stressed enough. Plus three further developers whose input was valuable: John Wagner, for suggesting various additions to my stories. His account bears this out. Kelvin Gosnell, for Tharg, his input on my later script drafts for prog one, and not least suggesting IPC produce a science fiction comic in the first place. And Kevin O'Neill, getting the visual tone of the comic right, visually creating Tharg, Walter the Wobot and so much more. Plus, of course, there were later developers, after I'd left.

There's a similar gorilla in the corner on *Dredd*. But it's actually really simple. John is the writer creator of *Dredd*. I'm the principal developer. As it stands, my development time on *Dredd* was considerable and unique and many people early on—and to this day —describe me as the co-creator of *Dredd*. I totally understand why they say this: after all I was increasingly committed to *Dredd*, above and beyond the call of duty, rescuing the character and getting the story and art right. But I try and repudiate the word "co-creator" whenever I can and I prefer the term "principal developer". And yes, Brian Bolland and Mike McMahon were also crucial visual developers.

I think there is a strong case for developers to be acknowledged financially in *2000AD's* highly unusual circumstances. The Suits might, predictably, say it was impossible; that it's "too complicated" and where to stop? It actually isn't complicated and you can stop. There is always a solution, if you *want* there to be a solution, and it's *already* happened on *Dredd*, thanks to editorial director Jon Davidge at Egmont.

So when the first *Dredd* movie came out, Jon Davidge paid not just John and Carlos, but also the key developers of *Dredd*: myself,

Mike McMahon and Brian Bolland. As well as Kevin O'Neill for the robot. Jon needed myself and Kevin to sign off on the movie, but that didn't apply to Mike and Brian. Jon acknowledged all of us economically, primarily because, as he said to me, he wanted to get it right. He wanted to do the right thing and to be fair to everyone concerned, and he discussed it with me in considerable detail. Good for Jon. However, on the second *Dredd* movie, only John and Carlos were paid.

It was a smaller budget and that has some relevance. When there's a *lot* of money involved, developers should be considered, at least from a moral perspective. Forget The Suits. It's the right thing to do and it's what fans expect. In fact, I'm certain fans would insist upon it if there was a Simon Bisley, Glenn Fabry, Mike McMahon or Clint Langley-based *Slaine* movie and that these artists would actually be rewarded *as well* as the original artist creator: Angela Kincaid, who only produced episode one, absolutely crucial and world-building as it was. Simon, Glenn, Mike and Clint clearly developed *Slaine* further. Clint, for example, brought a new widescreen cinematic realism to the character and also rescued it from the oblivion of the Dark Ages. That should mean something. The director or production company, recognising the importance of the relevant developer/s, and the expectations of the fans, would factor it in. This is feasible *if* there's a big budget. Jon Davidge's shining example proves it.

But I don't recall there ever being any acrimony or disputes between the key *Dredd* creators and developers over this matter. I think we've all been very supportive of each other. Thus, when the *Dredd Megazine* first came out, and was selling very well, John Wagner very generously passed some of his *Dredd* profits onto me on a semi-regular basis. It was his way of saying thanks. I appreciated the gesture.

That said, he didn't have to do it, and surely it is the publisher's responsibility, not the creators, to reward the developer?

There were now more exit wounds. After agreeing to create *Misty* next, I said to John Sanders that if I was going produce another successful comic for him, I wanted a financial interest in it. John said he couldn't get board approval. But if I had produced *Misty*, rather than being a later consultant creator, it would still be around today. There's no question of it. The female audience for comics was huge. Much, *much* bigger than the *2000AD* audience. *2000AD* launched with 200,000 copies weekly. *Tammy* once sold 250,000 copies weekly. *Jackie* sold over a million. Girls' appetite for mystery and the supernatural is greater even than boys' appetite for science fiction. It would have been a no-brainer.

So it was time for me to return to freelancing. To ensure *2000AD's* survival, I had edited and controlled the first critical twelve issues and planned the next twelve. I developed the most promising artists and writers and ensured that long-term plans were in place. But, before I exited, I needed to check that the editorial staff were suited to be part of the new wave.

I was about to make my most important decision about *2000AD*.

12. "DON'T MENTION THE SILVER SURFER!"

2000AD was my first experience of fandom. It was unknown on *Battle* and *Action*, which had a totally mainstream audience. Although John Wagner and I were never members of fandom, most of *2000AD's* other creators were—like Brian Bolland, Kevin O'Neill and Dave Gibbons. In the early days of *2000AD*, our audience was 90% mainstream fans and 10% "purist" fandom. By the early '90s, it was probably the other way around and sales started to suffer as mainstream readers, usually younger readers, felt alienated from the comic. The process continued in the late '90s and it took Rebellion's acquisition of *2000AD* to resolve the problem, with a recognition of purist fans (aficionados as John Sanders called them) *and* regular readers' tastes. Both factions have merged into one and seem content with the comic—an impressive achievement, largely due to current editor Matt Smith and his colleagues at Rebellion.

Definitions of fandom and how it applies to *2000AD* vary. But it's not actually complicated. *2000AD* should remain true to its subversive roots and that works well when fan favourite writers, like Alan Moore, produced *Halo Jones* and *D.R. and Quinch*. *Halo Jones* lives in the Rim: a fantasy version of a hopeless and hellish council estate, which she successfully escapes. A great concept. It reminds me of my own background growing up on a council estate.

D.R. and Quinch is about two alien dropouts, and both these stories are deliciously subversive. The same applies to Grant Morrison's excellent unconventional superhero *Zenith*, and many others. And when fan-orientated stories follow the stern rules of action and drama, with proactive heroes and heroines, and are accessible to readers of all ages—rather than just students or hard-core fans—they're fine. Even the odd arthouse story that breaks the rules is okay, because it can be supported by the other regular stories. There should be some experimentation.

Artwork is trickier. Fan favourite art is often not understood by regular readers. They literally don't know how to read it. There are notable exceptions like the fantastic work of Dave Gibbons and Brian Bolland, which is accessible to everyone. Equally, traditional comic art often doesn't appeal to either fans or regular readers. Hence the key role of Doug Church in disguising it. Then there are mainstream artists like *2000AD* stalwart Belardinelli who were disliked by fans but absolutely loved by regular readers and myself.

Fans are also more vocal than regular readers and this was to reach a point where the *NME* (a music magazine) was regularly pontificating on *2000AD* and what was good and bad in it. They called it "Toothy" and, inevitably, the comic became overly weird to keep NME and similar publications happy which, of course, was ridiculous. All this attention often went to *2000AD* editorial's heads and the comic started to change its identity to suit the cool staff on *NME* rather than the kids.

The solution is simple enough: you keep all these different factions in check and don't let any of them dominate the others and get out of control. Because they did, we paid a bitter harvest in the '90s when sales crashed.

On a personal level, both John Wagner and I adapted to the changing times. Gerry Finley-Day didn't—and paid the price.

Those responsible for this change of direction are understandably defensive and deny they have anything to do with *2000AD's* near-demise, so I've held onto a number of letters which cast some light on this. Here's one of them:

> I stopped reading 2000AD when I went to college at the age of 17. So this means I was a devoted fan for eight years. The final story I remember reading before I abandoned the comic concerned a character called Halo Jones who lived in an artificial city in the middle of the ocean. She had a robotic dog; or maybe the dog wasn't actually hers but it could talk and its teeth were very sharp. I didn't enjoy Halo Jones very much because there was too much going on; it was too cluttered, too cyberpunkish (for want of a better word). But the real failing was mine. The truth is that I had been left behind by an evolution in style. Comics in general at that time were becoming more urban, sassy, cool. I was still locked into the old ways. Halo Jones was beyond my comprehension. Deep down I still yearned for the traditional values of tyrannosaurs and bums.

This sums it up perfectly. Readers themselves felt *they* were to blame for not understanding the more elitist and niche strips. That they weren't cool enough. There were many other letters like this at the time. Others would feel too uncomfortable to voice their concerns in case they got shouted down by the "cool" readers. And they certainly would have been.

We lost so many readers, not because fandom was represented—it's great that it was—but because it prevailed. I recall at the time John Sanders having problems with *Halo Jones*, primarily about its sf dialogue, and expressing his disquiet to editor Steve MacManus. Those problems may have been resolved by the later serial where Halo goes to war. But if the other stories were in the tradition of the early progs, and thus the balance was right, then I like to think the reader above would be perfectly happy with *Halo Jones* being in his prog. You can't enjoy every story, after all.

It is difficult to keep a balance but Matt Smith does so on a regular basis. He and I both like tyrannosaurs. Not sure about bums, though.

I believe it's an endemic problem with sf fandom. I'm told there are similar conflicts around *Doctor Who* throughout its long history right through to the present day. When I started revising *Dan Dare*, I first became aware of this fierce energy around fandom. The Roger Dean reprint edition of *Dan Dare*—where they blacked out the margins—included the appeal to readers, "Pax Purists". E.g. "Please don't give me a hard time." Sensing my *Dan* might get a similar response, I went and asked John Sanders what I should do. Should I accommodate *Dan Dare* sf fans with my interpretation of the famous character?

His answer was, "Go for mainstream readers first and fans second. *If* you get it right, the fans will follow you anyway."

Wise, wise words, which should be set in stone somewhere. They've served me in good stead. Of course they are not what fans want to hear, but John is absolutely right.

It probably explains why *Watchmen* and the second *Judge Dredd* movie were not commercial hits. (The first *Dredd* movie didn't get it right for a mainstream audience.)

Not everyone will agree where *Dredd* is concerned. Some put the failure of the second film down to marketing, the age certificate, the 3D and the association with the Stallone movie and believe it *is* accessible to a new audience. I'm sure they are factors, too, but I still believe the principle expressed by John Sander is paramount. It's not one that makes anyone popular, though, which is why it's easier to ignore.

All too often directors want to please fans or themselves first and receive approval at conventions and don't think about the ordinary cinemagoer. So it's hardly surprising if *2000AD* editors fell into the same trap.

It's a trap DC Thomson's never fell into and their ruthless

recognition of the needs of the ordinary consumer led to the million-selling *Jackie*. So editor Gordon Small would reject any artsy, upmarket, Chelsea, Biba-style fashions in *Jackie*, because he would ask, "Could a young lassie in Dundee afford that jacket?" Good for him.

Some of these concerns were in my mind when I considered Nick Landau for the job of assistant editor of *2000AD*. Because Nick was a super-fan.

Up till now, at IPC, fans were regarded with so much hostility, only one staff fan member had actually "come out of the closet" and he was treated like a freak. I kid you not. To be fair, he was straight out of *The Big Bang Theory* and was endlessly criticizing everything everyone did, because it didn't match his fan criteria.

So I knew the very real dangers of employing Nick, and how John Sanders might think of him as another crazy fan.

Nick had just left film school and, seeing *2000AD's* potential, was keen to get a job on the comic. Reading his impressive CV, I thought he'd make a great assistant editor. He also seemed to have valuable connections and said he thought he might be able to get *Dredd* reprinted in the States.

I had one big reservation, however: he was also an American superhero fan, and I was determined to keep men in tights out of my comic. Any reader of *Marshal Law* knows my feeling on these wretched Corporate Gods. They represent and promote establishment values I despise. And, from a commercial point of view, despite all their hype, which could make you think superheroes are runaway successes, they *don't* actually sell well in the UK.

Finally, I decided it was better to have a fan who was passionate about comics, than some of the indifferent individuals who were also applying for the job. For instance, the son of a future managing editor. He informed me that he hadn't been successful at finding work in Fleet Street in "real journalism", so he had come to me instead. He didn't watch or read science fiction, he said, but he promised me he would do if he got the job. He didn't.

So it had to be Nick. I carefully schooled him in what to say to John Sanders for his final interview. I told him to play down his fan persona and to only show John some of his fanzines and not others and, whatever you, "don't mention the *Silver Surfer*". This was because John, too, shared my concerns about superheroes. He knew they were box office poison in the UK. Ensuring he left his motorcycle helmet and rucksack behind, I took Nick down to Sanders office and introduced him. John was impressed by Nick and he got the job

Probably everyone in comics knows that Nick went on to be publisher of Titan Books and owner of the chain of Forbidden Planet shops. And that he reprinted *Dredd*, *Nemesis*, *Slaine* and others as graphic novel collections. Titan Books and Forbidden Planet and Nick, personally, made a vital contribution to the comic's success. But there was so much more to this story, which I'll get onto shortly.

Nick steered *2000AD* towards fandom and, as I got him the job on *2000AD*, I guess you could say I'm responsible. Shucks! In my defence, I'd say there was no alternative.

The harsh truth is that, without Nick and Titan, there was no way *2000AD* would have prospered in those early days. We owe that to Nick. Without him, I doubt the comic would have survived.

But there was another person and another, potentially more mainstream, direction the comic could have taken.

Before I left *2000AD*, Deirdre Vine had also applied for the job of assistant editor. I was tremendously impressed by her CV, which included a genuine love for science fiction. Kelvin Gosnell, my editor designate, was equally impressed, so we hired Deirdre, alongside Nick. It was unusual for a female journalist to be interested in girls comics, let alone a boys' science fiction comic, so I was fascinated to see what she would come up with. In the few weeks I worked with her I could see she was going to make an important creative contribution to the comic.

Sadly, a few months after I'd left, John Sanders "promoted" her to the teen romance mag *My Guy*, even though she would have preferred to stay with *2000AD*. Editorial assistants were given no choice Subsequently she had a distinguished career in women's magazines as editor of *Woman's Journal* and *Aura*.

I've often wondered what would have happened if she had become editor of *2000AD*, as could so easily have happened.

13. IN THE SHADOW OF THE JUDGE?

Priority was increasingly given to *Judge Dredd* as it went from strength to strength. Other stories just didn't have the same strong creative teams.

Consequently, *2000AD* stories, at least, didn't always sustain the cool look and promise of my early episodes: *Mach One* and *Invasion!* and that is why they eventually came to an end.

Readers understood the subversive nature of the comic, right from the get-go, but I was never convinced the editorial did.

Thus, Richard Burton, later to be editor of *2000AD*, came to visit the *2000AD* offices in his role as editor of leading fan magazine, *Fantasy Advertiser*. He enjoyed *Flesh* and told me that he fondly imagined in my final episode, I would have the tyrannosaur Old One Eye dying at the hands of humans in a *King Kong* ending.

I was alarmed, because I thought its pro-nature theme was abundantly clear. We need to show that ultimately nature wins. Man can never triumph over nature as in *Kong*. And I thought, "You really don't get it, do you?"

Because in my final episode, Old One Eye, after triumphing over humans who lie in gored swathes at her feet, goes to the tyrannosaur's graveyard to die. *Of old age.* And sixty five million years later, her fossilised skeleton kills scientists in a museum, so even in death she is triumphant against humanity.

And then there was Christian assistant editor Roy Preston, who probably took over after Deirdre left. He changed one of my characters coming back from the dead because it was against his Christian beliefs. I guess Jesus has the monopoly. And on saving us too, apparently. Because he strongly objected to a caption, "Alien Messiah" in a *Cursed Earth* story where the rock-eating Tweak was being crucified by scientists.

Things weren't really working out to my liking. There was the sea-based *Flesh Book Two*, which although it had some memorable moments, with brilliant art by Belardinelli, lacked the heroes, the intensity and missed the subtext of my Wild West Book One. The artwork at the end by another artist was also pretty wretched and old-fashioned. As a result, *Flesh* disappeared from *2000AD* for many years.

Harlem Heroes was always popular, thanks to Dave Gibbons, especially with the hideous cyborg Artie Gruber, but now that we were no longer allowed to make it a death game, like *Rollerball*, it was hard for the writer Tom Tully to give it the ferocity he'd previously injected into the excellent *Death Game 1999* on *Action.*

Looking back, in theory there was still no reason why my plan for a comic with *all* number one heroes shouldn't have worked. The fact that today two of my stories from Prog One, *Savage* (*Invasion!*) and *Flesh*, have successfully returned to the pages of *2000AD* and are popular, tells you so.

I've no doubt *Harlem Heroes,* with the right writer and an artist like Dave Gibbons, would also still work today. As a huge fan of the original *Rollerball*, I've always regretted not continuing to write *Harlem Heroes* after my original script, with spikes around the goals, was censored. So in my French series *Sha* (set in a satanic New York called New Eden) I wrote a death game sequence called "Dwarfball", based on a concept by artist co-creator, Olivier Ledroit. It looks amazing, although it is not politically correct. But it *is* a Satanic New York, and it was for the French.

And then there's *Dan Dare*, which I anticipated would be especially popular, hence why I had it opening on the colour centrespread. I wanted Dan to have wider appeal, and therefore commissioned Gerry Finley-Day and Dave Gibbons to do a new incarnation of the character. I knew Dave's art would have better anatomy than Bellardinelli's and he would feature a more realistic protagonist. I felt Gerry, with a successful background as a war comics writer, would get the stories right. People are divided on his writing: professionals didn't like it, but the readers often did and still do. In the end, the professionals won. After I left, I heard Tom Tully had taken over the scripting and given him a power hand. I'm aware there are subsequent attempts to get it right, but of course the more you change writers, artists and realities, the more you can lose the readers' interest and I think that's how the character eventually died.

One reader, Gavin Aslett, wrote to me about Dare:

I bought 2000AD regularly from the age of 7 (prog 9) and Dan Dare was the main reason I bought it. A lot of people seem to not recognise that Dan Dare launched the comic and I consider the Belardenelli series to be one of the greatest the comic has witnessed.

The Dave Gibbons series was very captivating as well. Most of the people at school I went to were into 2000AD's Dan Dare and Judge Dredd did not really get popular until The Cursed Earth series in Prog 60. Dan Dare was badly treated by 2000AD and still does deserve a conclusion. I can't stand all these Eagle Dan Dare fanatics who pompously criticize the 2000AD Dan Dare version. It's a generational thing and the 2000AD Dan Dare reflected the 1970s kids were growing up in—hence that is why it appealed to me. I like the 1950's Eagle version but it is part of another nostalgic age. Worse still I can't stand all these

2000AD revisionists who never bought the comic in the beginning who tell us how awful Dan Dare was in 2000AD.

2000AD today is not the comic it was and frankly could acknowledge Dan Dare's contribution not only because it is just very disrespectful to the artists who gave the comic so much i.e. Massimo Belardenelli and Dave Gibbons.

Kind Regards,
Gavin Aslett

As Gavin's email implies, Dan's significance is often overshadowed by *Dredd*. He didn't fit, so his significance was played down.

The new *2000AD* stories, such as *Ant Wars* by Gerry Finley-Day, that replaced my original line-up were often not to my liking, but having left the comic, they were beyond my control.

However, now at least, the readers could see who wrote and drew the stories they liked or hated. This was down to Kevin O'Neill, who sneaked credits onto *2000AD* giving a bullshit reason to the managing editor. This changed the world of British comics overnight. If it wasn't for Kevin, no one would know Grant Morrison wrote *Zenith*. No one would know Carlos Ezquerra drew *Judge Dredd*. If anyone believes it would eventually happen, anyway, let me point out that's it's only *now* that the Beano are giving credits.

Technically, what Kevin did was a sackable offence and if the publisher had known where it would lead, he would have been in big trouble. Kevin was the man who changed the British comic industry forever.

But having our names on stories didn't have any immediate effect. Some rather average stories continued to appear and all the energy went into *Dredd*. This reached a high water mark, as Gavin says, with *The Cursed Earth*.

It was to be the most popular *Dredd* story of all time and it takes us deeper into the character of Judge Dredd.

14. THE CURSED EARTH

By now I'd written two further *Judge Dredd* stories, which I was happy with. *Neon Knights* and *Return of Rico*. *Neon Knights* featured a gang of Ku Klux Klan-style bad guys, a strange and sinister recurring theme in my work, which I seem driven to write about.

And *Return of Rico*, featuring Judge Dredd's evil twin, which also came from somewhere deep in my subconscious. It was a curious experience. Unlike my usual stories, I wrote it in a kind of waking dream, in a trance, like the words and plot were being dictated to me. I had no conscious idea where the story was headed. I was surprised by its power, emotion and conclusion. Looking back, I can see it's based on Jungian archetypes, the dark side of the self, that resonates deeply with all of us, and I'm sure this was why it was chosen as the plot for the first *Dredd* film.

It was in this story that I gave Dredd his first name: Joe. I'd never thought about it before, it was just the name that came into my head as I was writing it. I'll come back to this in the next chapter.

Kelvin Gosnell then asked me to write a *Dredd* serial to give John Wagner some time out, so he could catch up on other work. Kelvin did a great job setting the story up for me, with plot, hardware and artists, and thus making it economically viable for me to produce.

But then he had to go off to create *Starlord*, so Nick Landau was assigned to editing *The Cursed Earth*.

There were some great aspects to *Starlord*: the better quality paper and two successful strips: *Strontium Dog*, the story of a mutant bounty hunter by John Wagner and Carlos Ezquerra; and *Ro-Busters*, written by myself, visualized by Kevin O'Neill and drawn by Carlos Pino. But I'd said to Kelvin before I left, "Whatever you do, don't take on a second comic. It's too much work. Find your feet on *2000AD* first." There's no way that I could have handled two comics. *2000AD* had taken a year to produce, with endless problems to overcome, and a second sf comic required a great deal of thought to ensure its identity was sufficiently different from the first. But I doubt he had any choice in the matter. The pressure on Kelvin to bring out *Starlord* would have been enormous.

So, working alongside Kevin O'Neill, Nick was the *de facto* editor of *2000AD* and he closely monitored *The Cursed Earth*. He saw even greater potential in *Dredd* and focussed the best artists on it. Even though it was at the expense of the rest of the comic, it was probably the right thing to do, commercially at least. And he used his connections with Brian Bolland to bring him onto the strip.

Its success was due not just to the scripts and fabulous art by Brian Bolland and Mike McMahon, but also to Nick. He somehow managed to hold us all together, putting up with our angst, poor time-keeping and creative insecurity. This is a great skill, often not talked about or admitted, and frankly impossible in the harsh economic realities of today's world. Today's editorial staff simply don't have the time. But it can make all the difference if an artist is working round the clock to tough deadlines for poor financial returns. It's well know in the industry that subsequent artists would *crumble* when later, insensitive *2000AD* editors would chuck their labours of love, their imaginative magnum opuses, on a shelf, with a grudgingly muttered, "Thanks".

By contrast, Nick was a total enthusiast, he had a real and positive passion for great art and stories and would give detailed feedback, and this made an enormous difference to us. He was once actually admonished by management for being "too enthusiastic". I think I learnt my own artist bedside manner from Nick. It enabled me to inspire and develop some of Britain's finest comic artists, talking them down off the ledge on occasion, and I'm *not* being facetious here. In fact I got so good at it, Marvel comics editor, Margaret Clark once presented me with a gold card case and business cards inscribed, "Pat Mills. Artist Therapy always available."

Nick had even more patience; getting Brian Bolland to draw his episodes, which was a colossal achievement, as Brian was slow and needed regular encouraging. Nick deserves a medal for that alone.

Nick also had the patience to extract scripts from me, discuss and help me plan the great centre spreads for the artists, and encourage me to get ever wilder in my storytelling. For example, bringing back *Flesh* with Satanus in *The Cursed Earth*. Satanus was the son of Old One Eye, the monstrous star of *Flesh*. This proved to be phenomenally popular and I was delighted, as *Flesh* had always been one of my favourite creations. I also wanted to prevent the serial falling into the hands of other writers, who, even in recent times, don't seem able to keep their hands off my characters rather than thinking up their own stories. Thus I've successfully featured Satanus in his own *Dredd* saga, *The Blood of Satanus*, beautifully drawn by Ron Smith and the first "noir" *Dredd*. My plan was to create a loose *2000AD* universe where my characters, at least, could crossover and interact with each other.

I think there's potential in such a universe, which I've regularly used in my stories. If I'd had another three months or so to create the comic, I would have certainly made that one of its foundation stones. It would have been a lot of work but I'd run out of time, and other writers and editors were rarely interested. However, it has great commercial possibilities: you only have to look at Marvel and DC crossovers. I like to think our crossovers have been more sensitively handled and could still be capitalised on in the future, as long as the creators concerned are fairly treated, consulted and remunerated.

Readers often ask me about the dinosaur theme park I featured in *The Cursed Earth*. They have speculated that the writer of *Jurassic Park* (1990), Michael Crichton, may have got the idea from my story. It's possible, but I doubt it. I actually got the idea from a story in *The Year's Best Science Fiction No. 8,* edited by Harry Harrison and Brian Aldiss, published in 1976. Entitled *Paleontology: an experimental science*, it's written by Robert R. Olsen. It relates in some detail how DNA science is used to bring a T-Rex back to life, which is then kept in San Diego zoo. Inevitably, it escapes with predictable consequences. It's a very funny story, which I thoroughly recommend.

I also developed the origins of the Judges when Dredd discovers the American President incarcerated in Fort Knox for his war crimes.

The National Geographic inspired two *Cursed Earth* stories. I found a tamandua anteater in the magazine who was the basis for Tweak, beautifully imagined by Brian. And a stark metal tree in the nuclear desert, where nothing grows, depicted by Mike, also came from the *Geographic.*

I was short on time because I was working on other projects so a few additional, excellent episodes were supplied by John. Jack Adrian wrote a *Cursed Earth* tale featuring evil versions of brand name characters like the Jolly Green Giant. The corporations concerned complained and a public apology had to be made. After *Action*, it was obvious to me that would happen. It really was asking for trouble. Nick was nearly sacked over it, but for the intervention of Kevin O'Neill, who threatened to resign if he was dismissed.

But this was a great time to be working on the comic. I usually refer to this era as *2000AD's* First Golden Age, for which Nick and Kevin O'Neill are the principal architects. By the end of *The Cursed Earth* I was really into *Dredd*. And, while I was on a roll, I planned a major new *Dredd* serial about a civil war between Judges, inspired by some of the stories I had written for *The Cursed Earth*. But, at this point, *2000AD* took over *Starlord* and John returned to writing *Dredd*.

The Cursed Earth was especially popular because it presents Dredd as a hero, something that doesn't always happen or is not possible when he is in Mega-City. I followed the rules of drama here, which are very simple but all too often ignored in comics: make life hell for your hero.

And on a long-running story like this, I had to really think about Dredd. Who is he? Who am I drawing on for inspiration? So this is the right time, I feel, to discuss that very point. Where does John's *Dredd* come from and where does my version?

The Cursed Earth takes us to the very heart of *Judge Dredd*.

15. JOE DREDD

In both cases, we used *real life* role models on which to base our two somewhat different interpretations of Dredd. In John Wagner's case, Dredd is undoubtedly an alter ego of himself. His dour Scottish manner, combined with an early American childhood, admirably qualified him to create the Judge. The tower blocks of Greenock where he grew up, I'm sure have more than an echo in the city blocks of Mega-City, particularly in the new *Dredd* movie. His slow, monosyllabic responses are similar to, but less studied than, the late Clement Freud's. John's later writing partner on *Dredd*, Alan Grant has a similar dour Scottish character. Together, the two of them made for a lethal team with their optimistic and cheerful outlook on life (*not*) and were admirably suited to relate the appalling lives of the bizarre citizens of Mega-City. I still laugh out loud when I recall a John ending, where a perp explains it was the pressure of life in this terrible city that made him commit his heinous crimes. "I know, citizen. I know," says Dredd "sympathetically" as he leads him away to the iso-cubes. That is *so* John! A reader recently challenged me on my cynical conclusion and thought Dredd (and John) were showing a little heart. Ah, if only. It's making me laugh, all over again!

I think there was a similar identification with the hero in John's very successful *Darkie's Mob*, in *Battle*, now reprinted as a Titan Book collection *The Secret War of Joe Darkie*. It's a serial about a group of irregular soldiers fighting the Japanese behind enemy lines and led by the mysterious and very bald Joe Darkie, it was a tough story, the toughest story *Battle* had ever run, and Darkie's ruthless character has much in common with Dredd. The journal style in the story was inspired by *The Private War of Nicola Brown* by John Cornforth and Esteban Marota, a well-written and beautifully drawn anti-war serial about the Crimean War, which John and I worked on when we were editorial staff on *Romeo*. It would also inspire the letters home I used in *Charley's War*. When *Darkie's Mob* came to a powerful and emotional end where Darkie is killed, John shaved his head. He told me it was because he wanted to see what the top of his head looked like, but he said to someone else he did it because he'd lost a bet. Everyone on *2000AD*, however, was convinced it was because he was in mourning for his alter ego, Darkie.

I didn't think I can claim Dredd was an alter ego of mine, although I must be in there somewhere. But I had equally strong role models to draw upon: two of my teachers who inspired my version of Dredd, especially in my *Cursed Earth* saga. They were also the basis for Torquemada—*2000AD's* most popular and evil villain—in *Nemesis*. Describing how and why they inspired me is going to lead us into some dark and deep waters, which tell us something about the nature of Dredd and the heroes and villains we love to hate.

I don't wish to shatter anyone's illusions. I'm aware how important Dredd is, personally, to many readers. Certainly, in the early days, there was at least one reader who used him as a role model to direct every aspect of his entire life. He described in a letter how whatever was happening to him, big or small, he would ask himself, "What would Judge Dredd do?" And respond accordingly. I believe he is still at large.

There's a good *Viz*-style cartoon strip in this idea. Or a tee shirt: "WWJDD?"

But this use of role models and the blurring of reality and fiction is not uncommon in comics and is certainly a theme of all my stories, as you will have noticed. I recall seeing Peter Cushing on TV, telling us that he based his life on Tom Merry, the principal character in the *St Jim's* stories that appeared in the boy's weekly paper, *The Gem*. And it presented real problems for me on the characters Finn and Claudia Vampire Knight, as I shall relate later.

But, if you prefer to believe that comic book characters are—or should be—entirely fictional constructs, or you don't want to know about the reality, then I strongly recommend you skip the rest of this chapter, which is about characters from *my* school, St Joe's.

In the words of Lemony Snicket, "Look away."

The teachers were De La Salle brothers at my old school, St Joseph's College, Ipswich. The two in question were Brother James and Brother Solomon. They were "Prefects of Discipline", responsible for administering corporal punishment, which gives you an idea where this is going. Brother Solomon was to leave the teaching order under a cloud—you can probably imagine what kind—and later became mildly famous as the pop star known as The Swinging Monk. He then returned to St Joe's as lay teacher Mike Mercado and was at it again, of course. And despite countless allegations against him he was never charged with the crimes he committed.

Where Dredd is concerned, my main inspiration was Brother James, although all the brothers fascinated me. They were like cops, or *Batman*-style avengers: black-robed, fanatical figures. They were seemingly incorruptible; stern; driven by some higher power, and I was in awe of them. I imagined them sleeping in some kind of vampire-like hive: rather like the young John Hicklenton imagined Dredd slept in a cryotube. They appeared to have no lives outside the school and no interest in sex (or not legal sex, at least) having taken strict vows of chastity. Hence Torquemada's famous words "Be Pure! Be Vigilant! Behave!" The smallest infraction of discipline and we would be punished severely. Dirty shoes? The cane. Talking? The cane. Smoking? The cane. You don't mess with these guys. They are the Law!

But Brother James Ryan was the scariest. He was driven by

religious zeal, with a fanatical love of the Lord, which inspired my idea of Dredd's fanatical love of the Law. Hence an early *Dredd* episode, where he sits reading a giant volume on the Law in his spare time.

James wore a long black robe, Himmler-style, steel-rimmed spectacles, and had aesthetic, angular features. He was as menacing as Brother Solomon, from whom he took over as Prefect of Discipline.

One day he entered my classroom to find a thirteen year old boy talking. A great kid with a surly punk attitude to life that reminds me of Mike McMahon. James seethed with anger and sucked air through his clenched Clint Eastwood teeth as he sent another boy to fetch a size ten plimsoll from the cloak room. I would later *directly* draw on this incident for the fury of the scene in *The Cursed Earth* when Dredd razes the town of Repentance to the ground.

Then, in full view of the rest of us, James went to work on his victim, who was the younger brother of our English teacher *and* the son of the school doctor. So no favouritism there. All are equal in the eyes of the Law.

He raised the slipper high above his head and took a spin-bowler's long run-up towards his bent-over victim, whom he had carefully positioned at the far end of the raised wooden dais. His shoes thundered noisily across the bare floorboards, his black robes flapped wildly around him, before he administered a savage blow to the boy's posterior, raising a cloud of dust at the point of impact. Returning to his starting point, he took several more high-speed, bowler's run-ups to his victim, thrashing him without mercy, before the poor kid collapsed in a heap on the ground, whereupon—as we watched, quaking in fear—he stood over him and rained more ferocious blows onto his crouched and cringing, sobbing form.

In correspondence with this old classmate, he has confirmed my account and revealed his defiant, punk attitude eventually led to his expulsion. That doesn't surprise me. Neither Brother James nor Judge Dredd would tolerate defiant punks.

We should have gone to our classmate's defence, and I still feel bad that we didn't. The Brothers relied on terror tactics to control us, and how often do the citizens of Mega-City rise up against the Judges and give them what they also richly deserve? The Brothers and the Judges are the Law!

But one kid did actually fight back.

Here's an excerpt from an old boy's vivid description of this later uprising:

I have one wonderful memory, that of an American kid from the Bronx. James wanted to beat LM the student (who is now a prominent US human rights lawyer). At the end of the class we were all thrown out. (Then) James did his usual attack of kicking and punching. LM beat the sh....out of James with a few dozen boys watching and cheering. The result was that we never saw LM again.

I would love to have been there. Perhaps Sylvester Stallone should have played LM rather than Judge Dredd.

LM's first name was Louis. He memorably once said, in classic Stallone style, *"You think you're hot shit on a silver dish, but you're just cold piss in a paper cup."* I like to think *that's* what Louis said to James, just before he beat the shit out of him.

I think it's why readers love it when heroes like Chopper defy Judge Dredd.

One old boy described James as "totally detached with a stand-offish manner, never accepting any excuse for anything." Does that remind you of anyone...? That's *exactly* how I saw Dredd. He also said James liked cricket. Although, curiously, James always appeared on the cricket or rugby pitches wearing his black robes. He never changed into sports gear like the other brothers did, when he would have looked normal and "one of us". I suspect it was to maintain his "hard man", distant image. And just as James never took off his black robes, so Dredd never takes off his helmet.

There was also an element of black comedy about James, which also made him perfect for Dredd. Here's how an old boy describes a typical incident:

> *Who was it James threw out of chapel? I remember his punching* stopped *when the bell went off for the Consecration of the Host and then* resumed *immediately afterwards. The victim went straight through the doors about four feet in the air.*

That's like a crazy scene out of *Fargo*.

In an early rewrite of John Wagner's first *Dredd*, I had the Judge rescuing a perp from a fire, only to then execute him. I wanted to capture that obsessive nature of James/Dredd.

A De La Salle Brother described Brother James in his obituary in 2011 (now no longer accessible on the DLSB website) as "Timid and shy by nature." Well, of course.

Still in the world of fiction, we need these figures to inspire *fear*: Darth Vader; Batman; Judge Dredd; Marshal Law, but that fear has to be *real*, which means it should come from a real person, otherwise it's off the peg: it's *fake*.

When Dredd/James enters a room, we want to *feel* the fear.

But mixed in with that fear, I felt admiration for James, too. Misplaced, as it now turns out. And it's the same for Dredd: we fear and yet *admire* him.

How far you see Dredd as good or evil depends on your perspective and which interpretation of Dredd—the relatively heroic figure of *The Cursed Earth* or the Lawman of Mega-City—resonates with you. There are inherent contradictions in his character and hence why I chose my teacher with his own contradictions as my role model for my Dredd.

I've chatted to an old school chum of mine about James as my role model for Dredd. He's a successful comic book artist and is familiar with *2000AD*. He remembers "the Black Monks", as he calls them, and James in particular, and this is his opinion:

"Can't help thinking Jammy was a third of the size of Dredd, but ten times nastier!"

So our Judge Dredd *isn't* as scary as Brother James. He still has a long way to go. Perhaps it's just as well.

Another old boy recently asked me if Dredd's first name came from the name of my school: St Joe's? As I introduced the name when my muse was driving me to write that strange Rico story, I'm sure it was.

We *dreaded* Brother James of St Joe's. So: Joe Dredd. Yep, that's him.

16. CECIL B. DEMILLS

I wrote *Ro-Busters* for *Starlord* as a favour to Kelvin Gosnell, who was the comic's creator. Somehow, I'd promised him a story and I couldn't get out of it. The new managing editor, Bob Bartholemew, rang me up with a terrible story idea which Kelvin wanted me to develop. Bob was the man who was proud to say he shut down the original *Eagle*. He sat behind the famous *Eagle* desk, originally the property of the Reverend Marcus Morris, who created *Eagle*.

Kevin O'Neill and I were so fascinated by this desk, we feature a fictional version in *Serial Killer*, where our managing editor sits behind the legendary *Homework* desk. *Homework* is an excellent educational magazine for nice middle-class boys, with *Treasure Island* in Latin and articles such as "How to revise over Christmas". In fact, I originally wanted to go further and have a pulpit as well, but we decided that was too silly. We also planned to have a companion magazine *Housework For Girls*, but decided—once again—that it would be too silly.

Bob's idea featured ageing World War Two officer veterans with super-powers. They were from all three armed services and at least one of them had been seriously wounded in World War Two. They formed a disaster rescue squad, combining their powers with

Thunderbirds technology. Bob's first suggested plot was the disaster squad journeying to the Earth's core to plug a dangerous escape of lava, with an alien lurking down there at the centre of the planet.

Ignoring his idea, my version was called *Ro-Busters* and featured a muppet-like, robot disaster squad of foul, working class machines who say things like "Big Jobs!" and "Bog Off!" It will come as no surprise to you that Bob loathed it, which was a good sign.

It took me three weeks to develop. Kelvin and Kevin O'Neill helped with technical details, and Kevin designed all the hardware and robots, which makes him the co-creator. Originally, Kelvin sent the script to Brian Lewis to draw. *Starlord* was on glossy paper, after all, not like that nasty bog-paper *2000AD*. But when Brian saw its epic nature, he turned it down, sending it back saying, "Who does the writer think he is? Cecil B. DeMille?"

It then went to Carlos Pino, who did a good job, because he faithfully copied Kevin's robot designs. It really should have taken me the mandatory six weeks to produce, because after writing it as a twelve page self-contained story, there was a change of plan and the serial was cut back to six pages an episode. This leads to all kinds of pacing problems, especially on a Cecil B. DeMille epic. So I should really have taken the story back and re-designed it to suit the new format. But there is only so much time I can devote to subsidising publishers, so I let it go. A pity, because I knew the new format was wrong for it, and it's why I started to lose interest in the series.

When *Starlord* was "matched and despatched" into *2000AD*, I gave it another shot, but increasingly I was looking for a different and better format. So the stories moved away from the original disaster squad concept, that was proving too complex and unwieldy for a six page serial. The story of my brief success with copyright and the creation of the *Terra Meks*, I've already described.

Meanwhile, I'd been working on yet another epic: *Mekomania* that I would eventually draw on to develop *Ro-Busters*. This epic was a robot history of the future. Drawn by *2000AD's* finest artists, we had Nick Landau acting as our agent to find a publisher at the Frankfurt Book Fair, so we could be free of the oppressive British comics system. Big O, Paper Tiger, Dragon's Dream and French publishers, including Dargaud, were approached. All seemed to like it, but none, unfortunately, signed on the dotted line.

Yes, *France* came first for *all* 2000AD's founding fathers. Not Marvel or DC Comics. After all, *2000AD* was heavily influenced by French comics. They were my role model although you'd barely know it looking at *2000AD* today. Not America—apart from the great Warren Comics. If *Mekomania* had succeeded, there would undoubtedly have been a British Invasion of France instead.

In fact, that original subliminal French flavour to *2000AD* may still cause some market resistance to the comic in the States. After all, French comic books—despite their genius sf writers and artists—have never sold particularly well in the States, and I fear never will. Although they've certainly influenced Hollywood films: sometimes officially and at other times they've just been blatantly ripped off, which doesn't seem to bother anyone. I guess it's "homage", although I'm sure the French writers and artists would appreciate some financial thanks, too.

I'm not sure an American super hero audience likes what they probably see as "obsessive" backgrounds in French comics. But I, too, am keen on "obsessive" backgrounds, starting with Mega-City One and have always insisted on them in *2000AD*.

It took me three months to produce opening episodes and characters for *Mekomania* and, for the record, the line-up, all beautifully illustrated, was:

George, a story about the first robot to have emotions who falls in love with a scientist. I adapted aspects of this for a later Hammerstein story in *The Black Hole*, drawn by the great SMS. Art: Brian Bolland.

Triumph of the Robots, where the machines triumph over humans and require them to go back to their former, uncivilised state by removing their clothes. There's a wonderful page by Dave Gibbons where a robot tyrannosaur towers over naked humans in a *Close Encounters of the Third Kind*-style scene. (It had just appeared at the cinema.) The French editor that Nick showed the page to shrugged his shoulders with studied Gallic indifference at the nudity. "We are French. This is not a problem." I used this Naked Encounters idea later in *Nemesis*, where the Terminators are sent to the Planet of the Spiders. Intelligent alien arachnids watch over these now naked fascists.

Goldrod, a noir plot about a Bogart-style detective and his super cool robot buddy called Goldrod. Art: Ian Gibson, who gave it a fascinating faerie-like quality. I later adapted the characters for a proposed *Emap* comic with Brian Talbot but this also proved abortive. But I adapted the plot—about time anomalies—for my first *Marshal Law* story.

Grille, a robot-human civil war story. Art: Mike McMahon. It featured a super cool Spaghetti Western-style robot hero.

Armageddon, a robot Messiah, beautifully imagined and paced by Kevin O'Neill. The incredible chariot design, controlled by steampunk levers, features later in *Marshal Law*.

Alas, I don't have any of the pages. Apart from never collecting comics, I also never collect artwork—I like to travel light—so I'm afraid I don't have a loft with masses of old artwork and scripts. Some of the pages would have been returned to the artists, others I probably gave away.

But my musings on a robot future also gave rise to *Metalzoic*, a bizarre robot future where Amok, a huge robot mammoth, his robot harem and accompanying bull robots, are hunted by robot tribesmen. Yet another ambitious epic. Once again, beautifully imagined by Kevin, it was later published by DC Comics. And once again, it was another all-rights deal, the curse of Anglo-American comics. We nearly got it reprinted recently by DC and Rebellion, but ran into cost problems, which scuppered the re-coloured version. I think everyone was rather worn down by the painful negotiations. So I guess nobody at Rebellion or DC would now be interested in the black and white version of *Metalzoic*, which appeared in *2000AD* and was absolutely adored by the readers who are continually asking about it... "Hello...? Hello...?" I guess not.

On *2000AD*, I now developed *Ro-Busters* into a further epic set on Earth and Mars with future war, monsters and seven great robot characters: the *ABC Warriors*. I just had so many robot ideas running through my head, in particular a story about a robot called Mongrol, built from different machines by the beautiful and tragic Lara. That "Beauty and the Beast" story also seemed to come from somewhere deep within my subconscious.

Kevin O'Neill and Mike McMahon were commissioned to illustrate the *Warriors*. Then the brilliant Brendan "Mad Max" McCarthy was added to the art team. It was a great line-up, so it looked to me like we could have another *Cursed Earth* on our hands. The *ABC Warriors* would take over from *Ro-Busters*.

At this point, Kelvin Gosnell was still the editor. I still remember when he saw the artwork for Mongrol. That scene where the ape-like robot is tearing a vehicle in half and grunting, "Mongrol rip bogey buggy in half." Kelvin—hopefully in a good way—was shocked, and exclaimed, "What the hell is *that*?!!" Just the kind of reaction comics should have.

So all was looking well for my new series and then Steve MacManus succeeded Kelvin, I think while he was away creating *Tornado*. Unfortunately, the story was scheduled for publication far too soon. The timing was too tight for Kevin, so he dropped out and ultimately it only left Mike as the regular artist. This resulted in extra artists being drafted in. As we're talking about Dave Gibbons and Carlos Ezquerra, it wasn't too painful. Dave was great and Carlos also did a fabulous job. Once again, I brought back *Flesh* with armoured T-Rexes on Mars, continuing the theme of an interconnected *2000AD* universe. However, it wasn't Carlos's regular story, which he doubtless would have preferred to be drawing, and that is why he signed the *ABC Warriors* credit card "L. J. Silver". So, editorially, it just wasn't getting the TLC that Nick had provided on *The Cursed*

Earth. I was able to paper over the cracks by writing stories to fit and suit the individual artists but it wasn't what I had intended or was promised, so I decided to bring the serial to an end. Later I relented, and considered writing more episodes so it could be ongoing or return after a break. But Steve told me he wasn't interested. *The ABC Warriors* were finished.

This kind of aggro was unheard of on girls' comics, or *Battle*, where everyone knew what they were doing and I could produce relatively well-paid work of quality with far less stress. So I remember vividly saying at the time, "I swear I will never work for this guy again." Those weren't my exact words, of course.

Thanks to Steve, it would be several years before the *ABC Warriors* would finally return in their own right with *The Black Hole*, illustrated by Simon Bisley and SMS.

Titan Books introduced me to Simon and said there was a great comic artist from Oxford, currently working on a building site, who just needed a little directing and maybe I could help? They showed me some of his early work. I caught the next train to Oxford. We sat in a café, where Simon observed some of the university students at adjoining tables and loudly gave his opinion of them. I don't remember his exact words, but I think there were generally four letters in them. We got along just fine.

Simon's art on the *ABC Warriors*, and his appearance in the comic, was a game-changer. Since then they have gone from strength to strength and are currently being lovingly illustrated by Clint Langley. And, as I write this, Simon Bisley is producing a Joe Pineapples story in colour. And has been—for the last two years. Fingers crossed, but I think it will happen.

I also wanted stronger sf stories in the Warriors. Kelvin Gosnell had tried to bring more science fiction into the comic, he had a great and inspiring vision, but it wasn't possible to bring to fruition and I'm still sad about this. He really wanted to see some of those classic sf writers' work portrayed in comic form. Other publishers have tried and generally failed, but I do wish we'd had the time to do it and to get it right. To find pure sf that would still appeal to younger readers. Kelvin had succeeded admirably by serialising Harry Harrison's *Stainless Steel Rat*, because the Rat is an action hero. But much sf, by definition, is cerebral, rather than dynamic and it's hard to find artists who can portray it in a popular culture style. And then, so many years later, I found someone who, in my opinion, does exactly that and ticks all the boxes.

This first pure sf artist rejoiced in the splendid name of SMS. But this was decades ago, so there was no danger of anyone thinking he was a text message. His style is unique, but—for some—a slow burn, an acquired taste. He contributed regularly truly beautiful sf comic strip stories to the prestigious magazine *Interzone* and had worked with the acclaimed sf writer Iain M. Banks. I was blown away by his art.

Despite the readers' and editorial's understandable preference for the fantastic black T-shirt art of Simon Bisley, making his fabulous debut art appearance on the *ABC Warriors*, I also wanted SMS onto the series. I did this so that I could write cerebral as well as biker action episodes. If I didn't write some episodes with subtext, I would have just got bored and lost interest in the Warriors. I was following *The Cursed Earth* principle of using two contrasting artists. The results by SMS were incredible and opened up vistas of how really challenging sf *could* appear in *2000AD*. An Escher style city, for example, which SMS beautifully depicted in the *Warriors*. Who else, amongst *2000AD's* action artists, would even be interested in drawing such a fantastic concept which requires the artist to be marinaded in hard-core science fiction?

But, once my *ABC Warriors* series was over, editorial simply faded SMS out, probably because he didn't command an instant fan following like Simon. I remember the incumbent Thargs, Richard Burton and Alan McKenzie, telling me they found SMS too high maintenance and didn't like him abbreviating his name. That seemed to be a big problem for the Mighty Ones.

But that potential for a new audience was there. It takes time for a subtle style to grow on the readers. For them to get used to a new approach. This can apply to us all and it certainly applied to two of *2000AD's* most well known contributors, Alan Moore and Grant Morrison, both of whose preliminary scripts had been put on ice by an insecure and uncertain Tharg until assistant editor Alan Grant insisted they be used.

While I'm on the subject of blocking creatives, Neil Gaiman, too, was also blocked as a writer. You might imagine from his interview on the *2000AD* documentary that he was a regular contributor, but I'm told he only wrote four Future Shocks. One excellent Future Shock he wrote was drawn by John Hicklenton, John's first work on the comic. It's a little puzzling why Neil should be blocked and didn't go on to write serials for *2000AD*.

So why was talent usually blocked? Control? Jealousy? Potential rivals when staff go freelance? That certainly played a role in some cases. But it was often also down to shortage of time and shortage of staff. I have great, *great* sympathy with those last two reasons. It takes so long to develop new writers and artists, especially if they are unreliable, disappear in the middle of a story, or are high maintenance and the problems in their lives suddenly become your problem.

But blocking is a claim many readers and other writers and artists have made over the years. Of course, all rejected contributors will claim this in all areas of publishing and it can seem like sour grapes. But I'm very aware of it and the tremendous difficulties in getting Tharg's approval for an artist. For example, I had trouble getting the brilliant Glenn Fabry into *2000AD* because they weren't sure about his anatomy. Apparently.

Coming back to artist SMS, I think it was because his art was so different to the norm, so his face didn't fit with "comic people". But I still think he's fantastic, with an appeal to a *wider* audience, who don't actually care about artists having some kind of orthodox comic heritage, where influences of Jack Kirby, Neil Adams and others can be noted and approved of by pundits. I don't have a comic heritage either, and neither do many people who have succeeded in comics.

I really want to see SMS make a comeback. I do hope he'll be given a break now. I loved his work on *ABC Warriors* and now, it seems, many readers do, too. It was a slow burn, but I do believe we have ignition.

17. BE PURE! BE VIGILANT! BEHAVE!

Inevitably, I relented and returned to working for Tharg McManus and *2000AD*, primarily because I wanted to collaborate with Kevin again, so we cautiously dipped our toe in the water with a one-off. We were very impressed by the work of the French artist Caza, who would design endless high concept one-off fantasies. Our idea was that each story should be wildly different to the next but with an over-arching hero: *Nemesis*. It was to be comic rock and roll, hence our sub-title: *Comic Rock*.

The first story was *Terror Tube*, because I wanted Kevin to recreate his brilliant Travel Tube system in *Ro-Busters*, which Bob Bartholemew had tried to scrap as he "didn't understand it". It introduced Torquemada and was phenomenally successful. Another story followed and—before we knew it—we were both back in the Nerve Centre.

Then Kevin drew an astonishing and wildly imaginative steampunk *Nemesis*, without any doubt, the greatest comic book steampunk art of all time. This story forced me to really think through the whole saga and world and explain Torquemada's motivation which was to wipe out all alien life. My necessary six-week development time had been mercifully spread over a long period. But Kevin could no longer afford to work for *2000AD* on their slave wages. I think he was living off corn flakes at the time. So he left to work for America. Luckily, I headhunted Bryan Talbot and he continued in the same style. I loved his Victorian Brick Moon!

Furthermore, he actually suggested he'd like to draw the *ABC Warriors* and could they be included? I was thrilled. Because for a long time Steve/Tharg had been telling the readers, in response to their anxious questions, that the *ABC Warriors*, the future war story they loved so much, would be returning soon. This was being somewhat economical with the truth. He never asked me at any time to return to the Meknificent Seven and—in any event—no one wanted or was available to draw the series. I think Mike McMahon had gone back to *Dredd*. So had Carlos, or he was working on *Strontium Dog*. Dave was drawing *Rogue Trooper* somewhere around this time, Gerry Finley-Day's future war story, commissioned by Steve. Tharg had possibly seen from the *ABC Warriors* the potential in future war. For me, featuring the Warriors in *Nemesis* was a way—the only way—of honouring Tharg's empty promises to the readers and bringing the Warriors back, just as I'd brought *Flesh* back into the comic.

Frank Plowright, journalist and organiser of UK comic conventions, once interviewed me about *Nemesis the Warlock* and said how he envied *Nemesis* co-creator Kevin O'Neill and I our Catholic childhood, because it clearly influenced and inspired our work. I hadn't realised it showed, but of course it does and especially on Torquemada, the Warlock's greatest enemy.

And also on *The Redeemer*, a successful series about a similar deranged fanatic I co-wrote for Games Workshop. In the Redeemer's case, he went around with blazing coals in a brazier on his head, like you do. His monk-like assistant, Malakev, has to keep the fire going. The Redeemer's catchphrases were "Scourge and Purge" and my favourite: "If it doesn't hurt, it doesn't count."

So I should talk more about the characters who inspired me to create Torquemada, develop *The Redeemer*, and my version of *Judge Dredd*. Those De La Salle Brothers had always impressed with me their black robes and puritanical vows of poverty, chastity and obedience. My older brother, Terry, was more street-wise. He'd discovered that the Brothers ate posh food, smoked and watched telly, and kept a good wine cellar. He was very insistent on that point. I guess he must have sampled it. There's a Youtube clip from the film *The Devil's Playground*, which shows the DLSB in such a relaxed mode.

Another old boy recently described to me how the Brothers all went off to the golf course with first formers in tow as caddies. They owned five shotguns. Two .410 guns and three twelve bores. Two of the twelve bores being expensive West German guns.

If I'd known all this, I would have been shocked. Wine? Fags? Golf? Hunting parties? Surely not! These weren't ordinary human beings. They *must* exist on a strict diet of bread and water, accompanied by constant prayer, before regular self-flagellation, as recommended by Christian saints, then suspend themselves upside down, like bats, from the rafters of their Hive, before, suitably refreshed, going out to do more "good work".

I saw them in fantasy comic-book terms, like the cartoon strips in the movie, *The Dangerous Lives Of Altar Boys*. "Good work" was Torquemada's euphemism for his genocidal onslaught on the Galaxy. Already, in the back of my mind, I was creating the future basis of my evil monks in *Nemesis the Warlock*. I guess such comic book fantasies are common amongst kids. Graham Linehan, co-creator of *Father Ted*, told Kevin O'Neill that he used to daydream about the Blitzspear flying down to his school playground to rescue him.

I know the feeling. I could have used some rescuing myself. But there was only the classic *Dan Dare* in my day, and Colonel Dare was a signed-up member of the establishment (originally a space *chaplain*) so he wouldn't have listened to my complaints.

It's why I made sure my comics would be different and have role models kids could identify with. It's why even today I write *Defoe, The Last Leveller*, for *2000AD*. Defoe is the last of Britain's first revolutionaries, but most history teachers never tell their pupils about these great heroes. For me, it is so important for readers to have heroes who fight on the side of the oppressed.

Even if the Blitzspear never actually managed to land in that school playground. Sorry about that, Graham.

Brother Solomon was primarily my role model for Torquemada and Brother James the basis for Dredd. Brother Solomon, like James, was a "Prefect of Discipline" and was responsible for administering corporal punishment. Errant boys, sometimes after an apprehensive wait of several days, would nervously appear before him in a room set aside for the purpose and present him with tickets detailing their crime. He would read their offences, hear their excuses and then pronounce and carry out sentence, inevitably guilty as charged. This required them to prostrate themselves over a desk for a classic caning. He, too, was judge, jury and executioner.

I used the idea of that delay and the sense of dread it engendered in boys for a *Judge Dredd Blood of Satanus* story. The perp has been told by a busy Dredd to report to him later at Justice HQ for punishment, but he is far too scared to go, even though his girlfriend tells him he'll only make things worse by not turning up. Monday passes and there's no sign of Dredd. Tuesday, still no sign of Dredd. Wednesday and the perp starts to relax and think Dredd must have forgotten him. Thursday and he knows Dredd has definitely forgotten. Friday and the perp celebrates how he got away with his crime. Saturday, and Judge Dredd kicks down the door and comes for him.

We won't go into detail on Solomon's crimes here. I detail them in a Roll of Dishonour, on patmills.wordpress.com, along with the misdeeds of other "Black Monks" like Brother James and Brother Kevin, my Latin teacher. Their wrongdoings are detailed and corroborated by endless testimonies of survivors on my blog and elsewhere online.

The Christian fish has a shark's fin on its back.

I've sometimes wondered why I have Nemesis saying Credo! (Believe!) as the warlock's sign-off. Why would an alien demon speak in Latin, of all languages? Why, to annoy Torquemada, of course.

My primary version of Torquemada, Solomon, suddenly disappeared in mid-term with no official explanation, although we all knew the reason. Brother James wrote a glowing tribute to all his "good work" in the school magazine that year. Rumours were rife he'd gone to a De La Salle establishment in Jersey, which we believed was a reformatory for Brothers who messed with kids. Certainly, there was an establishment there run by the Brothers. We would joke about shipwrecked sailors staggering onto the rocky coast of Jersey, only to see all these Brothers descending on them, so they would hurriedly turn and flee back into the sea. We needed such trench humour to survive and, of course, you can see that in most of my work.

Subsequently, Solomon went on to teach at St. Joseph's College, Beulah Hill, where he was also thrown out, before returning to my old school as a lay teacher and being thrown out yet again. A Beulah Hill old boy angrily relates online *"as if there weren't enough very strange, totally weird, 'Christian' Brothers, they brought in Brother Solomon."* He characterized him as "detestable, monstrous, evil, brutal". Solomon was a serial predator, a lesser version of Jimmy Savile.

Distinguished, tragic poet Paul Wilkins, in his book *Truths of the Unremembered Things,* wrote about his experiences at the hands of Solomon and his poetry makes for chilling and sad reading.

Solomon was eventually dismissed from the order and went into showbiz as a pop pianist, calling himself Mike Mercado: The Swinging Monk. He had a couple of minor hits. If you Google him, you'll find him with a hood and a toupee, because he was bald. I mention it because the photo shows his smile, which reminds me how Torquemada was sometimes depicted, leering at the readers with that same Savile-like, knowing grin.

Fellow old boy, ex-MP Chris Mullin, two years older than me, remembers Solomon "all too well." Chris is the author *A Very British Coup*, one of my all time favourite novels and a brilliant Channel 4

TV series (dramatized by Alan Plater). Chris tells me that Solomon/Mercado "ended his days playing the piano on a pier in a south coast resort."

In fairness to St Joe's, I should add that, today, the current school has no connection with the "Black Monks", and I'm sure is an excellent establishment. As Chris wrote to me:

"Have you been back there since you left? It's a very different place. The Brothers are long gone, the school now takes girls—inconceivable in our day."

But, with my recollections in the back of my mind, I made Torquemada as warped and perverted as I could.

I hope this doesn't shatter anyone's illusions about Torquemada? I'm afraid creating characters is *not* just about having a vivid imagination or drawing on movies or books. All great fictional heroes and villains are based, directly or indirectly, on someone, or a combination of *someones*, whether the writer chooses to admit it or not. I think if you're going to create villains they should be genuinely evil: I've no time for pantomime villains. I'm sure that this is why Torquemada regularly won awards as British comics' favourite villain: because readers sensed this monster was *real*. And yet at the same time I mocked him, I enjoyed humiliating and defeating him.

So did the readers. In Prog 602, on the letters page, there's a cartoon by G. Green of Enfield depicting Torquemada as a beehive. With the caption: "Be Pure! Be Vigilant! Beehive!"

Mel Brooks has a similar humorous approach in *History of the World Part 1* where he plays the Grand Master torturing the Jews. "You can't Torquemada anything."

Nemesis the Warlock was *my* catharsis. It was *my* poetry.

18. KISS MY AXE!

Slaine was created by myself and my then wife, Angela Kincaid. It certainly took us both at least six weeks each to develop, and it was worth it. The character still appears in *2000AD* to this day.

I'd looked at Robert E Howard's work and Michael Moorcock's *Elric* and *Corum* and hugely admired their stories, but I wanted something different, something more subversive, in keeping with the tone of *2000AD*. Then I saw that Moorcock was referring to Celtic legends in *Corum,* and that led me to Irish legends, notably the Kinsella adaptation of the great Irish saga *The Tain.*

My mother came from the west coast of Ireland, so I'd grown up on Irish history. As a kid I'd read everything I could get my hands on about Michael Collins, Parnell, Wolf Tone and Eamon De Valera. Eamon is my middle name: I'm named after the Irish president. But up to this point, I knew nothing of Irish mythology, probably because it's wild, punk, pagan and sexy, so I felt really cheated. *Slaine* was my way of completing my Irish and Celtic education. The time travel stories that came later were a necessary part of further exploring the Celtic diaspora, in all its complex forms from the Britain of King Arthur, to the Scotland of William Wallace to the Holy Grail mysteries of Cathar France.

Angela and I based Slaine on Ray Morgenson, a "King Mod"

straight out of *Quadrophenia*, whom we both knew and liked. From Bury St. Edmunds, he was a powerful, cool guy who worked in the building trade. So Slaine is muscular and real, not an impossible, pumping-iron figure. But we knew Ray from a long time ago, so we also based Slaine specifically on Jack Nicholson, and I bought a photo-book of the actor as a reference source. I still think that's the best role model for Slaine, but subsequent artists have all, directly or indirectly, based the character on themselves, and that also usually works, although I prefer the Jack Nicholson look, myself.

In the early days of *2000AD*, all characters wore helmets and never smiled, whether it was Dredd, Rogue Trooper, Strontium Dog or Hammerstein. So for at least a week I insisted Slaine should wear a helmet and Angela came up with some great designs. Then I suddenly realised he would be better without one, hence that scowling image of him in Episode One, where he's saying "Kiss my axe", aimed, deservedly, at me, rather than Slaine's enemies. But Angela also has him smiling and looking handsome, two concepts that were hitherto unknown on *2000AD*, bringing much-needed female energy and perspective to the character and the comic.

Angela had shown an interest in us producing a character together, primarily as a social thing. *2000AD* was a club, and artists regularly hung out and supported each other. That didn't materialize here. Not one of my peers rang up Angela to offer encouragement and support. So, for this reason and—even more likely—because I was driving her up the wall with my endless changes, she only drew episode one and then bailed. Her experience with *2000AD* editorial was also not a happy one and they actually toned down her violence in one scene. So she returned to illustrating books for young children and had a hit with her impressive *Butterfly Children* (originally written by me). There were books, merchandising, and even a musical.

The majority of readers, the mainstream—but not the fans—loved her work. All the key design elements in the character and world are there in her first episode. I did this deliberately to ensure she wasn't gazumped: a very real danger, because it was clear she was already resented by my colleagues. The story topped the charts, the first story to ever beat *Judge Dredd* since the *Robot Rebellion*. Nobody rang her up to congratulate her. It was the first comic strip she had ever done and it beat them all. Imagine what might have happened if she had felt sufficiently supported and encouraged to draw subsequent episodes. It would be hard to minimize her amazing achievement, and to explain it away, although I'm sure her critics doubtless still do. The readers rated her, but purists really don't care about the readers, only their own minority orthodoxy. My answer to them, then and now is: Kiss my Axe.

The gap between the mainstream majority and an elite minority was now widening, with serious implications for *Slaine* and ultimately the wellbeing of the comic. I turned down two hot fan favourite artists on *Slaine*, approved of by purists, because I knew, despite their huge talents, they would have taken the character away from the "illustrative" look I was after. This was largely inspired by the popular French *Conquering Armies* by Gal and Dionnet, recently reprinted by Humanoids, and about to come out in paperback. It's disliked by British fan-orientated artists and—at this time—they were determined that their artistic vision for the comic should prevail, even though it was at variance with my own, and the majority of the readers. It lead to many angry phone calls with them.

I chose Belardinelli to continue *Slaine* and the readers responded well to my choice. But never the fan minority. Despite my passionate pitch for Belardinelli, Nick Landau refused point blank to reprint Massimo's *Slaine* stories and it was only really in the Rebellion era that his work and Angela's have been reprinted and given the respect they were due.

Mike McMahon's *Slaine*, notably on *Sky Chariots*, is now deservedly regarded as a classic. His style was very different and I—rather nervously—asked Angela's opinion. Appraising it as an artist, she rated it highly and that was good enough for me. But the majority of readers, initially, felt otherwise, which came as a shock to me. Today, thanks to Rebellion, the two opposing views on *Slaine* are reconciled, but it was quite traumatic at the time and for many years afterwards.

As the pressure from fans and their importance grew ever stronger, I eventually bowed to it and parted with Belardinelli. Thanks to a tip-off by Bryan Talbot, I found artists Glenn Fabry (Preacher) and David Pugh to continue the saga. Their work also reconciled the two factions and is amongst my many favourites. Glenn's characterisation on *Slaine* is truly sublime and David's savagery is unsurpassed.

Simon Bisley followed on the *Horned God* and his incredible and beautiful interpretation was so successful, sales of *2000AD* actually went up, although there was no bonus for either of us. In fact, some of his valuable artwork mysteriously went missing from the editorial office. I'm surprised they never tracked it down. Perhaps they should have called in someone from the official police magazine next door to assist them. But *Slaine* opened the doorway to Europe for *2000AD*. *Slaine* has appeared in beautiful foreign editions in France, Spain, Italy, Czech Republic, Belgium, Holland, Poland as well as in the United States.

More fantastic artists were to follow including Dermot Power, later a designer on Star Wars and Harry Potter, Clint Langley and currently Simon Davis.

But the elitism continued. The fandom tail was now definitely wagging the mainstream dog and this was a direction many editors, following in Nick's footsteps often pursued, preferring the acclaim of fans to the approval of regular and younger readers. So we lost thousands upon thousands of them, who would often write in and bitterly complain that the comic was becoming too cool, as I've exampled, or "up its own ass", as one of them described it to me.

Whatever you may have read elsewhere, this—and the lack of rights—is the ultimate reason the circulation would eventually drop and why we lost our younger readers. With a little clever footwork and talent it's possible to keep *everybody* happy: young and old, purist and mainstream. There's no reason to ignore *any* faction. Games Workshop, who started roughly the same time as *2000AD*, have successfully done this and gone from strength to strength.

Other explanations for the drop in circulation are often complacent excuses. It was never about video or computer games taking over, or new generations of kids losing the comic habit. It's not easy to spot changing trends, but publishing is never easy, and there's always a way. The old regime trotted out similar pathetic excuses to John Wagner, Gerry Finley-Day and I when we started the new wave, which revived comics. "Nothing works. Boys' comics are finished," was the lazy credo back in 1975.

Now not just *2000AD* but other British comics were slowly being destroyed by similar forces and this time there was no cure. Only *2000AD* and a handful of D. C. Thomson comics have survived.

19. COMICS CLINIC

Meanwhile, *Judge Dredd* had grown in popularity, particularly with the breathtaking *Judge Death* saga, drawn by Brian Bolland. Merchandising and reprints followed. We'd hear stories of *Dredd* and other *2000AD* characters being published in foreign editions, but with none of the profits being passed onto the contributors responsible, and this increasingly became a source of bitterness to everyone.

Sometimes, it would seem to me the writers and artists were regarded not as the vital basis of the comic but somehow as *the enemy.* Our requests for a fair deal were constantly ignored, along with our suggestions to make the Galaxy's Greatest Comic even greater.

Thus, back at the beginning, Kevin O'Neill discovered Star Wars poster rights were available *for nothing!* Seeing the huge potential, he investigated further and passed the info on to the bosses, telling them that *2000AD* must do it. He was informed that IPC was too big a company to handle "such an unimportant project".

Grievances reached such a point that I devised a one-off story, with contributions by the artists concerned, entitled *Tharg's Head Revisited*, in which I scripted their complaints, as a way of putting pressure on management to change. Two of these pages are particularly memorable. Unfortunately, John Sanders saw *Tharg's*

Head just before it went to press, pulled the two offending pages, rang me up and gave me a massive bollocking. I pointed out that Brian was highlighting how *Dredd* was a merchandising hit, thanks primarily to his art. "Tell Brian that *Dredd* makes no money," John said. "It makes no money, *at all.*" I duly passed the message on.

Brian's page has subsequently appeared and shows Dredd riding an absurd cockhorse, surrounded by ludicrous examples of *Dredd* merchandising. The other page by Mike McMahon is even more contentious. Entitled *Dredd and the Bloodsuckers*, it showed Dredd in *The Cursed Earth* on the road to a city named Catharsis. Dredd hears strange sounds coming from underneath a stone. He turns it over and underneath are blood-sucking parasites feeding off the blood of a fantasy version of McMahon. Dredd considers crushing them, but, after a moment's reflection, decides, "No. Don't want to dirty my boot." This was a clear reference to the way Mike's incredible and iconic images of Dredd had been disgracefully traced over and used again and again by other artists for their own covers. This was particularly inexcusable as Mike became sick, and editorial should never have permitted it. Ultimately it was *their* responsibility to put a stop to the practise. Shame on them.

Plagiarism is a sensitive issue. One *2000AD* writer, who we were told was going to be "the next Alan Moore" (and I read recently was even being lined-up to be the next *2000AD* editor), allegedly lifted an entire sf story and ran it as his own. I guess if you are going to do that, at least pick an obscure sf author. Not Philip K. Dick. Perhaps the writer in question wanted to be "the next Philip K. Dick." Needless to say, the readers pointed out the blatant copy.

Editorial's bullish response was hilarious. We were loftily informed in a circular from Tharg that there are, in fact, only seven basic plots in the world; and therefore, inevitably, there will sometimes be similarities between writers' works because of synchronicity. But, as a *2000AD* writer responded—I believe it was Alan Grant—it's one thing for the plots to be identical, but when the *words* are the same as well, this is stretching synchronicity to intriguing new levels of science fiction.

The horror stories coming out from *2000AD* at this time were numerous and the exact details are not always known to me, not least because I and other creators have broken the rule of *omerta* and spoken out about editorial wrong-doings. So, in response, the Thargs have become understandably secretive as the years have passed.

Here are three examples:

- There was the film *Hardware*, based on a *2000AD* story by Kevin O'Neill, which he didn't know about, until the readers alerted him. But it wasn't just concern about it being made into a film. The questionable circumstances around the original *2000AD* script prompted Kevin to write a letter to *Time Out*.
- There was the appalling story of how the Fleetway comic archive of original artwork—100 years of British popular culture—was brutally disposed of in skips with the knowledge and assistance of Tharg and no more sensitivity than the store men who once used classic artwork to block up drains.
- There was also the Fleetway Film and TV fiasco, where Egmont and *2000AD* were so enamoured by Hollywood producers and their pitch they actually *funded them* to sell our stories.

Kevin O'Neill and I had already worked with the Americans involved and we did well financially on our *Marshal Law* film option with them, because, after years of dealing with Hollywood people, we know how to play hard-ball. So we were insiders and we knew there would be problems. Correction: we knew it would be a disaster. Concerned for *2000AD's* wellbeing, Kevin generously made a special point of phoning a top guy at Egmont and alerting him to the *difficulties* they would be facing.

Naturally, he was ignored. Why should a publisher ever take any notice of a mere comic book artist or writer? No, better to listen to those hotshot Hollywood producers.

It was an embarrassing disaster. Our own contacts in tinsel town said they cringed at the ludicrous Fleetway advert in *Variety* that announced the *2000AD* character invasion. After years of hype, I'm only aware of one result. *Strontium Dog* was optioned for one pound. Or was it one dollar?

But worse, Tharg was feeding this Hollywood fantasy nonsense to the readers, telling them their favourite comic characters were well on their way to the screen.

Needless to say, we, the creators of the characters in these proposed films, were not consulted or credited on the final film pitches that went to the States. Tharg "forgot". Again.

The entire story of Fleetway Film and TV is actually worse, but that gives you the flavour. When Dave Bishop interviewed me for material for his articles on *2000AD*, I asked him to include details of the Fleetway Film and TV scandal. He told me it was too soon, and the details too sensitive, so I refused to co-operate with him further. I don't think you can have it both ways. If you're going to write a supposedly hard-hitting insider's story about *2000AD*, you can't miss out the worst story of all, simply because it may put your own role in a possibly negative light.

Inevitably, in response to so many years of poor money, unfair treatment, and incompetence, creators went elsewhere. Many left to work for America. Brian Bolland and Dave Gibbons were amongst the first to go. I recall bringing this up with John Sanders at the time and saying he *had* to offer them a better deal to hold onto these two masters of comic book art. John shrugged and said it wasn't possible. He told me America would always call the shots.

In my case, I was never that attracted to work for the States. Although I have worked for Marvel and DC Comics, it's rarely been on superheroes, unless I can show some truth in them. Thus I co-wrote an occult thriller, *Batman The Book of Shadows* (artist: Duke

Mighten), about the lonely people of the night and what happens to them, with Batman as the King of the Lonely. So while my peers headed for the States, I went to France and built a career there. France was, after all, where I drew my inspiration for *2000AD*. After Manga, France is the world leader in comics. Their stunningly beautiful comic books are in huge demand and I can actually see my most successful series, *Requiem Vampire Knight*, in supermarkets. Because in France, comics are not just for fans, but for *everyone*.

But it didn't have to be like this. We should not have had to search for work in other countries, and regard another culture as somehow superior to our own. All the answers, all the possibilities, all the opportunities for talent, should be here in Britain.

As proof, consider the equally British Games Workshop, which started around the same time as us, in the mid 1970s, with fantasy games aimed at a similar audience to *2000AD*. Though not known for giving creators intellectual property rights either, Games Workshop had a dynamic policy of expansion, which has resulted in a high street empire; the Birmingham exhibition stadium is filled to the brim every year with young enthusiastic fans; and new generations are constantly replacing old generations of fans.

Just as in France, and throughout Europe, new generations of kids discover comics and sometimes replace the previous generation if they outgrow them. It could have, and should have been like this for *2000AD*.

We could have been Comics Workshop. Instead, we ended up becoming Comics Clinic.

In fairness to the various outpatients, I should say many artists will have fond memories of working for Steve MacManus, who created an excellent social and working environment for them, which greatly helped their work. Prior to the Comics Revolution, it was unheard of. Writers and artists worked in lonely isolation. On *Action* I encouraged three artists to actually set up their studio in my office. That supportive trend continued on *2000AD*. Often it was the only way to get—and hold onto—hot artists.

Sometimes it could be overwhelming, though. Hence those therapy cards printed by Margaret Clark. I mentioned the cards to artists at a Guardian Master Class I gave on comics and I chuckled to myself as my anecdote went down like a lead balloon.

It wasn't what people want to hear, but the relationship of a writer and an artist is not impersonal, and is often the difference between success and failure on a strip. Especially on *2000AD*. Indifference doesn't usually work.

So artist therapy was a part of my life. One *2000AD* artist phoned me up and seriously told me he intended to commit suicide. By pure coincidence, I could hear a chainsaw buzzing in the background as he spoke. I arranged to meet him the next day in London to try and talk through his troubles. He was definitely in a bad way, trying to step in front of taxis and buses. We went to a restaurant and, as he knocked glasses onto the floor and insulted the waitress, I would have been a little more sympathetic if he hadn't also insulted a member of my family. I saw him safely onto the underground and hoped he'd survive. He has.

Another desperate artist told me he couldn't work unless he had a girlfriend and so I asked my own girlfriend at the time if she had any attractive single friends I could introduce him to. A third artist made anonymous phone calls to me late at night, even though I recognised his voice immediately. He cursed and threatened me. I believe it was because my comic projects were a rival to his own, although he was never articulate enough to be sure.

When I later had to rescue rival comic *Toxic!* from oblivion when we lacked an editor, I had to become the stand-in *de facto* editor, and hired a secretary, Oz, primarily to deal with such high-maintenance artists.

My friend Oz, a comic expert in his own right, has a gentle, calm manner and knew just how to handle them. He was fantastic. One artist screamed hysterically down the phone at him because he didn't like his colourist's work. Wonderful, kind, understanding Oz would calm him and the other *Toxic!* artists down with their various complaints, which were often absolutely valid. He could talk them all down off the ledge.

Later, he became a social worker and today works with clients with mental health issues.

Emotional challenges will always be there for creatives, it's the nature of what we do, but it would have been some comfort to us if we could have been *rich* and crazy.

20. FILMS AND TV SERIES

All of the key *Dredd* creators received some payment for our contributions to the first *Judge Dredd* movie. Credits were harder.

Kevin and I refused to sign away our rights unless we got a by-line, and the filmmakers finally agreed to our insistent requests. But they had the last laugh. If you have a magnifying glass, our names are all down there in micro-type (or they used to be), somewhere after the carpenters' credits and before the Dolby sound logo.

Finally, the first *Dredd* movie, with a version of my character Rico as the main villain, had hit the screen. The arguments about the weaknesses in the first movie and the suitability of Stallone to play the Judge sometimes take away from the tremendous achievement of it happening at all. Getting a film made is no small feat, so I think we have to cut them some slack, even when they get it wrong.

Personally, I was excited as I walked around the incredible Mega-City set at Pinewood and saw Carlos's fabulous starscrapers turned into reality. And the fantastic ABC war robot based on Hammerstein, created by Kevin O'Neill and myself. I won't let anything take away from that boyish excitement I felt at seeing these characters from *2000AD* brought to life.

After all, for years there had been plans to do a *Dan Dare* movie and this was generally held to be the most likely British hero to make it to Hollywood. Entrepreneurs like Paul De Savary spent a fortune trying and failing to do so. Dare was always held up by media pundits as an example of how comics should be. *Dare* is indeed a brilliant strip, one of the few classic British comic strips I admire. But it was in an expensive, middle-class, educational comic.

By comparison, *Dredd* was from a despised, cheaply printed, subversive, violent, working-class orientated comic with a bad attitude that everyone wanted to die. It was the peak of the comic new wave that began with *Battle*. Instead, in the best tradition of classic boys' comic endings, we'd come "forward from the back streets", to beat the teacher's pet to the Hollywood accolade.

As to why the first film didn't succeed, there are a host of possible factors which are well known: too many rewrites by too many writers; solid oak dialogue; the casting of Stallone as the Judge; Dredd removing his helmet, and so forth. But I think there's also the nature of *Dredd* itself. I think they understood *Dredd* from the outside, not from the *inside*. There was no internal comprehension—whether they went for my interpretation of Dredd in Rico and *The Cursed Earth* or John's original, hard-hitting version.

Fortunately, Alex Garland remedied this in the new *Dredd* movie. I understand he worked closely with John and it shows. Karl Urban is also utterly convincing as Judge Dredd. What a voice and what a profile!

It's been a hit in the UK but not in the States, which is disappointing. I'm reminded of my friend, Dejan Kraljacic's words: "By comparison, American superheroes seem compromised. *Dredd* is more radical, more punk rock, more on the edge. But he's too alternative-tough for America and not artistic enough for Europe."

Perhaps American cinema audiences like their compromised superheroes too much and *Dredd* is too cool and tough for them. I know the writer's intention was to reach the mainstream, but it didn't feel to me like they were prioritised. But it's surely necessary to appeal to those American twenty-somethings first, who may have barely heard of *Dredd*.

It's a tough one. I've sometimes wondered if that Nosferatu-like sense of dread that is built into the character's very name has sometimes been lost sight of. To build up that kind of suspense in a comic really eats up the pages so it's difficult. And you need the right noir artist to pull it off. I've had at least one strong *Dredd* story ruined by pedestrian, middle of the road art I would never have commissioned: *Birthday Boy*, where a perp sticks lit candles in his flesh. Potentially, he was a Pinhead: instead, he was a damp squib.

It's discouraging when editors waste strong stories in this way. Fear and suspense requires careful, slow, dark, Sergio Leone-style choreography, which takes considerable thought and often more than one draft to get it right. All too often we have to slam into the action and it's actually the easier option and what editors seem to prefer, so why risk time and effort being innovative. "A sense of dread" was certainly my intention in the *Blood of Satanus* story I described, where the perp is so afraid of his appointment with Dredd he just cannot face him. So Dredd comes to him. Doubtless there are other stories that explore this fear, but action always takes priority and that's what comes through in the film. I don't think of Dredd in a 'Nosferatu' way anymore. I really don't think I played this up enough in the early *Dredd* stories in *2000AD* so it's my bad. But hard, cool, slick action, by comparison, is a crowded field and there are plenty of other contenders in the cinema.

Despite the internal comprehension of the second movie, we still have to relate to the characters and from talking to non-*2000AD* fans, who are members of the target audience who love movies with guns, action and sf, they simply didn't *care* enough about the characters. Comedy might have been one way to reach them. Doubtless there were reasons for not going down that road: *Robocop* was influenced by *Dredd* decades before. But I recall talking to a friend who knew nothing of *Judge Dredd*. I told him about John Wagner's fabulous Judge Cal story and about Aaron A. Aardvark, who had chosen his name because he wanted to be first in the telephone directory. Judge Cal has decided to execute everyone in Mega-City and decides to do it in strict alphabetical order, beginning with Aaron. My friend fell about laughing. He got it instantly.

Similar drama rules apply to television, now in everyone's minds with the news there's to be a *Dredd* TV series. The promotional art is fabulous. It looks like they've got it right. It's a huge and exciting achievement and congratulations to all concerned. In some respects, TV is less problematic than film. So there's every chance it could work really well. There's the time and space and budget to introduce the world properly to a mainstream audience and still remain in harmony with the *2000AD* readers.

Fans of *Dredd* have been regularly contacting me to say how I must be thrilled it's finally happening. What many of them mean is that they think I will be doing well financially from the *Dredd* TV series. The answer is no. I haven't been paid anything for my role as the principal developer of *Dredd*.

My insistence that I didn't receive any payment for the last *Dredd* movie is often met with surprise and cynical disbelief. Similarly, some people also seem to imagine that I'm a producer on this TV series— even though it's clear from the publicity that I'm not, and who the producers are. One writer has already been in touch wanting to send me his outline for a proposed episode of the series. Once again, I'm not involved on the writing side of the *Dredd* TV series in any way, either as an editor or a writer, so, any other TV writers out there: I wish you well, but please don't send me your outlines.

Even so, I am genuinely thrilled about this success and it should mean that ultimately other *2000AD* characters will follow and be turned into films or TV series. My guess would be *Strontium Dog* and *Rogue Trooper*, because they seem closest to Rebellion's heart and are possibly the easiest. If it's TV, perhaps *Flesh*. I'm not sure the TV series *Terra Nova*, also about time travel, makes any difference one way or the other. *Savage* might be tricky because of those pesky Volgans. *ABC Warriors*—an all-robot cast—is maybe a harder sell, despite the success of *Transformers*. *Nemesis* is possibly too dark for a regular audience, but has cult and cartoon potential.

The success of *Game of Thrones* is in *Slaine's* favour. There has been film and TV interest in the character in recent times. A couple of successful film directors have said they'd love to direct a *Slaine* movie. Google *Slaine: The Horned God film*, a short, demo film by Miguel Mesas and you'll see just how cool it can be.

But making movies is an assault course and there are always hurdles to overcome. I can tell you that *Charley's War* was optioned a couple of years ago by an experienced and successful TV production company, but it hasn't gone forward, despite the fact we are in the World War One centenary years. I believe it's because *no* anti-war films or TV series have appeared in the centenary years.

I'm not overly disappointed, because neither I nor the estate of the artist, Joe Colquhoun, were paid *any* of the option fee received by Egmont (the copyright holders) and would not have received any money if the TV series had gone ahead.

But another *2000AD* "cousin": *Accident Man*, by Tony Skinner and myself, which we do own the rights to, is finally being made into a low budget film, after ten years of tough negotiations by Tony and myself.

Such is the world of British comics and the realities of movies and TV series.

21. THE INVADERS

Let's return to the British comic invasion of the States. So many went to work for America: Dave Gibbon; Brian Bolland; Cam Kennedy; Alan Moore; Grant Morrison; Garth Ennis; Andy Diggle—the list is endless. And even myself on *Metalzoic, Marshal Law, Punisher 2099* (with Tony Skinner), and *Ravage 2099* (also with Tony). *Ravage*? One of Stan Lee's creation for Marvel? A *superhero*?!

I should say at this point, if you love superheroes, you may want to skip this chapter. In fact, I'm impressed you've actually got this far, and haven't thrown my Secret History out of the window.

Once again, in the words of Lemony Snicket, "Look away."

To be fair, I was persuaded into writing *Ravage* after a meeting in New York to discuss an exciting Marvel superhero *2099* crossover. It was a splendid, very friendly, hospitable and high-powered event. I guess if you're a superhero writer it's a dream come true. Present were: Stan Lee; Warren Ellis; Peter David, and other writing legends. I assume it was exciting for the others, but I found the crossover artificial, overly-calculated, and uninteresting. It's a commercial device designed to encourage readers to buy extra copies but I couldn't feel any truth, any heart in it. I was so bored by the meaningless and contrived plot-line and so overwhelmed by the strident views of the forceful Peter David, I actually nodded off.

Fortunately, Tony Skinner was there, too, and held up our end as the *Punisher 2099* writers. Somehow, he could make sense of the tortuous plot, which felt like advanced algebra to me. "So if Spidey fights Punisher *here* and meanwhile Doctor Doom clashes with the X Men *there,* while Ravage tracks down the Punisher, then Spidey's battle with the Punisher ends on the first cross-over , because, hey, how about this? In the second issue Doctor Doom reveals that the X Men are actually … " It was the very antithesis of how I write. But Tony's British repartee effortlessly outclassed Peter David's conversation-dominating, fast-talking, New York wit, and he won their frequent verbal duels, somewhat to the latter's surprise. A Brit who could actually talk faster, wittier and sharper than a New Yorker? You never see that in the movies. That kept me amused and awake from time to time.

After the meeting, Stan Lee asked us if we would take over *Ravage* from him. It had made money on the early issues but sales were now dropping. Stan thought we might be just the guys to do a great job on the character. He was very persuasive.

But that night I thought about it, looked at *Ravage* and the thought of writing it made me feel deeply depressed and almost physically ill. It would be like writing *Yellowknife of the Yard* all over again. My muse was not happy. It was against everything I stood for. I went round to Tony's hotel room in a dark state of mind and told him my concerns. "I'm really not sure I can face *Ravage,*" I said.

Thankfully, Tony bailed me out, said he'd be happy to do it alone, and did a great and professional solo job of writing a character that was already well past its sell-by date when we took it over. He's a complete professional and I really believe could write *Thomas The Tank Engine* one day, *Friday the Thirteenth* the next and *Ravage* the day after. But before I get too snooty about *Ravage,* Tony and I were taken aback by a later incident at NY airport. It was on our next trip over to the States where we met an American at the airport who was thrilled to meet two Marvel superhero writers. Naturally I didn't tell him I also wrote *Marshal Law,* superhero hunter. He excitedly told us he loved *Ravage* so much, he bought three copies of it every month so he and his family wouldn't fight over who got to read it first. That was a humbling experience for me and I wish I could say I finally saw the light and understood the joy of superheroes, but I'm afraid not.

The whole Brit invasion of American comics began when DC Comics held a splendid party at the Savoy to invite British creators to work for America. They really pushed the boat out for us and nothing was too much trouble. But many of us acted like the Bash Street Kids at that shindig, and I'm sure I was amongst them. Some of the stories of what happened are memorable but not actually repeatable. There was a little more to it than "quiet interviews." I'm told the Brits' Bash Street Kids approach continued in subsequent years and thus there's that widely-known story of a *2000AD* artist supposedly biting one of the female DC execs bums at one such event. I wasn't there to witness it so I can't tell you why the artist would want to. I've heard the story from several *2000AD* creators, so it definitely has a basis in truth. I assume alcohol was a factor.

Jonathan Ross once asked me, "Why do you hate superheroes so much?" I answered, "How long have we got?" To understand why I even *physically* react against the idea of writing superheroes, I need to explain my thoughts about them.

For me, they're rather more than vacuous poseurs, more than just harmless entertainment not to be taken too seriously. They are the acknowledged icons of America; their superpowers are symbols of their country's super-technology, often they are proudly emblazoned on the sides of their super-weapons. A superhero's clean-cut, red laser rays are a reassuring metaphor for the realities of MOABs and depleted uranium which harms American soldiers as well as enemy targets.

Stealth bombers have awesome powers that are the equivalent of *Superman* and they're invisible, too. Well, not quite. I'm reminded of the occasion when the United States bombed Belgrade and one of their Stealth bombers crashed in Serbia. The Serbs, with their dark sense of humour which is even darker than our own, stood on one of the target bridges with a sign, "Sorry, America. We didn't know your planes were meant to be invisible."

In Belgrade, I've seen a book with graphic photos of the mutated babies caused by depleted uranium. I doubt such tragic photos will ever be seen in Britain and the United States. It's a far remove from the beneficial effects of mutation in the *X Men*.

Even though in comic book versions superheroes seem to be endlessly defending their country against "terrorists" or "crazies" or super-villains, in the real world the values they represent are the threat. *They* are the Invaders.

In superhero comics, corporate bosses, weapons manufacturers and all-powerful tycoons are transformed into superheroes. They are portrayed as benign, amusing and cool benefactors, looked up to in awe as Gods.

I try to counter this in *Marshal Law*. As the billionaire superhero Public Eye says as he looks out over his dark city, "I've pissed on you all and told you it is raining."

I should say in fairness to both Marvel and DC Comics, they look on *Marshal Law's* depredations with great good humour and DC have released the Marshal's adventures as a deluxe edition.

But the fact that comic propaganda has succeeded so well, in the States at least, so that ordinary people see their masters as heroes and don't value their *own* heroic quests, is Orwellian. Many of us really are a product of our rulers' carefully planned social programming.

I'm glad I took the red pill.

I feel so strongly about them, it even affects my dreams.

So a few years ago, an American comic journalist asked me for British fanzine information about Jack Kirby, about whom I know absolutely nothing, other than he was a hugely talented creator and a great guy.

I gently explained this to him, but he insisted that maybe I could get in touch with my friends who, he was adamant, would have the Jack Kirby information he was after. Of course I knew they wouldn't.

I had the most extraordinary dream that night. In it, a group of splendidly cloaked superheroes, making sure they were colour-matching, rushed down to breakfast, running on one leg towards me, in full "Crisis on Infinite Earths" mode, full of their own self-importance, with their mandatory gritted teeth and clenched fists. Courageously fighting for ..? Well, nothing in particular, really. Crying out "Aiee!" as they leapt through the air to seize a packet of cornflakes, desperately diving for the fridge to grab the milk, heroically helping themselves to toast, and then, with one final effort, hurling themselves at the cooker to scramble eggs.

Mercifully, that's all I can remember; I woke up with a start and couldn't understand why I found this nightmare so disturbing. Then I realised it was because something was clearly missing. Or someone. A cereal killer. *Marshal Law*. He would have shoved their heads in toasters, fried their asses and turned this Breakfast of the Vanities into a *Bonfire* of the Vanities.

The two polarities: what superhero comics stand for and what *2000AD* stands for, would be a regular source of conflict through the '80s and '90s. We would lose many contributors to the States and sometimes it seemed that creators were only working for *2000AD* so they could gather material for a portfolio to show DC. When I found a new artist, I would judge how long I would have him before he was poached by DC. Competition is inevitable, but I didn't see the Galaxy's Greatest Comic as a training slope for Vertigo, so I didn't care to see Vertigo-style stories increasingly appearing in the comic.

Doubtless many readers felt the same way and things could get heated between these two rival teams competing for British readers, a competition identified at the very beginning of *2000AD*, when Kevin O'Neill wrote and drew an excellent Future Shock where a superhero comic fan meets Tharg in the Nerve Centre and the differences between the two genres are fully aired.

It was also brought over to me at a comic convention where the Eagle Awards were being presented. I was nominated for favourite writer and so was Grant Morrison for his DC Comics work. I was voted the winner and, as I went up to receive the award, I was dismayed to find myself being roundly booed by the superhero fans, even as I was cheered on by *2000AD* fans. I'd never come across such rudeness and so I was a bit slow off the mark. Looking back, I should have given the superhero fans the finger from the podium.

Afterwards, Angela told me how she heard two DC execs in the audience reacting to the disappointing news. Making sure Angela could hear them, one of them said loudly to the other, "Well, of course, the Eagle Awards don't really count anymore."

The Invaders are also bad losers.

22. CRISIS

We now come to *2000AD*'s companions and rivals that were to influence the comic's destiny, for better or worse, commencing with *Crisis*, which ran from 1988 to 1991.

Before Egmont, *2000AD* was owned by Maxwell. There, Steve MacManus planned a comic for older readers. In association with Igor Goldkind, a successful promoter of graphic novels like *Watchmen* and *Dark Knight*, they came up with a fortnightly comic consisting of just two stories. This was to become *2000AD's Crisis*. It didn't have a single strong theme, which, as I've previously demonstrated, is essential in a comic. Anthologies, with contrasting stories or even "something for every one", are still beloved of comic professionals. But audiences usually don't like them. This feedback, painfully collected from my own past mistakes, is disbelieved to this day and probably always will be. So the price is paid at the box office. *Crisis* was designed to appeal to cool, older readers with more sophisticated and relevant stories for a modern audience. But that is not a theme.

One story was *New Statesmen*, about a group of superheroes, clearly influenced by *Watchmen* and aimed at that fan market (Writer: John Smith, artist: Jim Baikie). The other was to be a story about the politics of food and Steve and Igor suggested a female protagonist.

Possibly they were thinking of the success of *Halo Jones* because they wanted the *Halo* artist, Ian Gibson, to illustrate it.

As it was about politics and they were offering me a rights deal, how could I refuse? I called it *Third World War* and decided to try a radically new story technique. It was a more freestyle version of director Mike Leigh's approach. I consulted a small cast of young people and asked them how they would respond to certain situations if they were conscripted to work in the Third World, letting the cards fall where they may, rather than prescribing the plot, which I think Mike Leigh does. It worked very well, except, possibly, for Trisha, my Born Again Christian character. As I didn't know any Born Again Christians well, I sometimes had to fake her and some readers have said she wasn't as real as the other characters. I'm sure they were right and perhaps my loathing for her showed, which is a mistake. In drama, the more sympathetic you make a character you secretly loathe, the more effective your message.

My real-life role model for Eve, the main character, told me she would kill herself rather than be a "government hooligan" and I duly mentioned a suicide attempt. Ian Gibson wasn't keen on this as he felt it gave a bad example to young people. I totally respect Ian's view, but I needed to maintain this new level of realism, so Ian dropped out and Carlos Ezquerra became the art co-creator.

Of course, readers who like adult superheroes and readers who are interested in the politics of food make for uncomfortable bedfellows, one is likely to be a casualty of the other and this is what happened. *Third World War* was more popular than *New Statesmen*, which was dropped from *Crisis*. Really, the idea of the two stories being put together was actually unfair to both. Unfortunately, that's what happens when there is no theme.

In the dumbed-down times we currently live in, where so many escape into science fiction and fantasy, *Third World War* must seem bizarre and unlikely. Who cares about the politics of food today? Well, people actually did at the time. And it wasn't just about charity, which can have a questionable side to it. Many readers who had grown up with *2000AD* were becoming politically active. It was a time of strife and change, and young people wanted to understand why so many of the world's population was starving. Why weren't these charities' requests for money making a difference? There were endless books on the subject on sale in popular bookshops. They rightly pointed out the IMF and the transnationals were responsible. Susan George's seminal works *A Fate Worse Than Debt* and *How The Other Half Dies: the Real Reasons for World Hunger* were popular and very readable bestsellers.

So Steve and Igor were absolutely right in considering world hunger as a basis for a story. As I'd written the long running anti-war saga *Charley's War*, it was clearly perfect for me.

And readers were pointing out to me the obvious flaw in science fiction or satire: that it can run away from reality or mask its message so effectively that no-one knows or cares.

I recall, in particular, two students who had visited Israel and were appalled by how Palestinians were treated as an underclass. The gist of what they said to me, was: "Why are all you writers hiding behind science fiction to get across your message? Using robots and mutants as a metaphor for slaves? Featuring monsters like Torquemada when you really mean Norman Tebbit and Thatcher? Why don't you stop pissing about and start telling it like it is?"

So I did. The series worked. It was joined later by the very popular *Troubled Souls* by Garth Ennis and John McCrea and the daring masterpiece *Skin*, about a skinhead who was affected by the drug thalidomide. Passionately written by Peter Milligan and beautifully illustrated by Brendan McCarthy, like other *Crisis* stories it drew on real life for its heroes.

Crisis led to me writing about other ordinary heroes: antivivisectionists, black freedom fighters, prison survivors, ecotage, British soldiers who deserted, and teenagers experiencing the Troubles in Northern Ireland. Often, I would write in co-authorship with these ordinary heroes.

The commercial success of *Charley's War*, a story about a not very bright, but heroic soldier, shows it *is* possible to make the lives of ordinary heroes more attractive than men in tights.

As John Lennon says, "A working class hero is something to be."

There were so many more ordinary hero stories I would have loved to have produced. Eventually, Amnesty commissioned me to write an Amnesty issue of *Crisis*. And there were also plans for me do something with Campaign Against Arms Trade. For Amnesty, I wrote about the death penalty in South Africa and Palestinian youth in the Gaza Strip. Both were illustrated by Sean Phillips. One Palestinian kid was so beaten up by the Israeli forces, Sean showed him lying there with his legs and arms at twisted angles.

When it appeared, the watchdog organisation, the Jewish Board of Deputies, complained to Robert Maxwell that this kid's limbs were in the shape of a swastika. No concern about the kid himself. Or no interest in the story: a damning indictment of the brutality of the Israeli forces. It was like the Board were looking at faces in the fire and seeing what they wanted to see. But they couldn't try their usual anti-semitic allegations, which often successfully shuts us all up, because the three key organisers on the project were Jewish. Sara Selwood, Dan Green and Igor Goldkind. They couldn't all be dismissed as self-haters. Surprisingly, Robert Maxwell, of all people, and hardly a self-hater either, told the Board to get lost. I can get behind his response.

I featured other controversial stories like the British suppression of the Mau Mau. It was so horrifying, and showed the true nature of the British army in Kenya in such powerful and graphic scenes (artist: John Hicklenton) that the "old school" printers threatened not to print it. But we got it through and I'm proud to have shed light on at least one aspect of our country's evil colonial past.

That is the problem, of course: we have been so conditioned by Orwellian programming, we react badly to the truth. It's too toxic for us, so it must be wrong. So when John Hicklenton was once commissioned to draw the famous damaged teddy bear for Children In Need, they thought his Pudsey bear was too disturbing. Like it had been slammed up against a wall. But isn't that the whole point? Certainly John thought that was the point: that his bear should portray the dark truth of violence against children.

The story of *Crisis* is really too long for this book, so let me cut to the bottom line.

Despite Herculean efforts by Steve and Igor, sales dropped for several reasons—possibly because I introduced black leading characters. Surprisingly, we discovered many of our right-on readers had negative views about black heroes fighting the Third World War here in London. Writing with a black co-writer (the late Alan Mitchell), we showed authentic aspects of black culture that were not to many white readers' tastes. It sounds unlikely, I know, but this was made very clear to me. It's a pity, because we had some funny as well as tragic scenes that could only have come from working with a black writer. For example, a black guy being investigated by Social Security, and his hilarious excuses, based on Alan's time working for that government department, made for a great comedy scene.

But many readers preferred it when the Third World War was safely far away in South America, not on the streets of Brixton.

Artist changes also affected the story. Some were good, some bad. Other stories and the overall mix would also play a part. *Third World War* was just one story, after all. Finally, there was a rather desperate decision to turn *Crisis* into a cappuccino comic with reprint European comic strips. Then it died.

Certainly Steve was incredibly supportive of what we were doing on *Third World War*. There are plenty of anecdotes, but they'll have to wait for another time.

Thank you, Steve, for your support, which I value to this day. As you said, maybe *Third World War* was just too far ahead of its time.

But *Crisis* lasted long enough to prove there *was* interest in, and a market for, this kind of comic. Far longer, in fact, than the relatively conventional *Toxic!* that followed, with its dark but still fan-orientated mix of adventure stories.

The relevance for *2000AD* is that editorial became wary of stories with a strong political subtext. I had to tone down my stories, especially in the forthcoming Dark Age.

The new direction, for a time, was cappuccino comics like *Revolver*, not comics of the streets. Again, *Revolver* lacked a theme. Being "cool and hip" is simply not enough. It died.

Increasingly, as *2000AD*'s circulation started to drop, editorial would desperately try to find new directions for the comic. They tried to make it like *Deadline* magazine; like a poor man's version of *Vertigo*; like a glorified fan magazine, and finally like lads' magazine *Loaded*. They seemed oblivious to a golden rule, which applies to all publications, and I always believed was set in stone: publications should never suddenly change direction because it will alienate your existing readers and not attract new readers. Change, if needed, should be careful and gradual.

They didn't understand that we didn't have to be like anyone else. Just to be ourselves.

It was thus inevitable that *2000AD* moved away from its subversive foundations, which so many readers cared about.

Many of those responsible for the changes had never really liked or understood those foundations anyhow, and simply tolerated them as long as the publication was successful.

I've always felt that was an English perspective. Scotland, where I learnt my trade, is undoubtedly the true home of popular culture comics. It is in their blood. They love comics. It's why there are an astonishing number of Scottish creators in comics. And why so many great comics came out of DC Thomsons. Black comedy and subversion come naturally to them, which is why I always felt at home there. There is more than one Frankie Boyle in comics. And creators from the other Celtic countries also have this attitude. Maybe it's that sense of the "Celtic other", of being the underdog, that fuels it.

By comparison, England often has a more arthouse approach to comics. It's the cultural home of the graphic novels or "fat comics with bits of cardboard round them", as they are sometimes called by their critics.

While there's no snobbery or elitism in Scottish comics, there certainly is in England, and it was now seeping into *2000AD*.

———

In some respects *Crisis* and *Third World War* may have made things worse. It may have further polarised readers of *2000AD* into separate camps. Thus Mark Dawson, author of the best-selling John Milton spy thriller series and Beatrix Rose assassin series (optioned for a film/TV series) remembers that he liked *Crisis*, whereas his brother preferred *2000AD*. This split would add to the challenges the comic faced.

Readers are always asking me when *Third World War* may be reprinted. I'm sorry to say there's no progress, despite my endless reminders to all concerned. My take on it is that the series is caught in an endless "Groundhog Day", first between Egmont and Titan, which went on for at least five years, and now with Rebellion, who own the rights.

Titan say they want to do *Third World War*, but significantly, it hasn't been scheduled. If they don't run it, then, theoretically, Rebellion will eventually publish it.

My prediction? It will disappear without trace, following an endless soft-shoe shuffle between the companies. Why? Because in their hearts, I don't think either of them *really* want to do it.

Because it's not safe fantasy.

One long term *2000AD* fan, John Ottaway, commented, "With the current rise in the number of food banks in the UK, droughts and crop failures being caused by Climate Change and an Orange Terror Clown in the White House, who denies it is real … I think a war about food, is very relatable today. *Third World War* is definitely due a reprint."

Thankfully, there are still outlets where *Crisis* and *2000AD's* subtext still resonates. I'm giving a talk at Marxism 2017 on July 8th on the "Politics of *2000AD*" with Sasha Simic.

In the past, science fiction and comic writer and *2000AD Nemesis* fan, China Mieville has given talks at Marxism. Also, Professor John Newsinger, who wrote *A comic history of Russia's Red Year 1917,* which I wrote the introduction for. And *The Dredd Phenomena: Comics and Contemporary Society.*

So it's good to know there are some kindred spirits out there.

Similarly, *Scarred for Life*, the darker side of the pop culture of the '70s, by Stephen Brotherstone and Dave Lawrence, gives a positive account of the subtext of the Comic Revolution, which would, eventually, reach its high-water mark with *Crisis.*

Not everyone has taken the blue pill.

23. TOXIC!

2000AD's brief and only rival was the full colour *Toxic!*, which ran for 31 issues from March 1991. With my *Accident Man* (co-written by Tony Skinner) as its lead character, and with full colour artwork, a publisher finally gave creators our rights. A group of us, John Wagner, Alan Grant, Mike McMahon, Kevin O'Neill, and myself had been invited to produce it, with further popular creators coming on board later.

The first challenge was the title. As no one else had any suggestions, it fell to me to come up with one. I finally came up with *Toxic!* I discussed it with Kevin and we felt the title accurately suggested the comic's theme. John and Alan okayed it. I don't think they were especially keen, but they didn't have an alternative title as far as I was aware. And why should they? None of us were interested in being editors again, not after all the grief we'd experienced, and a title was usually an editor's job. However, there was no editor and it was certainly not a job I wanted. I'd rather herd cats. The first editor we commissioned didn't want the job either, the second was sacked, so I then had to step in and run it for a while before a replacement was found. Otherwise, the comic would have gone down the toilet.

Then *Toxic!* ran into financial trouble and I organised a successful artists' debt collection party to get most of us paid. The hilarious story of our surprise raid on the publisher's office is not strictly relevant, but I am happy to send you the account if you're interested. See the end of the book for details.

Toxic!'s impact on *2000AD* was considerable. They were scared of it, and copied us by going full colour, too, often to *2000AD's* detriment. One of my sources is adamant that *2000AD* editorial were also being given confidential information about *Toxic!* by an insider on our new comic. Payment rates, contract terms, sales figures and so on. I know this has been denied, and I haven't a second source to confirm this story so I won't elaborate. But my source is usually correct and insists we had an "enemy within". This is, after all, the Secret History of *2000AD*, so I'm not going to write a sanitised version and leave it out.

Toxic! was also more lurid and once again, *2000AD* felt they had to be lurid to compete with us. Again a mistake. They had so little faith in themselves or my original vision that they felt they needed to be like *Toxic!* instead. That's important and helps explain the Dark Age that was to follow.

My own and Kevin's top story on *Toxic!* was *The Driver*, by David Leach and Jeremy Banx, about the foul-looking, bald-headed driver of a road train, laden with nuclear waste, who drives across America, crushing all in his way, to dump the waste on a sacred Indian reservation. My favourite scene is where he's had his elbow out of the window of his cab for hours and dead flies have accumulated on it. He looks down, gets a knife to scrape the flies off, and casually eats them off his knife. It still makes me chuckle. It's not really a *2000AD* story, though.

I equally loved their *Dinner Ladies From Hell* and *Detritus Rex*, but, once again, the tone was not *2000AD*. Other stories possibly were: *Brats Bizarre* brilliantly illustrated by Duke Mighten, which I co-wrote with Tony Skinner. Living in a sentient house run by their dubious butler Bates, these teen superheroes indulged in every imaginable teenage excess, including chain-sawing each other's limbs off, because they would grow back. They had a very different attitude to their superpowers to DC's prim and proper Teen Titans. More recently, Channel 4's excellent *Misfits* did it bigger and better than us and shows the *Young Ones* potential in telling it like it is, but I still think *Brats* has something pertinent—and certainly offensive—to say, to challenge the staid world of superheroes.

And *Accident Man*: a story about a killer who makes his murders look like accidents, now, at the time of writing, a movie in post-production, starring Scott Adkins (Lucian in Marvel's *Doctor Strange*). It's a cousin to *2000AD's Button Man* assassin, which—I'm told—was the reason why the latter story was turned down by *Toxic!* Looking back, it was a pity *Button Man* couldn't have run when *Accident Man* was not in the comic, but that decision was beyond my control.

In response to this new New Wave, behind the scenes there was great animosity and apprehension at *2000AD* about *Toxic!* I think Steve McManus and his colleagues really believed we creators would finally break out of our British "all rights" prison with *Toxic!* And we nearly did. Again, it's too big a story to go into here.

As payback, after the death of *Toxic!*, for a long time at least, *Toxic!* artists were not given work on *2000AD* at a time when the Galaxy's Greatest comic could have used their considerable talents. That would teach the upstarts. Even at comic conventions *Toxic!* artists, like Duke Mighten and John Erasmus, were not given the respect and free entry passes they were entitled to, until I intervened.

Then, some time after *Toxic!* had died. Egmont called their young children's magazine *Toxic*. Who was the editorial overseer of Egmont's *Toxic*? Step forward Steve MacManus.

Using the same title could be seen as a little provocative. Or pure coincidence. I'm sure Steve will say it's coincidence, or even synchronicity, and that's fine. Because in *Accident Man*, I feature the killer's boss, called Clive, who also, by pure coincidence, has the same last two letters in his name as Steve.

Clive is a character whom I greatly enjoyed writing with Tony Skinner. He had an intense relationship with Mike Fallon, *Accident Man*, who was endlessly frustrated and annoyed by Clive's decisions and the grief it caused him. He sees Clive as someone who "dances in the headlamps" and invites trouble. Of course, that is also what psychopaths say. They believe their victims want to be chopped up into tiny pieces, so let's not take Fallon's views too seriously. He is Britain's answer to *American Psycho*, after all. But it does shed some light on how I felt at the time and how real people can inspire or suggest complex fictional characters, a long way from comic book stereotypes.

So here's a sequence from *Accident Man* about Clive, as Mike Fallon reflects on his boss:

> Clive is the contractor for "Them". He hands out the contracts. Decides who kills who. Most of us fantasise about killing him. He's Bambi, surrounded by the lions at the water hole. The hedgehog doing handstands in the road. There's a rumour going round he takes his holidays in Beirut. I think I'll save the Lebanese a bullet.
>
> Why do I always fall for it? I swore I'd never work for that weasel again. Must be something to do with the twenty grand. It's a mistake to think it was simply a foul-up. Clive's incompetence verges on the supernatural and is subconsciously calculated. Because people like him fight, too, using incompetence as a weapon. It's Bambi's way of biting you in the leg.

24. BY HOOK OR BY CROOK

There were other companion comics and magazines to *2000AD* that influenced its direction.

I had already devised several board games and a card game as marketing tools to accompany my *Battle*, *Action* and *2000AD*, memorably *Magnum Force!* for *Action*, where secret agents shoot their way around New York. John Wagner and I even devised *Go for Gold*, an Olympic board game for *Valiant*. They were an echo of the days when John Wagner and I worked for DC Thomson's and a group of us would play all-nighter, heated sessions of the board game *Diplomacy*.

So, with my gaming background, I created and wrote the comic magazine *Diceman*, with role-playing comic strips, featuring mostly *2000AD* heroes. It made money, but not enough for the publishers, so it was eventually cancelled. But it included my *You Are Ronald Reagan* with the hugely talented Hunt Emerson. This led to Titan Books publishing my *You Are Maggie Thatcher*, a dole-playing game, also with Hunt. The catharsis of writing about Thatcher made it worthwhile. The superb *Lower than Vermin: An Anatomy of Thatcher's Britain* was an inspiring source for me. It was written and drawn by cartoonist Martin Rowson, who tells me he grew up reading *2000AD* and found it equally inspiring. Thus the wheel had turned full circle.

A younger version of *2000AD* was also on the cards in the late 1980s. In response to the endless clamour for rights, Egmont finally offered creators copyright on their *Young 2000AD*, so I duly wrote a story about semi-intelligent dinosaurs, called *Dinosty*, partly inspired by the Royal Family. They are dinosaurs, after all. In fact I'd had the original idea right from the very beginning of *2000AD*. Clint Langley was the artist creator and when *Young 2000AD* never happened, the reader response to *Dinosty* was so enthusiastic that it ran in *2000AD* instead.

Clint and I hope to reprint *Dinosty* at some future point, possibly on Comixology, where an English language digital edition of my French *Requiem* saga appears.

I don't know if any other stories from *Young 2000AD* ever appeared in the comic or indeed what its real title was. But it was a relief that Steve MacManus recognised the need to appeal to kids before that market completely died.

Why *Young 2000AD* never got beyond dummy stage, I don't know. It does require huge commitment, talent and energy to make a comic work and I suspect there just wasn't enough of it around. Or, more likely, the company had no idea how to do it properly and wasn't prepared to pay anyone, like myself, who did.

So this fair deal, once again became a cul de sac. This endless battle for rights also brings us back to *Dan Dare* and new *Eagle*, a successful companion of *2000AD*.

Here's how the *Dan Dare Eagle* story rolled out. A year or so after I'd left *2000AD*, I heard from Tony Dalton, a film critic connected with the BFI, who told me he now had the *Dare* rights and would John Wagner and I like to do a film treatment of the character? He had studio interest already. With Star Wars riding high, we agreed.

We met Gareth Hunt, billed to play *Dan Dare* and also a great fantasy artist from the Young Artists group, Tim White, who had drawn some fantastic scenes for the proposed film. The brief clearly had to be "like Star Wars", not like the original 50s strip, and we came up with a strong storyline, on spec. For nothing, which was foolish.

We heard nothing more, the film project was dead, and then we learned that *Eagle* was being revived. *Dan Dare* was to be the lead strip with Gerry Embleton painting it. Would John and I like to write it? Of course we would. It was a way of using our detailed film treatment.

Only there was a catch. Dan now had to be the original Dan's great grandson. And there was also a confusing story about the original Dan Dare going through a time warp as a fighter pilot in the Battle of Britain. It had to somehow tie in with a film version and we understood Da Savary now had the rights again. Loaded down with this awkward extra, John and I made the best of it and our story was number one in *Eagle*. Readers liked our sf ideas—such as aliens with flying sharks on leads .

But Embleton eventually left, Ian Kennedy took over, John Wagner dropped out and I was left "holding the baby". By now, I was so appalled by the numerous changes to the *Dare* mythos, I decided —no matter how difficult—I had to get it right this time. I began by writing a heavily researched NASA-style version which, because it was illustrated by Ian, looked pretty good and stands up well today. Fans are looking forward to it being collected.

I then wrote man's first trip to the stars, with authentic details and some critical aspects based on the early astronauts, e.g. the appalling treatment of Ham, the chimpanzee, the monkey sent into space. Ham 2 features in my story.

Dare continued to go down well with the readers, and I decided to make it as close to the original as was viable. With tight deadlines on Ian, I'd made contact with a young astronomer and science fiction model maker, Julian Baum, based at Liverpool observatory. He produced some excellent planetary photographic landscapes and models, which were integrated into the strip, in the tradition of the original. But as the story moved back towards science fiction I couldn't see how to use his great talents further.

While Dan had been away on that first star mission, the Treens had invaded Earth and the Grand Canyon was the rebel redoubt (useful for star fighter Death Star-style scenes). The head of the United Nations Space Force was British and everything was as close as I could get it to the original, despite the burdensome grandson tag.

I also wanted to produce a credible backstory. I think it's a legitimate device to rationalise earlier notions with modern science— so I found NASA maps of the Venus continents under the cloud cover and used those as the basis for the continents of the Therons and the Treens on Venus. Heavy industrialisation by the Treens had caused a runaway Greenhouse effect, which explained the hellish atmosphere of the fire belt.

Increasingly I was drawing on the past, and becoming more fascinated with Frank Hampson's original. Whereas some *Dan Dare* stories by other original associates might be dated in story, art or character, I loved the vibrant energy of the original, which I understand was all down to Frank. So I worked some flashback scenes in, with tremendous help from *Dan Dare* fan Alan Vince, who sent me relevant images. I also tried writing the story in the minimalist style of the first *Eagle* adventure with its floating headshots. It's an excellent storytelling technique.

Dan and co. were victorious at the battle of the Grand Canyon and I now had to consider whether I should continue. The story was still number one in the comic, but I felt I'd done my penance for reviving the character. Unless I could make it closer yet to the original, there was no point in going on. This was not possible, and I walked away from it. I believe Tom Tully took it over.

With the benefit of hindsight, I've reflected on all these issues of rights and reviving characters. I think fan homage to a classic character like *Dan Dare*—as in *Spaceship Away*—is excellent. And there, it genuinely is homage. I think reviving writers' and artists' characters for reasons other than genuine (unpaid) homage, unless it's with the consent of the creators or their estate, is not acceptable. Even if it has the approval of the publisher. Creatively, *Dan Dare* succeeded in both *Eagle* and *2000AD*, but, morally, I should not have revived the character and I regret it.

Of course everyone has to make up their own mind, and there has to be an exception made for stories clearly *labelled* satire, but a simple rule of thumb is ... "What would Frank Hampson think of the revival?" If the answer is "not a lot", then it shouldn't be done, out of respect. I have little time for "re-imagining" or "new updated insights" into stories for supposedly more "sophisticated" fans—unless they're out of copyright, which means they're probably over a century old.

I've certainly made it clear I don't want some hungry hack "reimagining" (e.g. ripping off) my characters when I'm gone, and the word is out there to this effect. However, I'm pretty certain that, like past attempts to continue or copy my work, such "reimaginings" would just go down the toilet.

Therefore, any publisher's impositions in contracts that "we can do what we like with your story because we own it" are, in comics, at least, worthless. Most of the great *2000AD* stories, apart from *Dredd*, are now usually written by the original writer.

Editors are, thankfully, aware of the negative response by readers if they try passing them on to new creatives. They remember what happened when Gerry Finley-Day was pushed out and later Dave Bishop took over his well-loved *Fiends of the Eastern Front*. Dave's version just didn't fly with the readers.

Fiends, incidentally, is a story that Gerry still talks to me about reviving and ran an excellent idea past me, but I doubt it will happen. To achieve it would require a proactive approach that is not economically viable today.

There's more on this subject of "house characters" which I'll come back to later.

Meanwhile, there's also the finance side to using another creator's characters. This brings us to the case for remunerating Frank Hampson's estate, as DC Comics did in the case of the *Superman* creators. Doubtless, the large sums of money involved meant DC *had* to share their profits. Publishers, it seems, can be shamed into doing the right thing. But, as far I'm aware, it's never happened with Frank Hampson.

It's worth repeating that Leo Baxendale, as I've described earlier, fought for his rights and won. Frank Hampson, another older generation artist, lost, and was bitter about how he was treated financially on *Dan Dare* (now owned by a private company).

Later, John Wagner and I would also lose our battles, as I've described, and, I understand, the same thing has also happened to Alan Moore, with *Halo Jones*, and Grant Morrison with *Zenith*.

This problem is endemic in British comics, it's at the heart of what has gone wrong with them, and it's never going to go away, no matter how much it's ignored and how carefully publishers duck and weave around the subject, until a fair industry standard solution is arrived at, probably as in France, where comics flourish.

If you think this is merely the "punk" attitude of a '70s rebel, then let me conclude with a story I've heard from two different sources about Frank Hampson, whom many would regard as the ultimate British comics creator.

At a prestigious event, Hampson went up to receive an equally prestigious Mekon award from an IPC executive.

As he collected the Mekon statue, Hampson said to the executive. "I said I'd get this award, by hook or by crook. And I got it. From a crook."

25. "I CAN'T HAVE A WITCH WRITING FOR 2000AD!"

Tony Skinner is my dear friend and writing partner on *Finn*, *ABC Warriors* (*Khronicles of Khaos*), selected stories on *Flesh* and *Nemesis*, as well as *Shadowslayer* (Editions Glenat) for France, inspired by the life of Charles Fort (author of *Book of the Damned* who recorded strange "Fortean" phenomena) and *Accident Man, Psycho-Killer* (see Further Reading), *Brats Bizarre* and other serials for *Toxic!* Tony was also responsible for many of the pagan aspects of *Slaine The Horned God* and other *Slaine* stories. He was my main role model for *Finn*, too. Finn, a witch and an eco-warrior, was the most popular character in *Third World War* and continued with his own solo series in *2000AD*. And for America Tony and I wrote *Death Game 2020, Punisher 2099* and *Ravage 2099*.

So you can see from this impressive CV just how important Tony was to comics and to *2000AD*, in particular.

I would put my avant-garde, pagan friend in the same category as other writers who have led exciting lives and therefore have something to write about, rather than sitting in their back bedroom, imagining what life is like out there, and then writing about it. Of course that can work, too, but I think real life is always the better option. I sometimes attend pagan events with Tony and, it's fair to say, a magical time is had by all.

But the news that I was co-writing with a witch freaked out editor Steve MacManus. He actually exclaimed. "No! I can't have a witch writing for *2000AD*!" He refused to consider scripts from him. I think it was just a knee jerk reaction, because he soon relented. I'm not sure why. Maybe Tony put a spell on him...?

Personally, I'd found Tony invaluable as a consultant on *Slaine*. I've never regretted inviting him over my threshold, even if Steve didn't want Tony to cross *his* threshold. (It's mandatory for witches as well as vampires, apparently.) It was fascinating, and I felt privileged to witness magical ceremonies at first hand. ("*Come to the sabbat, Pat —but don't bring your notepad.*")

We both appeared on BBC TV's *Arena - Green Man* pagan programme about witchcraft. I had persuaded a reluctant Tony to appear, when he really wasn't that interested. Occultists are understandably wary of publicity when there is so much ignorance and hostility to them.

I'm on *Arena* with Simon Bisley walking round Rollright Stones. Then it cuts to a witchcraft ceremony with Tony. It's beautiful and meaningful, and, like anything from the heart, it is not a spectator sport for cynics. But it was also good promotion for *2000AD*.

Despite Tony's known contribution to *The Horned God*, a story that, thanks to Simon Bisley's art, actually increased *2000AD's* circulation, editorial on *2000AD* regarded him with unease, paranoia and passive aggression, a sample of which I will describe. I can begin to understand how widespread moral panics about witches led to The Burning Times and the trials of the Salem Witches.

A very distant ancestor of mine, connected through the myriad branches of my Irish family tree, was one of the Salem Witches. Susannah Martin (baptized September 30, 1621—July 19, 1692)—born Susannah North—was one of fourteen women executed for witchcraft during the Salem witch trials of colonial Massachusetts. Susannah was a long way away from me on the family tree, but it still doesn't endear me to people who give witches a hard time, as *Slaine* readers will know.

What makes Steve's rejection of witches even more surprising is that there are at least two other high-profile occultists who worked on *2000AD* around this time. One of them is Grant Morrison, who wrote the DC comics occult series *The Invisibles*. I understand he also met the Invisibles (magical entities) and regularly writes on chaos magic, which I believe he's an authority on. Alan Moore is also involved with the occult and has written on the subject.

We must attract magical people on *2000AD*: I can't imagine why. So it's okay to have known magicians working for *2000AD*, but not witches? That's going too far. I hadn't realized there was a class system in the occult world, too.

I assume my own interest in the occult must have been acceptable to *2000AD*, possibly because I kept a lower profile than my colleagues. They certainly never asked me *"Are you now, or have you ever been a member of a witch's coven?"*

My own interest included experiences involving reincarnation, UFOs and more. Thus, I met a UFO follower who contacted me because of my stories in *2000AD*. Through him I had a Close Encounter of a Third Kind. They didn't invite me on board and it was different to Spielberg's UFOs, but unexplainable in conventional terms. The "ships" I saw were like Wilhelm Reich's cloud-busting, embryo-like, organic UFOs, as photographed as "the critters" in the book *The Cosmic Pulse of Life*. Visually, I'm afraid they're a bit disappointing if you're expecting CE3K. I think Conan Doyle was the first to describe them in *The Horror of the Heights* (1913).

Whether you believe in them or not, it was certainly great material for stories in *Finn* and *Defoe*. I remember thinking this, as I was shivering on a hilltop and one of these "critters"—impossible to explain as a weather balloon, or any other man-made artefact—came pulsing over my head.

I also gave talks about my magical quests in the South of France, "Holy Blood and Holy Grail" territory, given at London's psychic questing conferences in Conway Hall. The quests provided material for my German fantasy serial *Torturer*, illustrated by John Hicklenton. And for later *Slaine* adventures.

"Magic", to use an umbrella term to describe a variety of esoteric phenomena, is really not a big deal to me or to Tony. It's something that happens from time to time, particularly if you follow the magical adage: "If you take an interest in the Unknown it will take an interest in you." Meantime, you get on with your life. As Finn says, "*When I'm not riding a broomstick, I'm driving a mini-cab in Plymouth. Guess which one pays the rent?*"

If you've witnessed unexplainable phenomena then you may well believe in magic. If you haven't, then you're absolutely right to be sceptical. And if you think it's all pretentious crap, that's fine with me, too. It doesn't require acts of *faith* like the Abrahamic religions. I see it as the manifestation of the magical workings of the subconscious, which our Matrix-style programming has conditioned us to ignore. Fundamentalists call this inner voice of the subconscious the voice of the devil and they are right. If people listened to it, they wouldn't waste time paying attention to Fundamentalists.

I'm attracted to paganism because it's doesn't have the same elites and elaborate titles of other magical systems. It's relatively democratic. Colourful clothes are still fun, of course, or, indeed, the lack of them.

My feelings about magical elitism are expressed through the *ABC Warriors*' characters Tubal Caine and Deadlock. Tubal despises Deadlock's elitist attitude towards "magick". Tubal believes magic is for everyone.

I believe it explains why I've always loathed Gandalf in *The Lord of the Rings* and why Tolkien's masterpiece has never appealed to me. I wondered why, ever since I was a kid, I hated depictions of superior, know-it-all, self-righteous men in flowing robes with long white beards telling me what to do. Maybe I'd had an unfortunate encounter with one in my youth and that's why I loathed them?

Then I suddenly realised I had. He's called God.

26. FINN

This extraordinary discrimination against witches would affect the story *Finn*, the spin-off from *Third World War* that began in *2000AD* in the early '90s. My experiment in using real people in *Third World War* rebounded on me—because, it seems, *Finn* had far too much reality for *2000AD's* taste.

I should mention that *Finn* is not completely based on Tony. My original *earlier* role model for *Finn*, before I focused on my friend, was an ex-army traveller who told me he originally joined the army because he had "a love of the green." And also because he had grown up reading war comics. A claim I've heard from other soldiers that led to me writing *Charley's War* in *Battle* to act as a counterweight. A strategy I'm proud to say worked. I've learned there were many young men who would have joined the army, but changed their minds because they'd read *Charley's War*.

My original *Finn* ex-army role model committed Greenpeace-style acts of ecotage (green sabotage) against polluters of the environment. I discussed the various techniques of ecotage, tree spiking and so on, and got his opinion on them. I had *Ecodefense: A Field Guide to Monkeywrenching* from the Anarchist Library, and we went through the manual together and he gave me an insider's view on the book.

If *Finn* Mark One hadn't been so busy "out there in the green", I'd have heavily featured green activism, which I'm sure would have been added to the list of subjects frowned upon by *2000AD*.

The *Finn* occult details in both the *Crisis* and *2000AD* versions were so detailed, it was clear they weren't from our imagination. One reader was sufficiently impressed by the *2000AD* version of *Finn* to contact me and ask if he could join Tony's community. He was accepted, and he is a member to this day.

Finn was always portrayed as a good guy, fighting against corporate and esoteric bad guys and—like typical *2000AD* heroes—fighting ruthlessly to achieve his aims. But some politically correct readers seemed to expect Finn to adhere to the high moral standards of traditional comic goody-goods like the original *Dan Dare* or *Superman*, and objected to some of Finn's magical practises and sacrifices. Some details we naturally hyped up for dramatic purposes. Just as I assume Grant Morrison does in his works of magical fiction. It's normal. But there must have been an underlying resonance about this story that bothered some readers.

So would these same people complain about *Breaking Bad* or *Nighty Night*, where there are equally questionable yet fascinating protagonists? The criteria, it seems, are depressingly different on comics, even adult comics. Anyway, they complained about *Finn*.

Finn certainly does look evil in his techno-pagan mask (an excellent original design from Angela Kincaid). We featured the origins of Finn and his mask in one story with some superb, fan-favourite Liam Sharp artwork. It's never been reprinted in a collected edition.

In the *2000AD* office, jealousy as well as fear of the occult motivated their response. One *2000AD* staffer, Igor Goldkind, admitted to Tony and myself that he was annoyed by Tony's meteoric success. He told Tony "you haven't paid your dues". He explained that Tony hadn't gone through an essential apprenticeship, writing endless *Future Shocks* first (like Neil Gaiman and Alan Moore) before finally being graciously allowed the privilege of writing a serial for *2000AD*.

In his eyes and in the eyes of his colleagues, thanks to me, Tony had unfairly jumped the queue. But, if you look at any of the arts, talent always jumps the queue. The more talent you have, the greater the jump.

We're back to that sad *British comic* thinking that Dez Skinn, creator of *Warrior* magazine, described to me:

I was around 25 when I was told that no matter whether my ideas were any good, I could not become an editor until I turned 30.

It got worse. Because then this concern about witchcraft in fiction spilled over into real-life.

A member of the editorial team started "filling in the gaps", and imagining what might happen at Tony's sabbats, at which I was supposedly present, too, and describing his fantasies to my peers as *fact*. How he knew, when he wasn't there, I cannot imagine. Remote viewing?

These made-up and damaging stories were lurid and not very pleasant, and really required a physical response from me, but, as always, I could never track down who started them. At that time there was a relatively large staff on *2000AD* and its associated publications. Everyone just denied they knew anything.

There were some indications they came from a *2000AD* editorial member who, around this time, propositioned a young female comic writer at a convention with the offer of a casting couch in order to further her career. She was understandably shocked, complained, and it's a matter of record that this guy was sent home in disgrace by Steve. Good for Steve. A pity he wasn't equally zealous in putting a stop to those damaging rumors. Presumably he believed the worst of witches and of myself.

Meanwhile, my witch friend was unconcerned. In fact, Tony has a great sense of humour about their paranoid behaviour. When a

French reporter once challenged him, "What's it like working under Pat Mills?" Tony replied, "*Well ... sometimes Pat is on top, but then we change positions, and I go on top.*"

When we were writing *Finn* we'd often laugh about our critics until my stomach hurt. It really was best to laugh it all off.

Finn made a successful changeover to *2000AD*, where he was also popular. Although one *Third World War* fan commented recently on Facebook: "Ahh the new tame Finn. Never as good as the Crisis version." As I explained in reply, this was because even then—in the early '90s—I was reeling from editorial censorship. I figured if *Finn* started off with more fantasy, I could always get back to social injustice stories later.

Even so, we covered some important subjects. Like identity-chipping the population. Two advertising Suits speculate how to sell them to the public. "*Do you really think we can persuade microchips being embedded in their backsides? They didn't take very kindly to our poll tax scheme.*" The Suits solve the problem by making the chips a status symbol. Shortly afterwards, Finn enters and kills them.

Then there was the power of the Freemasons, described in our version as Freemariners. Freemariners wear flippers and greet each other with "Hello Sailor".

And we covered details of the "total restraint technology" that Britain sells to the rest of the world. The information was authentic and given to me by an insider. So "*we can tranquilise, stupefy, nauseate or just scare the wits out of those who challenge our authority.*"

There was excellent fully-painted art by Jim Elston, and further first-class art by Jim with colouring by Kevin Wicks. Jim lived in Plymouth, where Finn was a mini-cab driver and we went down to meet him and talk about the character. Jim got it, and it shows in the art.

This was followed by the *Finn* UFO saga with more great art by Paul Staples. As Finn spends more of his time safely fighting alien monsters on the moon and inside UFOs, it's really hard, looking back, to see just what all the fuss was about. It was relatively tame, compared to *Third World War*. True, there was our suggestion that the biblical deity we know as Jehovah and Yahweh was actually a bug-eyed monster, but even the Egmont publisher thought that was rather amusing and jokingly said it confirmed his worst suspicions about God.

And then Dave Bishop took over.

Dave acknowledged *Finn's* appeal and told me it actually surpassed *Slaine* in popularity, which didn't surprise me. As *Slaine* is one of *2000AD's* top characters, that is praise indeed for *Finn*. Praise from the readers, that is. It was confirmation that my "Mike Leigh approach" to building stories and characters was paying off and Tony should also take the credit as the principal role model for *Finn* and my co-writer.

But then Dave refused anymore *Finn* stories without further explanation or debate.

He simply said "*No*".

I remember feeling at the time that Dave's decision surely had some undisclosed agenda behind it. Later, he claimed that the reason was because *Finn* was too similar to *Slaine*, but I don't think anyone's ever believed that. Slaine is a Celtic warrior fighting in a mythical Irish Bronze Age. Finn is set in modern-day Cornwall where he's a mini-cab driver. Slaine fights with an axe. Finn uses a sub-machine gun. Slaine fights mythical villains. Finn fights social injustice and aliens on the moon.

But it was an effective way of killing off a top story, without fuss, without an inquest, and without me asking awkward questions.

I think there are three possible explanations which lie behind that "it was too similar to *Slaine*" reason, which plainly makes no sense.

It may have been about cutting me down to size, which Dave certainly did, at every opportunity he could get. For example, when he took over, he sent all the writers a general circular with a long, bilious attack on us for our shortcomings. We all seemed to be to blame for why *2000AD* was in trouble, which Dave was now going to sort out "*in my usual hobnailed boot way*". There was no personal letter with it, or explanation. My copy of the circular simply said at the top "Mills". I think the creator of his comic was entitled to a little more respect.

A second reason could have been that Dave needed a reason to stop a witch working for *2000AD*. This had been Steve's concern and also that of at least one *2000AD* writer. This writer spoke out knowledgeably and forcefully to editorial about the "very real dangers of the occult" and, therefore, why thou shalt not suffer a witch to write. I believe he excluded *2000AD's* magician writers and, indeed, his own esoteric stories. They were safe, apparently. And then there was that member of Steve's team with his fantasy allegations. It was a behind your back, classic witchhunt, carried out in the best possible Kafkaesque taste.

Even though Tony hadn't soured milk, caused disease in cattle, or suckled demons at his breast. Or not as far as I'm aware. Although, when did a lack of evidence deter the worthy Inquisitors of Salem ?

A third reason could be that *2000AD* had become "too pagan". Because by now it was attracting a large, counter-culture audience. I was aware of this from London pagan circles, where I sometimes gave talks. They began when I'd attended one of the *Talking Stick* meetings where the legendary eco-campaigner and Neo-Druid leader, King Arthur Uther Pendragon, was due to speak. Unfortunately, he was arrested by the police for obstruction and was in the cells. So they asked me to step in and give an impromptu talk. They were great guys and had many excellent speakers who were activists, authors and occultists. I remember how thrilled and proud those Pagans were— before the Dark Age—when *2000AD* ran a cover with Finn and the headline: "Pagan Power!" (Prog 816, 1993).

There were other members of disaffected youth, Glastonbury New Agers, Travellers, Green Activists and Crusties, who regularly read *2000AD*. I camped out with some of them at a road protest in the West Country, and I know how much *2000AD* meant to them. Finn, with his long hair and counter-culture clothes, was a brother.

That was the whole idea: that readers could identify with a modern-day fantasy hero.

Perhaps, like Peter Lewis, the IPC traditional supplier of free gifts who objected to my iron cross gift because of its appeal to bikers, Dave felt "*We don't want to attract those kinds of readers.*"

My money is on this third reason, which could well have made sense from his point of view.

I can only speculate, but it could have gone something like this: *2000AD's* circulation is starting to drop. The staff worriedly look around for reasons. Some readers don't like *Finn*, they don't like the politics of *Crisis*. Even though it's popular with the majority of readers, "more popular than *Slaine*". But maybe it's still, *somehow*, the reason for the drop. So put an end to politics and paganism and that leaves the way clear for the *2000AD* New Universe.

For *Space Girls*, Grant Morrison's *Big Dave*, Vector 13, *et al.*

Playing devil's advocate, I think Dave may have just wanted a "normal" fan audience and felt that *2000AD*, despite its falling circulation, could afford to exclude or, at least, discourage the influence of counter-culture readers who didn't match his social criteria and were—in his view—changing the comic's identity. *If* that was his intention, he succeeded. There was no more Pagan Power. They left in droves. And if the remaining, ever-shrinking readership, once the comic had been counter-culturally cleansed, didn't care for *Finn*, well, that would have proved Dave right.

27. ESCAPE FROM REALITY

You might ask—why didn't you sort it out with Dave? I tried. I was so determined to try and understand what was really going on, I took the unprecedented step, for a writer, of taking an editor out for lunch.

I think it's maybe a Celtic thing (and a Russian thing, of course) to socialise with someone you're working with so they relax, drop their guard and come clean about what's really on their mind. Thus, on signing a contract, an Irish film producer made a point of plying me and Clint Langley with endless pints of Guinness, watching me carefully to ensure I kept up with him and didn't pour away any of the precious nectar, so "we can really get to know each other". He had reassured us however that, "*Whatever happens after midnight, never happened.*" That was a relief.

My similar "breaking bread" with Dave failed miserably. It was a pleasant-enough lunch and Dave is a pleasant-enough chap to talk to. But it really felt like I was having lunch with Judge Dredd. He never dropped his guard once. So I asked him outright: "*Where am I going wrong with you? What can I do to improve my stories for you?*", bracing myself for a serious critique of my failings. He told me that he felt I overused ellipsis marks. And that was *it*. So you'll see from somewhere in the late '90s, my stories often lack ellipses.

But with the end of *Finn*, effectively, my opportunities to write about issues I cared about were curtailed and I had to be careful what else I wrote in case it was deemed to be "polemical".

Whether they are consciously aware of it or not, there was then, and still is, a trend on *2000AD* to move away from "controversy" and realistic bad guys and to escape into the safer world of science fiction.

It's still hard hitting, on occasion, of course. For example, I featured the *Visible Man* dealing with a clerical sexual abuser, and I'm featuring arms dealers, and government shills in the forthcoming *Greysuit*.

There are other examples by other writers and artists. But, all too often, *2000AD* is set in the future or the distant past. My only current, "controversial" exception is my *Savage* saga where, from time to time, I'm able to pursue political subjects and write about what it actually feels like to have foreign invaders marching down or bombing your high street. It's surely the same for all of us, whether we live in Kabul, Baghdad, Gaza, or London.

I think it helps that I've made Savage a working class Tory who loved Margaret Thatcher and would love Theresa May. So it can be hard for me to get inside Bill's head, but I make a point of talking to similar characters for story material. I will regularly drink with them in ex-pat bars, to my wife's despair, listening to their often appalling views, nodding my head neutrally as I make mental notes to write it all down later in my notebook. I need to *know* the enemy. How his mind works and why.

Like Kris Kristofferson, I'll drink with the devil to beat him. And I *don't* believe that no one wants to know.

"And then I stole his song".

———

Readers were always aware of the counter-culture influence on their minds, not just by me but other *2000AD* writers. For example, Alan Moore writing about feminism in *Halo Jones*. Counter-culture was there from the very beginning of *2000AD* and grew as the readers grew. As writers, we have to be true to ourselves.

But I think David and other editors truly believed that "no one wants to know", at least on *2000AD*. They knew about this impact on the readers and genuinely didn't like it. Perhaps they felt it was going too far: stories like *Third World War*, which began with the song by the Dead Kennedys, "Kill the Poor" was the wrong direction for comics in their opinion.

And, in fairness to Dave, I'm guessing there was considerable behind the scenes pressure from some of my peers and some readers to "tone things down". It must have been hard for him to ignore, because they really can wear you down and be quite distracting. Dave should have taken a leaf out of my book when I started *2000AD* and put up that sign, "Piss off all *Heavy Metal* Fans".

I think this guess *is* accurate, because I was once sternly lectured by a prominent *2000AD* comic creator, whom I greatly admire, who is every bit as vocal and forceful as I am. It was a pity we had to fall out because I love his work, and he's a smashing guy, and we've made up since, of course. But he strongly objected to the politics in *Third World War* in comic book form and a heated and noisy debate broke out between us, sitting in the back of a BBC studio as we were waiting to be filmed for a documentary about comics. It became so intense I thought at one point they'd throw us both out.

I think I brought up how *Last Gasp* Comics of America, publishers of *Barefoot Gen* comics about Hiroshima, were the first to break the Karen Silkwood affair which led to the film *Silkwood*, exposing a nuclear scandal. And how this was the road I was taking with my *Third World War*, where any Third World injustice could feature.

Thus I later wrote an episode on the Nestle baby milk scandal after talking to the woman who led the campaign. In a *boys'* comic?! Oh, come on, Pat! Surely not? Google it and you may understand why. I'm fascinated and excited by how so many important subjects *can* be dramatised and reach a wider public and *Last Gasp* showed the way. Consider the enthralling film *Lord of War*, endorsed by Amnesty, exposing the arms industry, for example.

But my colleague insisted *"Comics should be about entertainment. Period."*

However, many readers would not agree with this interpretation of "Entertainment", which presumably means "And nothing else. Nothing controversial, nothing with political subtext, nothing that challenges the readers."

I've no idea why my critics would imagine I would ever apply their conservative values to the readers. When I started writing comics, my very first girls comic serial was a passionate account of the Irish Great Hunger. It does make me feel rather isolated. I'd always dreamed that other writers might come along and do what I'm doing, only different and hopefully better, so we could learn from each other, and we could establish a comics sub-genre where the lives of ordinary heroes could be told. I think *Skin*, by Milligan and McCarthy was a great step in that direction and there were others. But it was not to be.

Thankfully, the readers feel differently. They *do* want to know. They do want to be challenged. And they do want more than safe escapist entertainment, even if the opportunities today are somewhat proscribed.

This is a typical dedication a reader recently asked me to write on his copy of *Serial Killer*. *"Continuing to screw with your mind as an adult like I did your childhood. Pat Mills."*

28. COMICS BABYLON

At this time, *2000AD* were desperate for great writers, and they are still thin on the ground today. As a writer trained by the creator of *2000AD*, and co-author of *Punisher 2099*, Tony had huge potential. He could easily have had a successful solo career (as he did in American comics). And, as a powerfully-built martial arts and weapons expert who had met many strange and fascinating people in his life, he was a perfect writer for an action adventure comic.

It's one of the reasons *Accident Man*—with its authentic fight scenes—has been optioned as a movie several times. Finally a film has been made, by actor and martial arts expert Scott Adkins. Scott read the detailed fight scenes in *Accident Man* as a kid and realised someone knew what they were talking about. *That's* how films get made. I'm told scenes from the forthcoming film were recently shown at a comic convention and look amazing.

Tony is the British equivalent of Marvel's top comic creator Larry Hama, who has studied exotic martial arts and they feature in his work. It's why Hama's *G.I. Joe* is so well regarded. Just as Gerry Finley-Day knew what he was talking about in his military stories and it showed, so, too, did Tony.

So, yes, he should have been a key *2000AD* writer by now. But such larger than life characters are not welcome. Sadly, he would have been more successful if he'd been a couch potato who got his ideas from research online. Or if he'd been a writer who based his stories on ones by Philip K Dick. It's *2000AD*'s loss.

And, even today, the shadow of those snide, Salem-style whispers have left their legacy. Because *Finn* should have continued to appear as a regular *2000AD* character. Instead, it's never been considered, it's never talked about, and only a few *Finn* stories have been reprinted. When I bring the subject up with the current Rebellion guys, I've noted just how smoothly and quickly they change the subject. Unlike nearly all my other *2000AD* stories, *Finn* has never been revived or collected in album form, despite its success. Today, whenever I ask about a *Finn* collection, there always seem to be convincing reasons why it won't happen.

I'm also sure I would be given a convincing reason why I couldn't write any new *Finn* stories with Tony. Only, I wouldn't be convinced. There's still time to be proved wrong. My hat is waiting, with some ketchup to make it edible.

Back in the day, the problem was compounded because Tony was also a member of a successful and rather outrageous rock band. Perhaps that was also a problem for the comic young fogies. The band were featured on Eurotrash and similar TV programmes and Jonathan Ross enjoyed meeting them (of course).

But their fun attitude to life was just too much for comic pros. There was an amusing incident where Tony turned up with three sexily dressed young female members of the band at the annual British comic convention. It was pre-cosplay, so the girls stood out. Just a bit. Rather like that scene out of *Blowup* where two nymphets (Jane Birkin and Gillian Hills) have a romp with David Hemmings: the girls ended up retiring to a nearby hotel room with some comic fans and put a smile on their faces. And so what? We're not living in the world of *The Handmaid's Tale*. Yet.

But it was to the absolute horror of British comic professionals. An artist getting so drunk that he bites a DC Comic exec's bum, it seems, is perfectly acceptable in comic establishment circles, but not this. In the puritanical world of British comics this was a big deal. They should have heeded the words of Torquemada: Be Pure! Be Vigilant! Behave! *This* ... this was *Comics Babylon*!

It culminated, some time later, in one young and talented *2000AD* artist, who sported pink hair at the time, actually taking time out to reprimand me for "being involved with someone like that". Maybe he'd heard those Salem rumours and believed the malicious gossip. But it was clear it had been on his mind for some time and he felt a real need to confront me. Perhaps he wanted to protect the fans from anything that might distract them from reading comics, like *girls*. He said he was appalled by my nubile friends' "Seduction of the Fanboys".

It was none of his business, of course, but I really wasn't looking for a quarrel. So I responded diplomatically, shrugged my shoulders nonchalantly and said—as Tony Blair does—"that is a matter for them". I'm not their guardian, and those concerned had a day they might remember all their lives. I remember vividly that scene in *Blowup* from my teenage years (although I couldn't tell you a thing about the plot) and I wish I'd been so lucky when I was their age. It's surely an improvement on learning Klingon. But my youthful fellow professional just would not let it go. He would not accept my explanation, and I was guilty by association. He told me he didn't know how I could be friends with anyone who could behave in such an outrageous and libidinous way.

He meant the girls, I assume. I don't think the fans would actually have been attracted to Tony. Or, indeed, vice versa.

That moment, for me, symbolised the end of the new wave and the death of comic rock 'n' roll.

PART III

BEHAVE!

29. THE DARK AGE

The bad old comic days of the 1970s were now surpassed during the late '90s by the Dark Age.

I first coined the term shortly after Rebellion took over when I wrote about that era in a fanzine, and I've written about it since, from time to time. I'm mildly surprised that no one else has, but I felt someone had to speak out. Not only because the editorial decisions made in this era seriously harmed my career, as I've exampled, but also to ensure they could never happen again. And we can't all be the dutiful obedient robots Tharg really prefers, who keep our heads down and just "get on with our work". Keeping your mouth shut is bad for the body and worse for the soul. So the rebellious Ro-Jaws is my role model.

Perhaps it fell to me as the creator of the comic to say something. It was my baby, after all. I never discovered who first termed me "The Godfather of British Comics" but that seems to be my unwanted role. I'm not sure the term is accurate in the Italian sense of the word, which is all about "respect". Because, where the powers that be are concerned, I can dream on if I'm looking for respect.

Some creators would now be subjected to readers' unacceptable verbal abuse, which seemed to be encouraged by Tharg. Creative associations between writers and artists were discouraged, just as in the bad old days, and particularly in the case of *Slaine*. Editorial responses were terse, rude and, in one case, mind-boggling in its verbal abuse. I and other creatives often seemed to be seen as the enemy. Contradictions and abrupt changes of direction in editorial policy were the norm.

As far as I could make sense of it, violence and action was good, but subtext and any form of *2000AD* quirkiness, like eccentric speech patterns, was bad. Characterisation scenes—like the *ABC Warriors* appearing at a press conference when they returned to Mars—were frowned upon and scrapped. Authentic black guy dialogue, written with a black writer, was replaced without consultation, with a bastardised "fake the funk" white guy version, which I still can't bring myself to look at. Intense, "good value for money" action stories, like traditional pre-*2000AD* comics, such as Hotspur, were preferred. Self-contained story episodes, rather than true serials, were favoured. Yet in contradiction to this, novel drama structure—with the big pay off held back to the end of the serial—was insisted upon. So there could be nothing sensational to hook the reader in the first act.

Decisions on stories were abdicated and, instead, passed to artists to give a story the thumbs up or down. "Cool" also came into this equation somewhere, but I could never work out quite how. Possibly it's why they brought in Grant Morrison, the renowned writer of *Superman* and other superheroes, to give *2000AD* a cool makeover. It became clear to me that the new Thargs really didn't know what they were doing, but—chillingly—they believed they did.

I'm sure it wasn't the same for everyone and some excellent serials originated and prospered in this era: *Nikolai Dante* and *Sinister Dexter*, for example. And great artists like Jock also appeared during this period. The new Thargs certainly fostered a belief that they were a dynamic new broom, doing away with what they firmly believed were outdated stories and people, and replacing them with a brand new "cool" '90s vision for the comic. Their vision must have sounded convincing because there are still a few *2000AD* artists—poor souls—

who still fervently believe in that late '90s disastrous makeover to this day.

In fact, the Thargs were trying—and failing—to diagnose what had gone wrong with the comic; why the circulation was dropping, and apply angry, drastic and inappropriate surgery that just made things worse.

However, to be fair to Dave Bishop, there would have been great pressure on him personally to get it right. Egmont, having benefited from the *Dredd* film, were not especially interested in *2000AD* if it wasn't making money for them. They only bought Fleetway comics originally because they wanted the Disney license. As one of the Fleetway Suits they inherited, Gil Page, put it, "*2000AD* was the golden goose but it wasn't delivering anymore." So the knives were being sharpened to kill it.

And perhaps in trying to deliver, by creating a *de facto 2000AD* New Universe that largely did away with the *2000AD* Old Universe, Dave wasn't aware what happened when Marvel attempted a New Universe. It was a dismal failure. The decision to largely do away with the Old Universe and "the Old Guard" creatives would be like Marvel getting rid of all their favourite founding characters: *Spider Man, Doctor Strange, X Men et al.*, and the top creatives associated with developing them. As one new *2000AD* writer said to me, "*You're the old guard. I'm the vanguard.*" He was surprised by my colourful response.

The result was that the circulation continued to drop to worrying levels and this is the period so many readers refer to when they regularly say today, "I gave up reading *2000AD* in the late '90s."

It's been reasonably well chronicled in the film documentary *Future Shock!*, so I don't see the point in repeating everything here, as this is a personal account rather than a Wikipedia entry.

Also, I've received a written and generous apology from one of the editors concerned, Andy Diggle, so it would be churlish of me to go over that same ground in comprehensive detail. The apology provides closure for me. Thank you, Andy, I appreciate your letter, which resolves our differences and I wish you well.

On the documentary, Grant Morrison also seems to regret his role in *"taking over the comic"* at the behest of Dave Bishop. To quote Grant, it was *"great fun. I loved doing it."* But the radical changes he brought in were designed to react against "an older generation that we were deliberately annoying. I feel slightly ashamed about it now, but you know we were young."

I was barely aware of what Grant was doing, not least because coping with Dave Bishop's other strange requirements were more than enough for me. And Grant's changes really didn't seem to be aimed at me (he got rid of Tharg, for example), so I would have just ignored them. Possibly Grant was aiming at his fellow Scots, like Alan Grant, the writer who gave him his career break on *2000AD*. Or John Wagner. But I doubt John would have taken any notice of him, either. So the only people he was "deliberately annoying" were the readers, who were, indeed, very annoyed.

I'm not sure being thirty-something at the time justifies the excuse "we were young". I gather this would be seen by his fans as being a "bad boy". I wouldn't describe this as "bad boy" behaviour, in the true "punk" sense of the word. For me that often involves an element of genuine subversion and courageously fighting back against authority. Like the Sex Pistols describing the queen as part of a fascist regime and "our figurehead is not what she seems". I'm not aware of anything so impressive here. And the comic was already in serious trouble without a "bad boy" kick in the balls that nearly destroyed it.

I was also pleased to see Dave Bishop acknowledge that he'd got it wrong. So, in a vain attempt open up a dialogue between us, I thought one of us really should make the first move. So I tweeted directly after I'd seen the film at the National Film Theatre:

Great documentary on 2000ad! Includes a section on the dark days of the Dave Bishop/Andy Diggle era. I was most impressed by Dave who had the courage and integrity to acknowledge what went wrong on the comic during their era as editors. Thanks Dave - it closes a grim chapter. I appreciate it.

It opened the way for an apology from him, but it was not forthcoming. Still, if he had apologized, I would have had closure now and you wouldn't be able to enjoy this and previous chapters.

But, rather than going into his era in detail, I'll restrict myself to three items not covered in the documentary that are still important. The first two—readers letters and *Slaine*—because they seriously affected the *lives* of artists and a comic character I care about and the third, *Requiem*, because it led to bigger and better things for me, so I should really be grateful to Dave.

It was in this era that readers' letters became increasingly personal and aggressive towards writers and artists. Fuelled, I recall, by a comics pundit, one of my peers, in the *Megazine*, so bullets were flying at us from every direction.

I and other creatives concluded they were part of a deliberate editorial policy to cut us all down to size.

As the letters became more unpleasant, I just stopped reading them. I didn't regard them as worthy of my time.

But then I got some reader feedback of my own that I found quite disturbing. For some time, readers' letters seemed to be focused on criticizing *Slaine, The Grail War*. This was my Cathar story set in Langue d'Oc, a curious region of France renowned for its medieval castles and devastated in a savage crusade against the Cathar heretics. I'd had a spooky adventure there and given talks about it at Psychic Questing Conferences. It was so spooky, in fact, that the owner of the *gite* where my girlfriend and I stayed commented with a Gallic shrug, *"Such strange things happen round here all the time. C'est normal."* A bit *Rocky Horror Picture Show*. As the Holy Grail features strongly in the Cathar legends it had a good Celtic connection for a Slaine story.

The art, by Steve Tappin, was heavily criticized by readers, which was not justified. It's actually rather good. It's not Bisley, but the artist has taken care with his interpretation and produced very professional work.

Slaine travelling in time worked for many fans, but it wasn't to everyone's taste, and perhaps the Celtic esoteric themes in Cathar France weren't to the liking of a readership who by now had been been counter-culturally cleansed of readers interested in magic, following the demise of *Finn*. So I could see it was open to criticism and I decided to accept these really very negative attacks on the story.

But then I got further feedback from one local teenage boy in Colchester, a friend of my daughters. He always liked *Slaine* and he told me he was surprised by all the criticisms of the Grail War. He was no particular friend of mine (following one of those confrontations dads with teenage daughters sometimes have with boys), but he said he really enjoyed the story and couldn't understand why there was this avalanche of hate mail in *2000AD*.

Furthermore, his friends—all *Slaine* readers—seemed to have a similar view. It was that era where *2000AD* was avidly discussed and dissected by readers every weekend. And a couple of them had actually written to The Mighty One with their pro-*Slaine* views.

That a teenager I'd had to throw out of my house still liked my story gave me considerable pause for thought. I checked with other *2000AD* fans and the conclusion I came to was that the story and art had actually gone down okay. It wasn't the *Horned God*, but they seemed to think it was fine. Yet this counter-view wasn't being represented in the comic. Any feedback that was pro-*Slaine* was being withheld. So it felt like readers were being deliberately *encouraged* by Tharg to think of *Slaine* in a negative way.

But, you might say, what does it matter now? Who cares?

Well: the excellent artist Steve Tappin was a casualty of the affair and hasn't worked for *2000AD* again as a result. So yes, it *does* matter. For me, this was more than petty office power politics: people's *careers* were at stake.

Later, a new *Slaine* artist, Dave Bircham, was appointed, without consultation with me, by Dave Bishop. By now we had moved back to the bad old days of the 1970s, where contact between writer and artist was frowned upon and I had little choice but to accept his decision. I was very worried because this was the first strip to be produced on a computer and there was no recognition or interest in Slaine's complex visual heritage. So I made a special trip to London to discuss my concerns.

Dave Bishop smiled at me, "*Dave's never seen Bisley's Horned God.*" That actually seemed to him to be a good thing. Dave Bircham would create a new-look *Slaine*, and there would be new editorial rules for story and art. It would be part of the new look for *2000AD*.

In response to my fears, Dave simply said, "*Trust me.*" Foolishly, I did.

The story, *Secret Commonwealth*, appeared and there was, once again, a torrent of negative letters about both the art and the sternly editorially-directed story, where any Celtic esoterica and madness— the hallmarks of *Slaine*—were now rigidly controlled in the post-*Finn* era.

Once again, the art has some fine moments, as well as some questionable characterisation and rushed finishes. David Bircham is an extremely good artist. And, with some liason between writer and artist and editorial encouragement, I'm sure we could have made it acceptable to a readership that were still rather spoilt by the halcyon days of *Slaine* illustrated by Simon Bisley, Glenn Fabry and Dermot Power.

I don't know if Dave Bishop ever subsequently revealed his key role in the *Secret Commonwealth* debacle. But the relevant thing for me, then and now, is that once again, a great artist, Dave Bircham, never worked for *2000AD* again. Once again, a freelance's *career* was damaged by Tharg who, I'm not aware, has ever taken responsibility for it.

The hate mail also affected artist John Hicklenton and, I understand, other creatives. But Johnny's art will always be open to criticism; it has a strong counter-culture flavour, but also tremendous power.

I remember we produced a *Zombie World* serial for Dark Horse, which is a masterpiece of the grotesque, inspired by a trip we made to

London's catacombs where the Victorian dead are arranged in endless rows of neat, lead-lined coffins. We speculated: what would happen if they re-animated? We imagined a build-up of methane gas causes one coffin to explode and the corpse is plastered on the ceiling above, from where he can drop down, Dracula-like, onto his victims. Such breath-taking horror images blow many readers away. In my opinion, the risk of alienating more conservative readers was justified.

There were certainly conservative readers on *2000AD* and the *Megazine*. Once more the letters page, under Dave Bishop's guidance, were full of the most savage attacks on Johnny's art. I believe Johnny was drawing *Judge Dredd* at the time. Such venom is surely counter-productive, as it doesn't lead to better work. It just makes writers and artists angry and defensive.

Aware of the danger, I begged Johnny not to read the readers' letters, but *2000AD* was his whole life, and he felt he had to. He thought he could handle them. Incensed by their spite, he asked for the right to reply, and he got it. This just made it worse. If trolls know they're drawing blood, it will only encourage them, and that's what happened.

"*Why is Dave Bishop doing this?*" an angry Johnny would ask me. "*Did he have too many bog washes at school?*"

The hate letters continued after Dave had left. And, before they finally abated, there were still letters that should gone straight in the bin, especially as it was widely known that Johnny was sick; after all he had made the courageous and very funny Channel 4 documentary about his multiple sclerosis: *Here's Johnny*.

The letter that comes immediately to mind appeared in the Rebellion era: a reader described a collaboration between Johnny and Clint Langley as "ice cream covering shit". There was more, but I don't want to read it again in case I blow a gasket on Johnny's behalf.

It was a clear case of verbal abuse and it should never, *never* have been published. Shame on all responsible.

Johnny put on a brave face, but I know he was stabbed to the heart by such letters. *2000AD* meant everything to Johnny. It was his whole life. Even, sometime later, when he made that courageous, one-way flight to Switzerland, with his devoted partner Claire, he was texting me messages about comics and *Slaine* almost up to the end.

Slaine readers will know of Clint's moving and sensitive presentation of Johnny's art on *Slaine* . The beautiful, tragic scene where "the King falls".

A picture says a thousand words.

I wrote this piece to honour Johnny's memory. We love you, Johnny, and we'll never forget your incredible contribution to *2000AD*. For me and so many readers, you and Clint are *both* ice cream.

———

Reflecting on the Dark Age, it would be unfair to say it was all the result of one or two Thargs misguided policies in the late '90s. Prior to the Rebellion era, *2000AD* had been *endlessly* unlucky with its editors and it takes time for the impact of their decisions to have an impact on the readers and the circulation of the comic.

2000AD's ongoing success is primarily due to the incredible talent that constantly ran through its pages, the fierce loyalty of the readers, and the occasional good decision by an editor. There have also been some very cool covers which are usually down to the editors. But otherwise, I, and many creatives found the Thargs an obstacle to overcome or circumnavigate around who added very little to the comic. If you don't believe this, consider their subsequent careers and what they're doing today.

The notable exception is Nick Landau, as I've described earlier. As Nick and I always seem to be on opposite sides of the fence where comics are concerned and disagree about everything, that is hardly a partisan opinion.

And consider, by comparison, Dave Hunt, editor of *Battle*, who knew how to support and encourage creatives. Here's what I said about Dave some years ago in an interview with Neil Emerys:

"When Battle's editor Dave Hunt took him (Joe Colquhoun) off Johnny Red to do Charley, I knew it was going to work. I can't sing Dave Hunt's praises loud enough. He was the editor and it was an incredibly brave, dangerous, even foolhardy thing to do. Because Johnny Red was phenomenally popular. There is no editor in modern comics who would ever risk anything like that today. It could never happen. They are far too cautious—and usually Dave was! The significance and importance of Dave's decision cannot be emphasized enough. We all owe him an enormous debt of gratitude. He knew how to put creative teams together—a gift that few modern editors have."

If Dave Hunt had remained editor of *Battle*, I'm quite sure it would still be around today.

If only we'd had Thargs with his vision.

30. THE FRENCH CONNECTION

During the Dark Age, I submitted a new story idea to Tharg. I can't remember why now – maybe I was still foolishly optimistic that *2000AD* was open to new stories from me. But it clearly illustrates just how wretched the editorial process was at this time and how many other creators must have been messed around by Tharg. Entitled *The Resurrectionist,* it was a story about an inside-out Hell World, where time runs backwards and thus the dead come back to life. Where there is land on Earth, there is sea on Resurrection. Everything is reversed: good is bad; cruel is kind; fags are good for you, and so on. I'd had the idea since I was a kid and it was my way of making sense of the inside-out world I was living in, with mad teachers and a dubious religion.

It's what writers seem to do as a kind of catharsis. Thus, Richard O'Brien explored his transgender personality in *The Rocky Horror Show*. *The Resurrectionist* would become another black comedy vampiric world that mocks its demons in a similarly outrageous way.

As I developed it over several unpaid weeks, I was first enthusiastically encouraged by *2000AD*, notably by the American producer working with them on Fleetway Film and TV, who regarded *The Resurrectionist* as a premium story. She was full of enthusiasm for it. Then, suddenly, there was some behind the scenes change of opinion, possibly connected with the failure of Fleetway Film and TV or my outspoken criticism of it and the bullshit Tharg was filling the readers' heads with about it. Suddenly I was told *The Resurrectionist* wasn't working, no matter how often I revised it. Dave never formally turned the story down or even had the courtesy to discuss my final drafts. *2000AD's* interest in it just fizzled out. Instead, Dave vaguely claimed that time running backwards had already been used in a science fiction novel, and was therefore invalid in a comic strip. Utter nonsense. Of course time running backwards has been used in numerous sf novels: it's an sf sub-genre. As bullshit excuses for rejecting a story go, this has to be the most pathetic I've ever come across. The real reason was some kind of office politics.

But it turned out to be good news for me, because I then developed it with artist Olivier Ledroit for France as *Requiem Vampire Knight*, where it's a top bestseller, with various European and American editions as well as selling very well in digital English-language editions on Comixology.

So it led me away from the Puritanical world of British comics and brought me back into Europe where comic rock 'n' roll is alive and well. It reminded me that there was still life in comics; they didn't have to be as miserable, as humourless, and as wretched as they were during *2000AD's* Dark Age. I began working for Germany for Extreme comics, published by Bela B of the top punk band Die Ärzte along with John Hicklenton, Duke Mighten, and Simon Bisley. Bela's credo was that comics were all too often dull and boring and should be fun and I could not agree more. We had signings where the signing booth was turned into the padded cell of a lunatic asylum and we wore straitjackets. In further signings, we were behind bars on Death Row and took turns in the electric chair.

The French have similar professional cosplay ideas. I have great memories of being in a Paris Goth nightclub and Olivier and I emerging from coffins while actors playing Requiem Vampire Knight and a whip-cracking Claudia Vampire Knight patrolled the club.

Claudia proved so popular, we had a yearly competition for a reader to play her at events. The winner (whose entire back was covered in a tattoo of the beautiful vampire) was great, but she took her work a little too seriously, wanting to remain as Claudia, which presented us with some difficulties.

You see? This is what happens when you start to have fun in comics and stray from the boring Path of Righteousness. If only we'd heeded the words of Torquemada: Be Pure! Be Vigilant! Behave!

French comics treat their creators so much fairer. So how the French handle rights is directly relevant to the British experience and to the future of *2000AD*. To set the scene, on *Charley's War*—currently printed in ten volumes in the UK as well as in omnibus form, and in several European editions—you will doubtless be shocked to learn that neither I nor the artist's estate have received any money in royalties either from the copyright holder, Egmont, or from the licensee, Titan Books. Or from the foreign licensees. Yet I regularly promote *Charley's War* at numerous events and shops in Britain, Holland, France, etc., because I feel I have a duty to promote its anti-war message, despite not receiving a bean in royalties.

Neither Egmont, Titan, or foreign reprint publishers, currently feel they have a moral *duty* to voluntarily pay the creators because it is the right thing to do. Or indeed to reveal sales on my work. When I brought the subject of royalties up with Egmont years on *Charley's War*, on behalf of myself and the artist's estate, I was turned down by The Suits in no uncertain terms. All the license fees and TV option money on *Charley's War* stays in Egmont's pockets.

This attitude can change if all of us in the industry: writers; artists, and fans make publishers aware of their *responsibilities* and the importance of checking creators *are* receiving a royalty on their work. Then it's quite possible for them to factor it into their sums when issuing licenses or paying for them. The well-worn excuse that it's the other guy's responsibility just doesn't hold up anymore. There's no excuse for not paying creators.

Thus, after taking the *Charley* license over from Titan, and the girls comics licenses from Egmont, Rebellion is paying a small royalty to the relevant creators in future. That's excellent news. They're not under any legal obligation, but they recognize they have a *moral* responsibility. This is clearly progress, and the right thing to do. Bravo!

When Titan Books started publishing *Dredd* and other *2000AD* material, they also voluntarily paid a *very* small royalty to creators. This was primarily in response to *considerable* pressure from all of us, because they needed covers and introductions.

And possibly also because it was the right thing to do.

When Jon Davidge of Egmont apportioned significant sums from the first *Dredd* movie to the story and art developers, he did it unequivocally because it was the right thing to do.

John Wagner did the same for me on the *Dredd Megazine* royalties, because it was the right thing to do, although it was actually the publisher's responsibility, not his.

So in Britain we still have a long way to go. Starting with house characters and serials taken over by new writers and artists.

Currently, the original creators get nothing. So John Wagner and Carlos Ezquerra don't benefit from other writers writing or drawing *Dredd*, unless they have a very different deal to the rest of us.

For this reason, I was lukewarm some time ago when IDW Publishing considered producing *ABC Warriors*, almost certainly with another American writer. It would undermine my position; there's no financial benefit to me; and they could easily have got the characters wrong, especially if they "Americanised" the Warriors.

For the same reason, I was wary when *The Phoenix* showed an interest in *Slaine*. They wanted to do a "*Slaine* Light", but, thankfully, decided against it, so my hero was spared a makeover that would have made him suitable for Waitrose customers.

I did wonder about subverting its nice middle class readers with some challenging ideas, but I think I'm too far out of the closet to get away with it anymore.

The French solve all this easily enough: if another writer were to write my *Requiem Vampire Knight*, or the spin-off series, *Claudia*,

Vampire Knight, I would receive a percentage of his royalties. A financial interest concentrates everyone's mind wonderfully and ensures a suitable solution is found, agreeable to all parties. The same would apply if another artist took over from *Requiem* artist Olivier Ledroit. That's the industry standard in France, and I believe it's enshrined in law.

It's also the right thing to do. John and Carlos *should* receive a percentage of other creatives' *Dredds* in a similar way.

It would also make the idea of other writers taking over my popular characters at some point in the future worth considering

If the percentages are industry standard, it's not painful for anyone.

But in Britain and America there is a record of publishers owning characters devised by individuals, which then become "house characters" written and drawn by anyone. Publishers and editors have actively encouraged readers to see things this way, even though the end result is often a disaster.

But, as I've demonstrated again and again, I think they would often prefer a disaster to stop creators becoming too important.

Because it's always been part of a very British calculated policy of divide and rule to reduce our importance, which goes back to the era of no credits.

I've told my French publishing associates about Britain's Stone Age position on rights and industry standards (of which more later). I've explained how British publishers would like us to behave like Tharg's obedient robots in the Nerve Centre, and they look at me in utter disbelief. Because original comic book characters should be, under European law, the intellectual property of creators. In Europe, rights are more real, more precious and longer lasting than a Barrett home.

But, with Brexit looming, The Suits can now tell publishers they can safely ignore European law on copyright, which contradicts British law and was in the process of being challenged by creatives in various fields of publishing. I and other writers were carefully watching their progress and the outcome. It could have been a game-changer, notably on the increasingly important digital rights, which none of us ever signed away, as they didn't exist at the time. Therefore they can't possibly have any right to them.

But the French connection has now been broken.

31. RISE OF THE ROBOTS

When Rebellion took over, shortly after the Millennium, and the Dark Age came to an end, *2000AD* was close to death's door. I was so aware that it could be axed at any time, I took a voluntary page rate cut, and at least one of the comic's top artists did the same.

That *2000AD* survived, found its way again, and regained something of its original position in the market place, is an astonishing achievement. It's down to everyone at Rebellion, but notably editor Matt Smith.

His cure was simple enough, although it seems to have been beyond the abilities of at least three previous Thargs.

To make *2000AD* like *2000AD* again.

I guess it was easy for Matt, because he has no personal agenda: he doesn't want to be a producer for Fleetway Films and TV, or to use it as a stepping-stone to another publication, and he doesn't listen to those who want the comic to be like *Deadline*, *Vertigo* or *Loaded*.

As a result, the classic *2000AD* characters returned. Stories like *Flesh* and *Savage*, as well as *Greysuit*, my adult version of *Mach One*.

The cure is also possible because of one further important factor, hitherto missing: Matt and his colleagues *like 2000AD*. And they like it just the way it was.

I thought the documentary *Future Shock!* really didn't do justice to Matt's achievements. It was like they were taken for granted or weren't considered important, by comparison with the various high profile fan-favourites interviewed. Doubtless because these creators might find more favour in America, and help sell the documentary there. *2000AD* creators had such an impact on the world of superheroes, after all. But, from my soundings, I think the Americans themselves recognize the documentary is inappropriately skewed for their consumption. I thought the producers bigged up the sometimes unlikely impact the comic may or may not have had in the States. And who cares what difference our comic made to men in tights? That's *not 2000AD's* story, but a very different story that's clearly *piggy-backing* on our comic's success. The important thing is 2000AD is a *British* success. Here's what I wrote to the producers just after I'd watched the film:

I didn't think Matt's 14 years were emphasised in doc airtime … His truly incredible success contrasts with others' failures.

Now, for the first time, mainstream stories were reprinted in collections, thanks to the efforts of Rebellion's Keith Richardson and Ben Smith. Bellardinelli's serials, *Dan Dare* and others, were reprinted. This was unthinkable during the era when the fan-orientated Titan Books tail wagged the *2000AD* dog. Now the elitism I loath has gone, and all tastes are accommodated and all subjects are covered.

Apart, of course, from paganism (*Finn*) and politics (*Third World War*).

Matt's method is unique, and I haven't seen anyone else comment on it. I'm not sure it would work on other publications, but it clearly works on *2000AD* and I rather think it is the *only* solution. Because of it, we have had an uneventful, calm, *fifteen years* under his editorship which seem to have flown by because nothing awful happens anymore. There's no more chaos, and no more aggro.

Matt's secret? He simply doesn't emotionally engage with any of us.

At the same time, his grasp of storytelling is first rate, so he knows what he's talking about. He's also not a frustrated writer, so he's quite happy for our story visions to be different to his.

There's a downside, of course, to maintaining the very barest of contact with creators. I've never received a Christmas card or rarely even a Christmas greeting from Rebellion, they are *that* emotionally detached from their creators, but, as this method of keeping us all at arm's length works and there's no alternative, why talk about the downside?

This robotic approach is so successful, I wish I could program my own brain with it. However, I fear my muse would reject the software.

And emotional disengagement may well be the norm in these post-Millennial times.

Thus Kevin O'Neill and I visited one creative studio working on exciting sf stories, and we were both shocked to find it felt like a mortuary. At another creative funeral parlour, a studio boss asked a staff member to show me examples of what they were doing and then abruptly added, "*Right. Get on with your work now.*"

Similarly, a few years ago I considered working for a publisher who operated through an online database, with no personal contact. As I waded through the system, I came across a startling and fairly lengthy robot edict. Words to the effect: "Stories will be assessed by our out-source readers and rated accordingly. We do not have the time or the budget to respond to writers personally, to socialise with you, or have a drink with you to discuss your problems. That is not our function. If you have emotional problems, go and find yourself a therapist."

That's a long way from the traditional working methods of *2000AD* creatives in the '70s and '80s, where it so often seemed like *Life on Mars*. Hence why Kevin and I wrote *Serial Killer* in the *Read Em and Weep* series, to capture the insanity of those days.

I think emotional disengagement is infinitely preferable to the Dark Age of the late '90s. For instance, it took me a whole *decade* to recover from the *2000AD* Millennium "party" that was held towards the end of the Dark Age.

I was so wary of the "celebration" I was invited to, but I felt I had to take the risk, just this once. The comic had made it to the twenty-first century, after all, and it would be wrong if I didn't show my face. But my paranoia was justified. Sure enough, it turned out to be an ambush, where I had to buy my own drinks and a handful of *2000AD* creatives (actually just three) rather glumly "celebrated" our achievement in a dingy pub basement. I recall there was just one woman present.

And then a fanboy that Dave Bishop, or his companion, had invited and was waiting for me to turn up, was launched on me like a Rottweiler. Without introduction, the fan castigated me in intense and comprehensive detail about some "very serious" story continuity flaws in my *Nemesis* saga. The saga was now over but that didn't matter, it still required my urgent acknowledgement of just how far I'd fucked up, and I needed to show suitable personal contrition. To this fanboy personally. He simply would not shut the fuck up.

Just the kind of conversation you have at celebration parties, eh? When we should be saying, *"Hey, guys! 2000AD made it to the millennium! Isn't that brilliant? Let's get off our faces."*

I should have bought the fanboy a drink and poured it over his head. I will if anyone else ever tries it.

I wish I was being facetious, but in the austere world of British comics, many genuinely *prefer* such belligerent conversations to relaxing, having a good time and partying. Look at the response to Tony Skinner's efforts to party, for example.

So you can see the attraction of Rebellion's policy of emotional disengagement from creatives. For all its drawbacks, it's *got* to be better than this.

The Millennium "party" was also a huge culture shock after the rock 'n' roll of European comics, where comic people actually know how to enjoy themselves. In Paris, my French publisher and artist once looked at me with genuine consternation and admonished me for not taking money from the *company's* petty cash to book into a hotel with an attractive Goth designer I'd just met at a promotional event. "*C'est normal*," they said with Gallic shrugs and puzzled puffs of their Gitanes. I tried to explain I was broken from decades of working for British comics and I really should get back to my work now, but I don't think they understood.

A robotic, distant approach at Rebellion is also inevitable because, due to budget constraints, Matt is a one man band, running *2000AD and* the *Megazine*. That is seriously impressive. I have no idea how he manages it.

But it does means the era of high maintenance artists and writers mentored by guys like Gerry Finley-Day, Steve MacManus or myself, is over. Unlike the '70s and '80s, there simply isn't the time or the money to do it. Maybe it's a good thing.

Anyway, there was such a sense of *relief* that the Dark Age was finally over: it meant Rebellion has had a very extended honeymoon of good will from all of us. Maybe I should be sending *them* Christmas cards.

32. PAT'S MYSTERIOUS WORLD

Now in retreat in the bars of Marbella, I ponder on the riddles of *2000AD* and other comics.

And the challenges Tharg's mighty organ faces today.

One of the most crucial challenges, which is endlessly debated by readers, is how *2000AD*—or any comic—can get back those young readers we lost in the '90s.

And no-one knows how, it's as if everyone's lost the art, the ninth art.

The forthcoming *Dredd* TV series, with its potentially wide appeal, could be a game-changer and make pondering more than a hypothetical exercise.

I've done some research on younger age groups for girls' comics and *Charley's War* and the principle is pretty much the same.

To lure them back, without alienating existing readers, requires an accessible, longer length, blockbuster hero story or stories and a level of research and a quality of script and art that is not easily achieved.

This is assuming there is a genuine desire, which I seriously doubt. It involves really studying that audience and deciding if Tharg and his creators *like* and understand or *want* to understand younger readers.

From the way they have been neglected in the past, I honestly don't think so. I refer you to the typical reader's letter earlier in the book, where he felt he just wasn't cool enough for *2000AD*, and left.

Older readers are far more appealing to editors and many creatives. They enjoy the media attention and the boost to their careers. We can have great conversations with older more sophisticated readers at conventions. By comparison, younger *2000AD* readers were famously rude. One kid would pass our tables going, "Ugh! Don't like your story. Ugh! Don't like your story. Ugh! Don't like your story." And they could be so intrusive. Another kid sent everyone a questionnaire wanting details of our education and whether we lived in a private or a council house. So a sense of humour is required. Or perhaps a Super Soaker Revenge Zombinator to blast them, if they're too cheeky. That would sort them out.

Because I know kids are and should be at the heart of comics, I don't feel the same way as many of my peers. I enjoy writing for my current older readership, but I also like writing for younger readers. If I'm honest, it's because they're so damn difficult; it's such a challenge to get it right and it's incredibly satisfying when I have done. In fact, if you really pushed me, I'd probably say I prefer writing for a younger age group. Don't take too much notice of the character Dave in *Serial Killer* who hates his audience. He was inspired by W.C. Fields, who supposedly hated kids.

And I know it's possible to appeal to them, because superhero comics reach a wide age group. And Games Workshop hasn't fallen into the trap of only appealing to an increasingly ageing audience. In France, they continue to attract new generations, proving theories about computer games taking over are an excuse for typical British comic complacency. And from time to time I see great photos of lego versions of *2000AD* characters created by dads for their young sons, so they *are* out there.

About five years ago, I did a straw poll on kids, male and female, aged around eight to eleven in order to try and bring back girls' comics. I showed them copies of a number of girls' serials, including my own stories, and I valued their enthusiastic response. They were not interested in the writer or the artist, although they liked our end products and said they would buy the comics, in paper version or online. They saw the stories as timeless and had no problem with the staid but not particularly '70s fashions or the looks of the heroines.

Give them another two years and they might have been more critical. Thus I showed the same stories to my nieces, who are educated in France, and are a few years older. They thought the fashions weren't very cool and the heroine in one story "wasn't pretty enough". They didn't like her rather masculine short hair. Sorry, feminists. It was *Glenda's Glossy Pages,* art by Capaldi, my serial about a girl who has found a sinister mail order catalogue: a nightmare version of Amazon that gives Glenda anything she wants, but there is a price to pay. They also weren't keen on my "over-written" dialogue on *Glenda*. They thought the brilliant French-Canadian series *Belly Button* (published in France by Dupuis) primarily about teenage girls who stand around bitching about each other all day, was superior to all the British girl comics. I get that. I used to write a similar photostrip story (*9 to 4* for *Girl*) which baffled the script editor, Norman Worker, because he said to me, "Why on Earth do readers like your story? There's no action. The girls are just endlessly moaning and being really horrible to each other." I *knew* that's what readers wanted, because I'd studied my audience.

So we have to understand the complex rules and there's always more to understand, between genders, the changing times we live in, and the differences even two years can make. And sometimes I'd get it horribly wrong. Like *Shaney in the Shade* I wrote for *Pink*. It's about a teenage girl whose mum is more glamorous than she is. So there's incredible tension between them. Well, that was my thinking. Boy! Did the readers hate that one! "Kill it!" cried my script editor. Similarly, in girls comics, step-dads can be evil as Hell, but never good old dad. I love the challenge of new directions. But I think it requires too much money, time and effort to get right.

I fear the siren-call of fandom will always seem more important, as it has been in the past.

Another example shows the differences and the challenges of appealing to children. On *Charley's War*, Titan Books have photographic covers. Although they're beautiful productions, the covers themselves look dull, worthy, a little pretentious and are confusing when they're shown spine out. I'm also uncomfortable with the red poppy on them, not least because of the aggressive patriotism it can sometimes represent today. I would be in favour of the white poppy on the cover as it's an anti-war series.

I don't recall *ever* signing a copy of *Charley's War* for a UK boy. Adults, of course, in droves: it's a successful series that's done well for Titan and Egmont, if not the writer and artist who created it.

By comparison, the French covers have attractive bright, contrasting primary-coloured covers. So when I've signed copies in France, I've noticed twelve or thirteen year old French boys, spotting the bright covers, browsing through the books, liking what they see and buying them. So there was no need for the Zombinator. Because Joe's beautiful art and my story lured them in. *Charley's War* was always intended first and foremost for them.

It gives me one helluva kick to bring comics back to the audience for whom they *really* belong: kids.

33. THE GODFATHER

As no one else seems inclined to put their head over the parapet and speak out, I guess it's up to me, once again, to say something about the current financial state of play on *2000AD* where creators are concerned.

It's time to revisit the legendary *Tharg's Head Revisited*.

To set the scene, when John Wagner and I started, writing in a garden shed, by oil lamp, comics were already in economic recession. Because the money was so crap, we ended up typing a story on tracing paper, to the editor's fury. In fact, John estimated we had to think up a funny story every twenty minutes to make it viable for us to write cartoon strips for *Whizzer and Chips*. No pressure there.

The golden years, when one writer, Mike Butterworth (of Trigan Empire fame) lived in a moated Tudor farmhouse, and a fun comic artist owned a yacht from the proceeds of his work were over.

Mike Butterworth created and wrote the opening episode of *School of No Escape* for *Sandie*, around 1971. The money was already poor by this point, so when the managing editor John Purdie wanted changes made to a story on which Mike owned no rights, Mike quite rightly said no and walked. It wasn't worth his while. He could see the way things were going financially, had prepared his exit, and was already writing successful novels

John Purdie's response was predictable. Rather than offering this successful writer more money or a better deal, they simply let him go and employed John and myself to continue the story. There are always hungry writers who will take a "difficult" writer's place, and I regret now that we were part of that system.

It's the time-honoured way British publishers and editors deal with creators who stand their ground.

Thus Pat and Alan Davison—whom I rate highly as the Alan Moore of girls' comics—were "let go" because they had the temerity to ask for a by-line. As the editor told me, "I had to. I can't have freelancers telling me what to do."

Pat and Alan's absence was one of the reasons girls' comics crashed. But at least the editor had succeeded in keeping us all in our place. That's far more important to Suits.

A similar thing happened to me on *Charley's War*. I believe the Suit genuinely thought it was *better* for my controversial serial to crash with another writer than pay me a development fee to bring this number one serial into World War Two.

There's no way to wrap this up nicely. Economically, on *2000AD*, we are now back to those dark days.

Currently, page rates for writers and artists have been frozen *for over twenty years*. And we work on stories where we don't own the rights and royalties are minuscule, or non-existent.

It cannot be argued "The industry is in the doldrums. Times are hard", the argument always given by John Sanders: see below. That really doesn't fly anymore. Rates elsewhere on other comic books, which I've just analysed, show that the rates for a similar, low circulation comic with an equivalent cover price are at least 15% higher. (I've excluded from my calculation higher selling comics with an equivalent cover price where the rates would be significantly more.)

If we complain about the deal, the comforting thought for bullish publishers in the past has been that we're disposable and there's always someone who can take our place.

As comics publisher John Sanders once said, to my great amusement, "It's very cold out there on the street."

Requiem fans may notice my character Lord Cryptos similarly warns the defiant hero, "It's very cold out there on the moon."

But the days of attracting a new Bolland, Jock, Fabry, Moore or Morrison to *2000AD* are long gone. Creators with that kind of talent no longer need to serve a *2000AD* apprenticeship and instead they go straight to America or in some other creative direction.

So we're not quite as disposable as publishers would prefer us to be.

To survive financially, some artists now hold onto their day job, work *insane* hours, to the detriment of their physical and mental wellbeing, sell off their beautiful art cheaply and quickly, or supplement their income with drawings or selling books at conventions. Other creators find jobs elsewhere to *subsidise* their work for Rebellion and maintain their creative standards.

I've done this myself by taking on advertising work. The higher advertising fees enabled me to spend more time on *2000AD* stories.

The days when everyone relaxed at conventions, spent ages chatting idly to fans, and hung out at the bar, are gone. It's now an opportunity to supplement Rebellion's low rates.

These low rates mean there is a slow-down in production and the danger of a reduction in quality. Sometimes my serials can take two, even, astonishingly, up to *three* years to appear! Because the artists, quite understandably, prioritize *better* paid work elsewhere.

The incentive is simply not there.

The result? Readers lose interest because the story has lost momentum. They're picking up a tale left on a cliff-hanger *years* before and they've forgotten what was going on. They have to get back into characters and plot.

So a series that has taken me time, thought and great care, is canned as a result. This is what happened with *Greysuit*. It's a story I wrote back in December *2014*! The second part of a serial with complex characters and themes. So the *Greysuit* adventure, "Foul

Play", that began in July 2017, is the last one. It's a proveable casualty of financial neglect; a lack of investment in the creative team.

I've become frustrated by the endless delays, caused by the poor rates. So I've taken up writing novels instead, like *Serial Killer* in the *Read Em and Weep* series, or non-fiction books. Like this one.

Because there's a dynamic excitement and energy to the independent publishing world that was once there during the Comic Revolution. Now the muse seems to have moved on. In indie publishing, I can devise a project on which I own the rights, publish it within a few months, and, thanks to my wife Lisa's marketing, it can pay better than *2000AD*. There's a friendly and supportive online community of fellow creators who've gone out of their way to warmly welcome us and give us advice and encouragement.

I know other key creators have had to come up with similar ways of living with the low payments. But this means there's surely something wrong with the comic system.

If *2000AD* can't compete with the comic giants of America and France, it should, at least, be able to compete financially with one-man bands in the indie market, and offer a better deal for long-standing creators.

The development time on a completely new *2000AD* serial (up to six weeks) or for a story on an existing serial (up to three weeks) is still not paid for by the company.

The writer has to fully absorb the development cost. In the past, the Thargs understood this, as I've exampled, and efforts were made to share the financial burden, but no more. There's no time.

In response, some creators will cut corners and so it can become a speed exercise, once again, where writers used to boast, "I can create a new serial in two days". Yes, and in two years time, no one will remember it. It was the very thing I fought against when I started *2000AD* in order to produce *quality* stories like *Judge Dredd* and *Slaine*.

I assume Rebellion and *2000AD* readers would like *new*, classic, long-lasting serials like *Dredd*, *Slaine*, *ABC Warriors*, Robohunter and *Strontium Dog*?

Certainly in the past, readers would complain to me that they wanted such iconic *new* stories. They told me they wanted new *Slaines*, new *Dredds*, new *Strontium Dogs*. It explains why fans regularly fondly look back to those days and rarely mention current *new* stories with the same affection.

But prominent writers no longer create stories of *that* stature. They cannot afford such a huge investment of their time for free. As I've already described, it involves endless drafts, considerable thought, hunting for the right artist and what Mike McMahon once memorably and accurately described as "staring out the window time". Plus some hand-holding when things go wrong, which they invariably do. It's unfair that the development costs and risks on a story *not owned* by the creative team is born by the creative team alone.

It proves, once again, that there's something seriously wrong with the comics system.

Royalties should be part of the solution. They're not.

Royalties—in percentage terms—are below the comics industry standard, which applies to books, merchandising, films, *everything*. And that is: 50% to creators, 50% to publisher.

I recall vividly that the Rebellion contract was a past source of complaint from freelancers, who were mesmerized by its fine print. They didn't understand it, it drove them nuts to read its complex prose, and the more it was explained by Rebellion over the phone to at least one of them, the more baffled he became.

As one well-known *2000AD* artist put it to me, "It's a complete head-fuck".

In the end, they gave up.

I remember feeling the same way, but I ignored it at the time because it was still the honeymoon period and, back then, the Rebellion books and merchandising had only just begun.

I've just taken the contract out today, in May 2017, and had another look at it. It is certainly not as easy to follow as other media contracts and could benefit from different, simpler wording. Despite a lifetime's experience of reading media contracts, I'm personally confused by it.

Some areas need further explanation, including digital, and the only thing I can say with certainty is that the terms offered to creators are significantly below industry standard.

But, like other freelancers, I cannot afford a day or more of my time studying it and making detailed notes for explanation, which would then lead to subsequent explanations, eventually taking up to a week of my time. Or paying an accountant or lawyer to explain it to me.

But rather than ask Rebellion for a "Ladybird book" version for dunces like myself, my feeling is *it doesn't actually matter*—it's always what a contract *delivers* in real terms that counts.

Let me illustrate just how poor the current royalty system is.

After John Wagner, I must have the largest collection of *2000AD* reprint books currently in print and these include top-selling *Judge Dredd* titles, and various other successful collections, many with a high cover price. My stories notably sell as European editions, plus my stories and characters generate a sizeable amount of *2000AD* merchandising: mugs; tee shirts; figures, and so on.

Yet my current annual royalty payment is the same amount that I receive annually from comics platform Comixology for the English language *digital* version of my Requiem Vampire Knight series.

So just *one* reprint series of *digital* royalties on a French comic book that is not particularly well known in the UK and the USA, pays the same as *forty years'* worth of royalties on *2000AD* books and merchandising!

Given the clear success of Rebellion's books and merchandising, that doesn't seem reasonable.

There are an *endless* number of *2000AD* books on which I'm the main or sole writer and which are available as digital editions. The digital version of the best-selling *Slaine The Horned God*, for example, which gets 40 five star reviews on Amazon. Yet just *one* digital series I've *self-published* through Comixology gives me a higher royalty payment than *all* of them put together!

Rebellion also pay royalties just once a year, unlike other comic publishers, who pay every quarter (Comixology) or every six months (DC Comics, Titan Books and Glenat Editions). Amazon's Kindle Direct Publishing pays royalties once a month.

And the royalty statements do *not* show the number of copies of books sold, in paper or digital, unlike the statements of *every other publisher I've worked for*. So we have no way of knowing how well our books are selling or why royalties should be so surprisingly low.

Not only is there emotional disengagement, there is also information disengagement.

For a long time, there was the shadow of the Dark Age, and the recognition of Rebellion's fantastic achievement in rescuing the Galaxy's Greatest Comic. This gave them an extended honeymoon of goodwill. And the knowledge that *2000AD* was still not performing well a few years ago, as director Jason Kingsley told me at the San Diego comic convention.

Just as John Sanders once came down to visit myself, John Wagner and Alan Grant in Essex in the 1980s to answer our complaints in person, and told us *2000AD* was not performing well.

But the years have passed since the 1980s, and the comic's still here.

And the years have passed since San Diego, and the comic's still here.

More staff have been taken on, and comic merchandising is now at a higher level than when Brian Bolland drew his critical *Judge Dredd* in *Thargshead Revisited*, highlighting the creators' lack of a fair share of *Dredd* merchandising.

Now there are films, games, an impending tv series, and more. *If* the comic still isn't doing that well, the products it's spawned are certainly doing very well.

If the comic ever disappeared, it would have a major, negative impact on that merchandising, so the two cannot be separated from each other. They are closely connected. So clearly the comic is going to around for a long time to come.

The comic and its creators are the source of that wealth. So the time comes when the honeymoon is surely over. I had thought once that with the new success of *2000AD*, we'd all finally make shedloads of money.

Instead, we're back to the garden shed.

34. THE RIGHT STUFF

It's clear the long-neglected page rates need a major improvement.

It can't be right to wait until *2000AD*'s 50th anniversary, in ten years time, when some of us may not be there to celebrate it. That would mean rates would have been frozen *for over thirty years*.

There are also endless ways to ease the cost of development and thus act as an incentive for all of us to create new iconic characters, that will last as long as *Dredd*, *Slaine* and *Strontium Dog*.

But the best way is to pay royalties at the simple, easy to understand, recognised industry standard, applied by publishers large and small, of 50% to publisher, 50% to creators, divided between writer and artist equally.

It's regarded worldwide as the fairest way to share the publisher's risk and reward success.

The increasingly important digital rights also needs fair evaluation, especially given that they were never signed off on at the time. Also, because there is less work, less risk than a paper publication and a greater profit for the publisher: no shops and distributors involved. So some major publishers already recognise this and take *less* than industry standard for themselves.

We should all share fairly in the Galaxy's Greatest Comic's success.

Similarly, if major *2000AD* films, games and TV series happen, key developers on stories, as well as creators, need to be recognised financially, as they have been in the past, when the publisher knew it was the right thing to do.

Rebellion have broken the mould of British comics. They are the first publishers to actually *care* about comics. They've rescued *2000AD* from certain disaster.

They've also rescued the archive of legendary British comics and are reprinting classics like *Charley's War*, on which—unlike predecessors like Titan Books and the European editions—they're paying a *voluntary* royalty.

It would be great to think they will now complete that process and care about the creators. I don't think it's hard, and it's the right thing to do.

If there's a positive outcome for freelancers, there could then be a new chapter added to this book. Perhaps entitled "Pat On The Back"?

Or if I incur the wrath of the Beadle for daring to ask for more, maybe "Ex-Pat"?

Or it may just be ignored, by far the most likely option, which would be consistent with the company's carefully considered policy of emotional and information disengagement, distancing themselves from the creatives who have produced their huge comic success but don't adequately or properly share in it. But the problem won't go away and will still need to be addressed.

Because the chapter would be called, "The Truth Is Still Out There".

35. YOU ARE 2000AD

2000AD readers have hung on in there through thick and thin. Thank you for your support, patience, tolerance and enthusiasm. You *are 2000AD*, and, ultimately, it's because of you it's still around today, stronger than ever.

We've all of us survived that shocking era of "Great News Inside, Readers!" when a comic fell victim to the brutal policy of "Hatch, match and despatch". And we've come through later eras, where the comic could be steered into icebergs by panicking editors.

Perhaps uniquely, the comic and its characters belong to you. Publishers, editors and creatives are only its guardians. We can no longer be "bad boys" and do just what we like with it. We have to show it proper respect. And I'm sure you'll tell us when we don't. You usually do. We know the power of the readers and how, when Conan Doyle killed off Holmes, fans insisted he was brought back.

Reader power is a phenomena that inspired me to write a scene in *ABC Warriors, The Volgan War*, Volume 3 (beautifully depicted by Clint Langley). The architect Krøll has devised the nightmare city of Mekana as a vast eternal building site. Then, driven insane by the Martian Goddess Medusa, he tries to deface it with endless graffiti. We join the scene as the Mekana cops, the G Men, led by Inspector Sturn, catch up with him:

Sturn: Put the spray can down, Professor Kroll.
Kroll: No! *I* built this city! I have the *right* to *deface* it!
Sturn: It's *our* city now.

That sense of ownership means that readers want to write and draw for their comic in a personal and special way. No longer because it's a convenient stepping-stone to other comics.

So readers constantly ask me: what are the chances of getting into *2000AD?* For artists, I'd say it's harder now than the '80s, but not *impossible.*

But I'm not going to give you any bullshit. What I can usefully tell you is what *not* to do. So, a few years ago, I gave a talk about the need for more female comics and artists. An agent listening was so impressed by my passion, she set up a competition with a £1K prize to find an artist. Art student Fay Dalton won. Fay has since produced fantastic and glamorous work for the James Bond Estate (*Casino Royale*), Sony, Titan Books covers and comic strips for my *Megazine* series *American Reaper,* co-created by Clint Langley. If you Google her, you'll see why Clint and I are crazy about her work. She is amazing! I saw her as a future Brian Bolland, but, despite Herculean efforts by both Clint and I, we've been unable to get her comic work on *2000AD* at this time of writing. Now this top artist is busy elsewhere. In my opinion, it's Rebellion's loss. And yours, the *2000AD* reader.

But, looking at it positively, there *are* insights to be drawn from my failure to get her on board. Fay's glamorous work is a touch risqué, more than a touch retro, and is quite unique. That's part of its appeal. I fear those sexy qualities have worked against her. Remember the words of Torquemada as they apply to British comics. Other great artists with styles that suggest some counter-culture thinking I've also tried and failed to get onto my stories. Being *too different* seems to be the common denominator in my failure to be a facilitator.

So I think the style you need to adopt is exciting, dynamic, but *conservative* and "middle of the road". That *doesn't* mean pedestrian, or the D C Thomson's "front seat of the stalls" style that we did away with on *Battle*, *Action* and *2000AD*.

The artist Mike Dorey (*Ro-Busters* and *Hellman of Hammer Force*) once told me a great story of such old school thinking. He had to illustrate a ballroom formation dancing story for *Diana*. There were nine pictures on the page and he had to feature the full formation in every one! So count yourself lucky those days, at least, are gone.

Thankfully, on *2000AD*, there is no one "house-style" like Marvel, but the closer you can get to orthodoxy, without copying anyone—which has rightly incurred the readers' wrath in the past—the better your chances. It's not my heartbeat, but I assume it's what the majority of readers now want?

So *don't* be too different. If you have a maverick or an odd-ball style or you're following your personal artistic vision, as Fay and some past artists have, I'd say don't waste your time submitting work to *2000AD*. I very much doubt an artist like Kevin O'Neill—*if* he was starting out today—would get work on the Galaxy's Greatest Comic. The times have changed *that* much.

If you're thinking of writing for *2000AD*, it may be equally challenging, but again not impossible.

The good news is that editor Matt Smith has a truly impressive understanding of the rules of drama, which his predecessors often seemed to lack. So if you're following the rules, you may stand a chance.

I recommend you study your bible. Not the Abrahamic one, but a writer's guide. Mine is Robert McKee's *Story*, which I suitably adapt to comics. If you receive contradictory or confusing advice from editors, your bible will keep you on the Path of Righteousness. That's why I've noticed screenplay editors seem to hate McKee, because he often contradicts them. So never tell editors you read the bible (whichever one you choose), they don't like it. Keep that to yourself. There can only be one God, and that is The Editor.

I also have some advice on comic-writing on www.millsverse.com, notably about the Formula, which is the equivalent of McKee's

Principles of Storytelling. I prefer "Formula" because it's a more down-market term. If you look at crime procedure novels, they're often "Formula", which is why readers like them and they sell by the shedload. It's more honest for our market, it recognises our comic formula heritage, and it annoys the graphic novel chaps.

Younger readers, female readers and mainstream action readers are more my area of expertise, so I don't know how useful my advice is for *2000AD* where there may still be a tendency towards less subversion and more sf stories. And I have different views on story pacing to Matt, who generally favours a more condensed approach.

There's also the whole subject of the challenges of working with an artist, and vice versa. It's rarely talked about but can lead to grief on every imaginable level (and some you can't imagine) if you don't get it right.

So what do you do if you're a comic artist but can't—or have no desire—to write? And you don't like the look of the writers out there?

The great anti-war artist, Tardi, told me how he got over the problem on his *Paris Commune* by basing his work on a French classic novel that was out of copyright.

But what if you're a writer and care passionately about a subject, e.g. wild cities, crazy cars, hideous aliens—and the artist is merely lukewarm about them? Believe me, it will show in the final product, and the readers will often blame the story for not inspiring the artist.

So, having empathy with artists is necessary, whether we like it or not. It's no good giving them things to draw that they don't care about. It's a skill I certainly used to have, and possibly should write about further, although, as you will have already noted, it's a sensitive subject.

The state of mind of a writer and artist also affects the work. If either is depressed it will show, as I've seen on more than one occasion. I've seen happy, up-beat scenes I've written portrayed in a gloomy way, for example. Conversely, if either writer or artist is euphoric that will show, too, and may even be *worse*.

For example, there was a great series from the French publisher,

Comics USA. It was violent and successful. Then the creator's partner had a baby, and he wanted the whole world to know about his happy event. There was a sudden change of tone as he shared the joys of fatherhood with his readers, who weren't impressed. Sales dropped as a result. He was told to get back to the blood and gore, pronto.

I lecture on comics at universities from time to time, so maybe I should come back to comics writing in a future book, if anyone is interested.

In the past, I also used to co-write. Firstly, because it was fun and introduced me to worlds and cultures I knew little of. And it's more interesting drawing on people's real-life experiences than getting them from Wikipedia. Secondly, because it *democratises* writing. It reduces "them and us" pyramid thinking. I pass on hard-won skills and knowledge for others to use. And I've learnt from my co-writers, so it's a two-way street.

As you've seen, that approach was very firmly blocked and I would be discouraged from doing it again. As one editor told me, "You're a brand name. So you're diluting the brand if you co-write with others." I think that's true for other writers, but I do feel readers would accept a more counter-culture approach from me, as long as my co-writer was a kindred spirit. Anyway, those are the rules, and I have to abide by them. Today my stories tend to draw on more personal material and are thus solo-written, but I still miss that era. But, with the current low payment rates, there's no longer any slack in the system to make it economically viable for me to pay a partner.

However, I should take this opportunity to acknowledge and thank co-writers I've written with in the past, since the conception of *2000AD*, *Crisis*, and other comics: Tony Skinner, Alan Mitchell, Steve Earles, Bianca Veenstra, Debbie Gallagher, Kevin O'Neill, Kelvin Gosnell, Malachy Coney and Nathan Harris.

And, of course, John Wagner.

No overview of *2000AD* would be complete without talking about hand-lettering and its relevance for a prospective writer and artist.

The current system is another casualty of producing the comic on a low budget.

Because today's computer lettering often lacks the impact of original hand lettering as in the early days of *2000AD*. Consider, for example the hand lettering by Jack Potter on my original series of *Flesh*. It makes a significant difference to the final product. Jack's work made him a *2000AD* artist in his own right. Not just the words, but the *shape* of the balloons themselves. These are details a writer shouldn't have to add in his script but I have been forced to in recent years. Jack didn't have to be told, he knew what to do intuitively. There were other great letterers, too, like Tom Frame, whose words are a joy to the eye.

It seems wrong to me that modern lettering cannot compete visually with the superior hand lettering of the 1970s. We should be going forwards to bigger and better, but that's not the case where lettering is concerned.

Indeed, in recent years there were some computer letterers who readers and I saw were actually harming a story. Readers would write to me and complain about listless lettering and indifferent positioning. The letterers in question regularly made a point of ignoring my detailed and repeated instructions—often in red 16 point (as they deliberately seemed to miss them)—because it would have meant more work for them. So multiple balloons would be stacked one below the next, in the most horrible way imaginable, like a ladder, without thought or care, pointedly ignoring my careful and specific requirements. Pat's just the writer. What the fuck does he know?

The genius of hand-lettering, best exampled by the brilliant American letterer, Ken Bruzenak of *American Flagg* fame, would have been lost on them. Ken not only draws the most exciting sound effects, but can position multiple dense speech balloons effortlessly in a dynamic and readable way.

And then of, course, there's art supremo Dave Gibbons, whose hand lettering is so brilliant I daren't even look at it because it will just make me yearn for the classic days of yore.

Thankfully, the awful computer letterers I've described are no longer working on my stories.

But if the lettering today is done on a tight budget, it doesn't always give today's excellent letterers a chance to shine.

Personally, I'd like to see an exploratory return to genuine hand lettering. A comic art tutor agrees and at least one of his students uses real hand lettering. We both feel there can be an "uncanny valley" effect to computer pseudo-hand lettering. The reader senses on some level it's not the genuine article. It's not *quite* real.

They want to feel again the *passion* in the words, as was brilliantly demonstrated by Jack Potter, Steve Potter, Johnny Aldrich, Tom Frame, and others.

Google Bill Savage's "Laugh *this* off, Twinkletoes!" by the great Jack Potter, with page layout by the equally great *2000AD* art director Doug Church, and tell me I'm wrong. The words *shout* off the page. If we had similar great hand lettering today, we wouldn't be relying on slogans from yesteryear for cool tee shirts. It's the *punch* in his lettering that makes it work.

We miss you, Jack.

36. THE COMIC OF THE FUTURE

With the merchandising boom, the games and the forthcoming TV series, not to mention TV interest in other *2000AD* characters, it's reasonable to assume *2000AD* will be around to make its 50th birthday and beyond.

Today, it's an essential part of British popular culture. There are endless allusions to *Dredd* and *2000AD* characters in the media. My personal favourite, a few years after the Millennium, was a reference to *Nemesis The Warlock* in Coronation Street. I also recall one of the stars of *Men Behaving Badly* wearing a Nemesis tee shirt in that series. And the comic's influenced so many rock bands. Names that come to mind include the Mutoid Waste Company and the folk punk group The Men They Couldn't Hang who were influenced by *The Cursed Earth*. (The Lord Weird) Slough Feg, an American Heavy Metal band, take their name from my main bad guy in *Slaine*. That was one of those strange names that just came into my head.

Looking ahead, I like to believe the continuing success of *2000AD* and Rebellion's acquisition of the British comics archive will eventually lead to originating new comics, new books and exploring new directions.

I hope these will include stories with anti-establishment and anti-war themes: a cornerstone of the Comic Revolution. So I'd like to linger on some aspects of anti-war and "subversion" because they're what's most important to me personally and have driven all my stories and comics.

Thus I'm envious of the French, who can effortlessly publish a successful graphic novel about the Paris Commune. By comparison, when would any British company publish similar dramatic and heroic events, like the General Strike, in comic book form?

Because there is, indeed, overt, covert and subconscious censorship in the UK in every media, including comics. Thus the laid-back disinterest of cappuccino comic thinking also acts as a form of censorship.

I believe it applied to the exhibition *Comics Unmasked – Art and Anarchy in the UK*—held at the British Library in 2014 at the start of the World War One anniversary years. Whilst it included my science fantasy stories, it noticeably did not include the *most* political and controversial British comic strip of all, *Charley's War*.

When I "unmasked" the cappuccino comic curator on his anarchy shortfall, I was told the British Library hoped to do something separately on *Charley*. They never did.

In the library bookshop at the time, I noticed there were many books on World War One, but I couldn't find *any* on conscientious objectors, pacifism, or a critique of World War One.

For example like the classic *Hidden History, the Secret Origins of the First World War* by Docherty and MacGregor.

This makes a strong and carefully documented case that kindly, benign old chap Sir Edward Grey and the other British politicians, didn't go to war by "accident", as we are endlessly and *carefully* brainwashed in schools to believe, but rather it was the kind of "tragic accident" the comic character Accident Man specialises in—but on a grand scale.

It resulted in the *deliberate* mass-murder of a generation in pursuit of the imperial aims of "Perfidious Albion", as Britain is often known in other countries. In fact, our ancestors were actually *better* informed about the true nature of the war *a century ago* and how to protest against it, than we are today in the supposedly advanced, high tech internet age.

A university professor, annoyed by my expressing similar views during a lecture I gave, made a self-flagellation gesture at me. But I see what I write not as hatred of my country but rather flagellating a system that suppresses the voices of the many, and has sold us all short.

Comics are one of the few media areas relatively overlooked by censors, where the voices of real people may yet be heard.

2000AD is, realistically, the last comic standing to express those views, of people who challenge the status quo, rather than take the blue pill.

Today, many *2000AD* readers are in positions of importance in the media, and I like to believe some of our subversive themes at least just might have rubbed off on them. Many are well known. British actors, film and TV directors, musicians, producers, animators, a UK film studio boss (Lionsgate), heads of computer game companies, publishers, journalists, novelists, comedy writers, artists, television editors ... the list is endless.

The most important for me, though, is the CEO of a school. Reading his letter, I don't think he'll be receiving an MBE any time soon. And I rather think he'd turn down such an "honour".

As I'm a paid-up member of *Republic*, I can relate to that.

Here are excerpts from two of his emails:

Dear Pat

We've got a library that we need filling, and I am creating a section I would like to call with your permission, "Mills and BOOM!"... dedicated to yourself and others that engage kids through graphic novels with a decent message within them.

When people ask me how my moral compass developed, I always say that it was from *2000AD*! I learnt about fascism from Dredd, racism from *Strontium Dog*, feminism from *Halo Jones* etc and most people just think I'm weird saying this...

I'm now 44 and I've been working in education for many years, and have recently opened up a new school in my home town of Doncaster.

www.xpschool.org

Myself and Andy, our Principal are both comic readers, punks, and want our kids to be open minded, questioning and challenging. We've both refused invitations to Downing Street and Buckingham palace that arrived because we've opened a school.

I really just wanted to drop you a line to say thank you for all the subversive and subliminal plot lines and stories I've read over the years written by you! It worked!

I'm doing this because I just read your blog post about your disgusting teachers, James and Solomon! Schools don't have to be like that at all. Ours is fantastic!

I'm sure you get shed loads of fan mail, but whether you read this or not, I really want to say thank you from the bottom of my heart for influencing/informing me in the way you have.

Creating a world-class education free for our children is the most subversive thing I believe I could do.

Keep it up, and so will we!

Best wishes,

Gwyn ap Harri

A not so evil CEO

XP School Trust

Thank you, Gwyn.

So the foundations many of us laid in the '70s, '80s and early '90s as Gwyn has described, have their impact today and will continue to have an impact for decades to come. And Gwyn and co. are about to open a *second* school. "Spread the Word!" as Hammerstein would say.

Sometimes I wish I'd taken the blue pill like so many others, then I'd be quite content to write cappuccino comics or even—God help me—American superhero comics. Unfortunately, the muse that drives me (a story of writer motivation beyond this secret history) would never permit it.

Falling asleep in a Marvel script conference was a gentle warning by my muse to step back from corporate comic thinking. I have to take her seriously (the muse is always female). The warning may not be so gentle next time.

So my muse hopes that the rebellion that *2000AD* once stood for won't be forgotten in a desire for commercial exploitation of the comic by the hopefully appropriately named Rebellion.

Meanwhile, I hope the creators won't be neglected either.

I really believe commercialism *and* sedition can go together. Thus, on the extremely seditious *Marshal Law*, we had a range of merchandising which included boxer shorts. On the front of the shorts, the superhero hunter was holding a strategically placed giant bazooka and saying "Cover me". Unfortunately Marvel turned the shorts down. For some reason, they thought they were offensive.

I am optimistic about the future. But that optimism may well be misplaced. I've certainly got it wrong before. Google the next item I'm going to mention and you'll see just what I mean.

I recall vividly, after the *Action* debacle, that moment when the sales figures for *2000AD* came in and confirmed we had a hit. I realised that with *2000AD* using science fiction we had the perfect platform to make a difference to readers' lives. We had powerful characters and stories that could *never* be corroded because they were anchored in truth. They could *never* be modified, compromised or diluted by empty commercialism and the blind pursuit of profit.

I turned triumphantly to my staff and famously prophesied:

"You know what, guys? There'll *never* be *Judge Dredd* pyjamas."

I'll get my dressing gown.

Credo!

Pat Mills, May 2017

DID YOU LIKE THIS BOOK?

WE NEED YOU ...

Without reviews, indie books like this one are almost impossible to market.

Leaving a review will only take a minute: it doesn't have to be long or involved, just a sentence or two that tells people what you liked about the book, to help other readers know why they might like it, too, and to help us write more of what you love.

The truth is, VERY few readers leave reviews. Please help us by being the exception. If you bought *Be Pure!* online, you can leave a review at the retail site. Or you could leave a review at Goodreads, or on a blog, or even just tell your friends about us!

Thank you in advance!
Pat

Battle. Action. 2000AD. Misty.
The British Comics Revolution!

You've read *Be Pure*, now it's time to go deeper. The gloves are off in *Read Em And Weep*: the fictional saga of the Revolution that changed readers' lives. Based on the real-life comics and their creators, it's the story of *Blitzkrieg!* (Battle), *Aaagh!* (Action), *Space Warp* (2000AD starring Judge Dredd), and *Raven* (Misty) told over four novels starting with... *Serial Killer*.

It follows the fortunes of Dave, Greg and Joy – the young creators who spearheaded the Revolution – producing fiercely anti-establishment and wildly futuristic comics as they endlessly fight, rival and betray each other.

The saga starts with a depressed Dave working on the pre-Revolution *Spanker:* on stories like The Caning Commando, so ridiculous they are laugh-out-loud hilarious today. And girls' serials like the wolf girl Feral Meryl, with mysterious emotions far beyond his shallow understanding of the opposite sex.

Because Dave is emotionally shut down, thanks to the evil newsagent

who made his childhood a misery, and his mother's mysterious murder. He hates his life, and he hates his readers.
But then a chain of events as fantastic as his comic stories transforms Dave from a bitter and twisted editor into a defender of kids, disposing of the adults who harm them as he becomes a real-life... Serial Killer.

The 1970s – a dangerous time for kids. An even more dangerous time for adults.

Fast-moving, and with as high a body count as the comics themselves, you'll be hooked from the first page. Get *Serial Killer* now – because we all need a little vigilante justice in our lives.

GOODNIGHT, JOHN-BOY (Read Em And Weep 2)

Now Dave and Greg have created *Aaagh!*, the 'comic of the streets', and Joy writes about *that* great white shark. Every week it devours human prey - including the President of the United States when Airforce One crashes in the Pacific. *Aaagh!* so enrages the establishment, it's torn up on live TV - an event that actually happened! Dave and Greg fight back and their crimes lead them to be sentenced to the Siberia of comics: the *Laarf! Puzzle Specials*.

Joy rescues them by suggesting they create the thrill-powered *Space Warp*. Then, to her fury, Dave and Greg sell out and bring back Dan Darwin, a legendary space hero that she believes should have been left to rest in space.

Even deadlier than his comics, Dave continues his work as a Serial Killer, a secret vigilante who kills monsters that harm kids. And his next target is TV celebrity and 'national treasure' Fabulous Keen. But Keen, the ultimate monster, discovers Dave's identity and prepares a terrible revenge.

GRAPHIC NOVELS BY PAT MILLS

Accident Man, by Pat Mills & Tony Skinner, illustrated by Duke Mighten, Martin Emond, John Erasmus (Now a film starring Scott Adkins)

Marshal Law, by Pat Mills & Kevin O'Neill

Requiem: Vampire Knight, by Pat Mills & Olivier Ledroit

Charley's War, by Pat Mills & Joe Colquhoun

2000AD GRAPHIC NOVELS

Slaine

ABC Warriors

Nemesis The Warlock

Defoe

Flesh

Greysuit

Savage

COMING SOON!

THE GRIM READER (Read Em And Weep book 3)

- The final battle between the Geek Detective and Fabulous Keen. But who is 'the other party' involved in his mother's murder?
- More kids' vigilante justice against adult abusers. Is kids' rule okay? Or is it *Lord of the Flies* mayhem?
- The dark secrets of a comic book artist revealed, with terrible consequences for Dave.
- The dark secrets of a comic book editor revealed, with terrible consequences for Dave.
- The dark secrets of a comic book publisher revealed with … yes, you guessed it.
- Which stories will make the number one issue of the famous SF comic *Space Warp*?
- The Caning Commando returns with three new stories: *Bum Rap, The Cane Mutiny* and *The Dark Arssassin.*
- Can Dave save Joy from the terrors of 'The House of Correction'?
- Why is Greg acting so strangely? And why won't he walk down Fleet Street with Dave and Joy?
- Psychopath Tristan Morgan catches up with the Geek Detective to avenge his brother's murder.

Don't miss our news and updates: join our mailing list at www.millsverse.com and we will send you two stories, completely free!

ENTER THE MILLSVERSE

 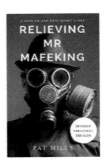

While Pat's working on his next book, why not join our mailing list and download a couple of stories from Pat while you're waiting?

Head over to www.millsverse.com to grab your stories, completely free.

RELIEVING MR MAFEKING

A long short story (c. 7000 words) from the *Read Em And Weep* universe.

What is the dark secret of Mafeking and Jones? What is waiting for Dave Maudling in the basement of the famous caning emporium? And what does Mr Jones really mean when he tells Dave that Mr Mafeking is 'no longer with us'?

Dave's tough new comic *Aaagh!* – known to the press as the 'eightpenny nightmare' – is so controversial, questions are asked in Parliament. But Dave naively believes all publicity is good publicity.

Then Dave is invited to visit Mafeking and Jones of St James's, the famous cane-makers. Lured by the prospect of receiving a bottle of ten-year-old malt whisky, he accepts, and is shown an awesome array of swagger sticks, swordsticks, bullwhips, riding crops and school canes.

But there is a nightmare waiting for him in the basement.

This is a tale of revenge, treachery and treason, with even more blood and gore than *Aaagh!*

THE ARTISTS' DEBT COLLECTION PARTY (Being an account of how the Toxic! artists, led by Pat Mills, did recover their unfairly withheld wages from the Publisher)

This true story short (just under 3000 words), written with Pat's trademark acerbic wit, is a companion piece to Pat's *Be Pure! Be Vigilant! Behave! 2000AD & Judge Dredd: The Secret History*, but it can definitely be enjoyed on its own.

FURTHER READING

These are most of the books mentioned in my text. Some of them were crucial, such as *Comix* by Les Daniels, which features a primary source for *Judge Dredd*. Others were character-shaping when I was growing up, like Stephen Leacock's *Maddened by Mystery or The Defective Detective.*

If you're interested in any of these titles, I've put this list up on my website at **millsverse.com/bepurefurtherreading**, with live links to Amazon, for your convenience.

- 1984, George Orwell
- Animal Farm, George Orwell
- The Blood Never Dried, John Newsinger
- Catch 22, Joseph Heller
- Charley's War, Pat Mills and Joe Colquhoun
- 1917 Russia's Red Year, John Newsinger
- Comix: A History of Comic Books in America, Les Daniels
- Concrete Island, J. G. Ballard
- Conquering Armies (renamed Armies), Dionnet, Picaret and Gal
- Corum, Michael Moorcock

- The Cosmic Pulse of Life: The Revolutionary Biological Power Behind UFOs, Trevor Constable
- The Dice Man, Luke Rhinehart
- Doctor Who, Song of Megaptera, audio play, Pat Mills
- Don Camillo, Giovannino Guareschi
- The Dredd Phenomenon: Comics and Contemporary Society, John Newsinger
- Ecodefense: A Field Guide to Monkeywrenching, Dave Foreman and Bill Haywood
- Elric of Melnibone, Michael Moorcock
- Erewhon, Samuel Butler
- The Exploits of Brigadier Gerard, Arthur Conan Doyle
- A Fate Worse Than Debt, Susan George
- Future Shock! The story of *2000AD*, DVD
- Gulliver's Travels, Jonathan Swift
- Flashman, George Macdonald Fraser
- Hidden History: The Secret Origins of the First World War, Gerry Docherty and Jim MacGregor
- How The Other Half Dies: the Real Reasons for World Hunger, Susan George
- Iron Council, China Mieville
- The Lord of the Rings, J. R. R. Tolkien
- Lower Than Vermin, Kevin Killane and Martin Rowson
- Maddened by Mystery: or The Defective Detective, Stephen Leacock
- The Making of Judge Dredd, Charles Lippincott, Jane Killick, David Chute
- Paleontology: an experimental science, Robert R. Olsen. In The Year's Best Science Fiction No. 8, edited by Harry Harrison and Brian Aldiss
- Requiem Vampire Knight Series, Mills & Ledroit (Comixology digital edition)
- Scarred For Life Volume One, Stephen Brotherstone and Dave Lawrence

- Serial Killer, Pat Mills and Kevin O'Neill
- Story, Robert McKee
- The Tain, Thomas Kinsella
- Truths of the Unremembered Things, Paul Wilkins
- You Are Maggie Thatcher, Pat Mills and Hunt Emerson
- You Are Ronald Reagan, Pat Mills and Hunt Emerson
- A Very British Coup, Chris Mullin
- Valerian, Mezieres and Christin
- Very Good, Jeeves, P. G. Wodehouse
- Voyage to Venus, Frank Hampson
- War with the Robots, Harry Harrison

Head over to millsverse.com/be-pure-further-reading/ for live links to all these titles.

SELECT BIBLIOGRAPHY

Wikipedia has a complete list of my books and comics, and the various editions, so I've only listed a selection here, the ones that are most pertinent to The Secret History.

If you look at the complete list, you may wonder–how on earth it was possible? The answer is the sweatshop conditions of British comic publishing means it was the only way to make a living. Although I'm still surprised myself by just how much I had to write to keep the wolf from the door. And, even today, with current poor rates and royalties, he still sniffs at the window. I'm not alone in my surprise: one member of *2000AD* staff once said to me, "You wrote all *that?* Why aren't you dead?"

One explanation is because all my stories contain elements of Truth, Justice and a non-Corporate American Way. And that fills me with passion and life-enhancing energy. If I'd chosen to write superheroes, I'd have been in my box long ago.

- ABC Warriors The Black Hole with Tony Skinner. Art: Simon Bisley and SMS
- ABC Warriors Khronicle of Khaos and Hellbringer with Tony Skinner. Art: Kev Walker
- ABC Warriors The Meknificent Seven. Art: Kevin

O'Neill, Mike McMahon Brendan McCarthy, Brett Ewins, Dave Gibbons, Carlos Ezquerra
- ABC Warriors: Mek Files 01 and 02. Deluxe collection of the three titles above.
- ABC Warriors. Return to Earth, Return to Ro-Busters, Return to Mars. Art: Clint Langley
- ABC Warriors The Volgan Wars. Art: Clint Langley.
- Accident Man with Tony Skinner. Art: Martin Emond, Duke Mighten, John Erasmus
- Batman: Book of Shadows (co-author). Art: Duke Mighten
- Charley's War. Art: Joe Colquhoun
- Defoe 1666 and Queen of the Zombies. Art: Leigh Gallagher
- Finn with Tony Skinner, unpublished. Art: Jim Elston and Paul Staples
- Flesh the Dino Files, Pat Mills, Kelvin Gosnell and others. Art: Ramon Sola, Belardinelli, James McKay and others
- Greysuit Project Monarch. Art: John Higgins
- Judge Dredd: The Cursed Earth. Additional stories by Jack Adrian and John Wagner. Art: Brian Bolland, Mike McMahon and others.
- Judge Dredd: The Complete Casebook Files One. The Return of Rico and other stories. With other authors. Art: Carlos Ezquerra, Mike McMahon, Ian Gibson, and others.
- Marshal Law. Art: Kevin O'Neill.
- Metalzoic. Art: Kevin O'Neill.
- Misty collection. Moonchild. Art: John Armstrong
- Nemesis the Warlock. Art: Kevin O'Neill, Jesus Redondo, Bryan Talbot, John Hicklenton.
- Psychokiller with Tony Skinner. Comixology. Art: Dave Kendal

- Punisher 2099 with Tony Skinner. Comic book format only. Art: Tom Morgan and others
- Ravage 2099 with Tony Skinner. Comic book format only. Art: Paul Ryan and others.
- Requiem Vampire Knight. Comixology.Art: Olivier Ledroit
- Ro-Busters by Pat Mills and others. Art: Kevin O'Neill, Dave Gibbons, Ian Kennedy and others.
- Savage Taking Liberties. Art: Charlie Adlard
- Savage The Guvnor. Art: Patrick Goddard
- Serial Killer. Text novel with Kevin O'Neill.
- Sha. Art: Olivier Ledroit
- Slaine The Books of Invasions. Art: Clint Langley.
- Slaine The Grail War . Art: Steve Tappin, Nick Percival and Belardinelli
- Slaine The Horned God. Art: Simon Bisley.
- Slaine The King. Art: Glenn Fabry and David Pugh
- Slaine Lord of the Beasts. Art: Raphael Garres, Greg Staples, Dave Bircham and others
- Slaine The Treasures of Britain. Art: Dermot Power
- Slaine Warriors Dawn. Art: Angela Kincaid, Belardinelli, Mike McMahon.
- Third World War in Crisis. Unpublished. Art: Carlos Ezquerra, Liam Sharp, Duncan Fegredo, Sean Phillips, John Hicklenton and others.

ABOUT THE AUTHOR

Pat Mills is the creator of *2000AD*, now in its 40th year, and still writes for the Galaxy's Greatest Comic. He is also the creator of *Action*, and co-creator of the following: *Battle*, the girls supernatural comic *Misty*, *Marshal Law*, *Requiem Vampire Knight*, the anti-war saga *Charley's War*, described as "the greatest British comic strip ever created", and the black comedy text novel *Serial Killer*.

For *2000AD*, he developed *Judge Dredd*, and, with the artists, created *Mach One*, *Savage*, *Slaine*, *Harlem Heroes*, *Flesh*, *Nemesis*, *Greysuit*, *Defoe*, *ABC Warriors* and *Ro-Busters*. As well as *Third World War* for *2000AD's Crisis*, which led to the *2000AD* series *Finn*. Although he wrote *Punisher 2099* for Marvel, *Metalzoic* and *Batman* for DC Comics, and *Marshal Law* for Marvel Epic, he is one of the few British writers to be uninterested in mainstream American superheroes and prefers instead writing for the French comic book market with series like *Sha* and *Requiem Vampire Knight* (available in English language edition through Comixology).

His *Accident Man*, co-created with Tony Skinner, is now a film starring Scott Adkins.

You can get in touch with Pat in the following ways.
www.millsverse.com
pat@millsverse.com

Printed in Great Britain
by Amazon